Why South Vietnam Fell

Why South Vietnam Fell

Anthony James Joes

LEXINGTON BOOKS
Lanham • Boulder • New York • London

Published by Lexington Books
An imprint of The Rowman & Littlefield Publishing Group, Inc.
4501 Forbes Boulevard, Suite 200, Lanham, Maryland 20706
www.rowman.com

16 Carlisle Street, London W1D 3BT, United Kingdom

Copyright © 2014 by Lexington Books

British Library Cataloguing in Publication Information Available

Library of Congress Cataloging-in-Publication Data

Joes, Anthony James.
Why South Vietnam fell / Anthony James Joes.
pages cm
Summary: "Examination of the administration of President Ngo Dinh Diem of South Vietnam and
how the country survived all Communist attempts to overthrow it until the U.S. Congress allowed the
anti-Communist population to be conquered by the North"—Provided by publisher.
Includes bibliographical references and index.
ISBN 978-1-4985-0389-1 (hardcover : alkaline paper) — ISBN 978-1-4985-0390-7 (ebook)
1. Vietnam (Republic)—Politics and government. 2. Ngo, Dinh Diem, 1901–1963. 3. Vietnam—
Politics and government—1945–1975. 4. Communism—Vietnam—History—20th century. 5. Anti-
communist movements—Vietnam—History—20th century. 6. Vietnam War, 1961–1975—Political
aspects. 7. Vietnam (Republic)—Foreign relations—United States. 8. United States—Foreign relations—Vietnam (Republic). 9. Vietnam War, 1961–1975—United States. 10. Vietnam War,
1961–1975—Campaigns. I. Title.
DS556.9.J63 2014
959.704'3—dc23
2014030429

ISBN 978-1-4985-0391-4 (pbk : alk. paper)

♾™ The paper used in this publication meets the minimum requirements of American
National Standard for Information Sciences Permanence of Paper for Printed Library
Materials, ANSI/NISO Z39.48-1992.

Printed in the United States of America

To my life companion,
Christine Calhoun Joes.

Contents

Maps

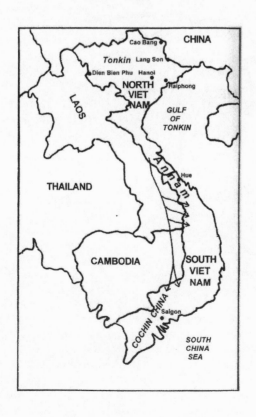

Maps

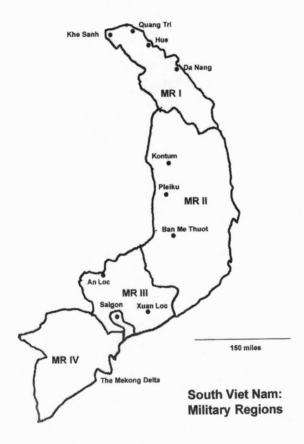

South Viet Nam:
Military Regions

Introduction

The Fall of South Vietnam

On April 30, 1975, heavy-armed units of the People's Army of Vietnam—
the North Vietnamese Army—crashed through the gates of the Presidential
Palace in Saigon.

For Americans, that was the end of what they called the "Vietnam War."
Actually, it was one major event in a series of wars that had lasted for thirty
years, and had involved not only the Vietnamese and the Americans, but also
the French, the Japanese, the British, the Soviets, and the Chinese, both
Nationalists and Communists.

Involvement in the latter period of the Vietnam conflicts agitated and
divided the American polity as nothing else had since Pearl Harbor, although
most of the agitation was confined to relatively unrepresentative groups in
American society.

This book does not offer yet another history of the Vietnam wars. Rather,
it presents key aspects of those conflicts that contributed directly to the final
conquest of South Vietnam by the Communist regime in Hanoi. Most of
these key aspects have been forgotten in the United States, or were never
clearly understood there in the first place.

A great deal of the literature on Vietnam produced by Americans might
leave the impression that its authors thought the Vietnam conflicts took place
inside the Washington Beltway. Relatively few authors suggested that the
outcome of the war had very much to do with the prowess of the North
Vietnamese Army (NVA), at that time one of the best armies in Asia, in part
because of the massive assistance that army received from China and the
USSR. And in the rare instances where American attention fell on the South
Vietnamese Army (ARVN), the treatment of it, almost uniformly, was curso-

ry, ill-informed, and dismissive. In fact, the South Vietnamese allies were often portrayed as being important contributors to the frustration of U.S. aims in Vietnam. Steeped as they allegedly were in corruption, cowardice, and incompetence, the repellant shortcomings of such allies were surely more than enough to justify the final American abandonment of the South Vietnamese.

The main purpose of this book is to demonstrate that these views of America's Vietnamese allies were and remain not the product of argumentation and debate based upon empirical evidence, but have resulted rather from mindless repetition of what were at best half-truths which have petrified into dangerous dogma. Specifically, this book will show that the widely-repeated and sometimes officially sanctioned American views about South Vietnamese President Ngo Dinh Diem, the South Vietnamese armed forces, the 1968 Tet Offensive, and the causes of the sudden collapse of South Vietnam in 1975 are gravely distorted or simply wrong. And clearly, "lessons" drawn from such distortions can continue to exert perilous influences on U.S. foreign policy.

Arguably more than anything else, the way the war ended damaged the American image of the South Vietnamese. As Dale Walton states, American evaluation of the struggle is profoundly affected by its perceived outcome,[1] and thus the image of the South Vietnamese would incontestably be much more positive today if the conflict had ended more favorably to the United States. But it is essential to understand that the arguments and judgments advanced in this book are completely independent of questions about the necessity or advisability of U.S. intervention in South Vietnam. That is, *whether or not it was a good idea for the U.S. to involve itself in the Southeast Asian conflict is irrelevant to a proper and fair assessment of the South Vietnamese allies.* It is the purpose of this book neither to defend nor demonize U.S. policy-makers of the period (although that cannot be completely avoided). It is rather to offer a measure of justice to the millions of South Vietnamese who paid the highest price for the abrupt cessation of U.S. concern for their country and their fate. Any attempt to help counteract the ill-founded and often cruel opprobrium heaped upon those millions, no matter how belated or inadequate that attempt, must surely be worthwhile.

Although a large number of the sources I cite in this volume make use of the latest Vietnamese documents available, I do not claim to introduce previously hidden information or to offer sensational revelations. On the contrary, I base my arguments on sources most of which are easily accessible to anyone with a serious interest in the fall of South Vietnam. These include the *Foreign Relations of the United States*; the official Hanoi history of the North Vietnamese Army; the papers and memoirs of Ambassadors Frederick Nolting and Ellsworth Bunker; *The Pentagon Papers* (which unfortunately need to be treated with circumspection); the writings of principal actors or commentators from several countries, especially France, South Vietnam, and North Vietnam; and the works of such acknowledged authorities as Anne Blair, Robert Brigham, Bui Tin, Phillip Davidson, Arthur Dommen, Dennis Duncanson, Peter Dunn, Bernard Fall, Ellen Hammer, Norman B. Hannah, Marguerite Higgins, Guenter Lewy, John T. McAlister, Mark Moyar, Don Oberdorfer, James S. Robbins, Lewis Sorley, Robert Thompson, Andrew Wiest, James H. Willbanks, James J. Wirtz, and Martin Windrow, among others. I have presented frequent and extensive quotations from these sources in order to reassure the readers of this book that even if many of the narratives, analyses, and conclusions offered herein differ jarringly from what they have read or viewed or been taught previously, the book is neither idiosyncratic or sectarian.

What Americans called North and South Vietnam emerged from the protracted conflict between the French Army and its numerous Vietnamese allies, on one side, and the Communist-dominated insurgency known as the Viet Minh, led by Ho Chi Minh, on the other. Chapter 1 explores the origins and development of this conflict, which resulted in the French leaving Vietnam and the partition of that country into a Communist North and a non-Communist South. It also addresses the widely (and often wildly) misunderstood "Geneva Accords of 1954." Chapters 2 and 3 deal with the emergence of Ngo Dinh Diem as constitutional President of the Republic of [South] Vietnam and the participation by officials of the American government in a military coup against him. That coup resulted in the murder of President Diem—an American ally—and eventually the massive intervention of U.S. military forces into what Americans today call the Vietnam War. Chapter 4 examines the strengths and weaknesses of the South Vietnamese Army (ARVN). Chapter 5 analyzes the famous Tet Offensive of 1968, which grew out of the North's realization that it was losing the war with the Americans and the South Vietnamese and therefore needed a dramatic stroke to change the course of that war. The Offensive was a very costly failure for the Communist side, but nevertheless persuaded influential opinion-makers and policy-makers in the U.S. that the American effort in South Vietnam had been unsuccessful and must be terminated. After Tet, the guerrilla aspects of the war receded and the Communist side launched an openly conventional effort by the North Vietnamese Army (NVA). Chapter 6 looks at the Easter Offensive of 1972, the supreme effort of the NVA to destroy ARVN and end the war. Like Tet, the Easter Offensive was a Communist failure but, again like Tet, it somehow convinced certain strata of American opinion that an independent South Vietnam was not viable. Chapter 7 presents the stunningly asymmetrical "peace" imposed by the U.S. and North Vietnam upon South Vietnam in 1973, and the subsequent slashing of U.S. assistance to its erstwhile allies. Chapter 8 explains the South Vietnamese decision, resulting from their abandonment by the Americans, to retrench their forces into Cochinchina (Saigon and the Mekong Delta region), and why that decision led to the rapid collapse of South Vietnam. Chapter 9 offers some final reflections on the fate of the South Vietnamese. The appendix then outlines a workable strategy whereby a South Vietnamese state could have endured for an indefinite period.

NOTE

1. C. Dale Walton, *The Myth of Inevitable U.S. Defeat in Vietnam* (Portland, OR: Frank Cass, 2002).

Chapter One

The Viet Minh War

Note: A principal purpose of this chapter is to demonstrate that there was widespread resistance among the Vietnamese people to the Viet Minh. For a much extended account of this conflict, with more detailed consideration of French strategy and tactics, see Anthony James Joes, "French Vietnam: A War of Illusions," *in* Victorious Insurgencies: Four Rebellions That Shaped Our World *(Lexington, KY: University Press of Kentucky, 2010).*

The country of Vietnam forms part of the great Southeast Asian peninsula that separates the Indian Ocean from the Pacific Basin, and links China and the Indian Subcontinent. Besides Vietnam, Southeast Asia includes the countries of Brunei, Burma, Cambodia, Indonesia, Laos, Malaysia, the Philippines, Singapore, and Thailand. In 1941, Imperial Japan was already well embarked on its program of extensive expansion onto the Asian mainland. The territories of Southeast Asia, most of which at that time formed part of the British, French, or Dutch empires, contained great quantities of rubber, rice, petroleum, and other commodities essential for modern war-making. The attack on the U.S. Pacific fleet at Pearl Harbor grew directly out of the determination of the Japanese Empire to establish its secure control over these invaluable strategic resources. As we will see, even before Pearl Harbor Japanese troops had taken possession of French Vietnam.

Present-day Vietnam has a population of over ninety-one million. But in the 1950s, it had only about thirty million. The country is 128,000 square miles in area, somewhat smaller than Germany, a little larger than New Mexico. Vietnam's long coastline is bathed by the South China Sea. Many Americans who went to Vietnam described it as the greenest country they had ever seen. Its northernmost point is on the same latitude as Miami, and its southernmost on that of the Panama Canal. From north to south—from above the great delta of the Red River to below that of the Mekong—the country stretches for a thousand miles, the distance between Rome and Copenhagen or between Boston, Massachusetts, and Jacksonville, Florida. But the country is like Chile or Norway: very long but notably narrow, at its narrowest 50 miles, and even at its widest, only 300 miles; for twenty years that narrow waist contained the demarcation line that used to divide the states of South and North Vietnam. The principal regions of Vietnam were Tonkin in the north, containing Hanoi, capital of French Vietnam and of the present regime; Annam in the center, with the traditional imperial capital of Hue; and Cochinchina in the south, comprising the Mekong Delta and bustling, beautiful Saigon.

A major thesis of this book is that South Vietnam's geography was its destiny. Two features of that geography were especially crucial. To the north of Vietnam lies China, a country that was to play the decisive role in the establishment of Communist North Vietnam, and then an essential part in North Vietnam's conquest of South Vietnam. And to the west of Vietnam lies Laos, the thinly-populated country with which Vietnam has its longest border. Laos was the key to the fate of South Vietnam.

Before Americans forces arrived in Vietnam, that country was the locus, from 1946 to 1954, of one of the twentieth century's major conflicts. On one side were the French and their numerous Vietnamese allies, and, on the other, the Communist-controlled party's army usually known by its short title as the Viet Minh. During that war the French lost thousands of their finest young men, and more money than they received under the Marshall Plan. In the end, the French withdrew from Vietnam, over which their control had begun in 1859 with the capture of Saigon, in those days hardly more than a large village.

WHAT WAS THE WAR ABOUT?

Why did France wage war for so many years in Vietnam? And why was the long French effort there unsuccessful? Undoubtedly, holding onto their investments and privileges in Vietnam had tremendous importance for a very small percentage of Frenchmen. For others, *la mission civilisatrice*—France's "civilizing mission"—justified, and even required, its continuing rule over Vietnam, and all other parts of its extensive empire. Thus while some Frenchmen viewed Vietnam through the lens of the crudest financial exploitation, others approached that country with truly altruistic motives: they would confer upon the Vietnamese the riches of French culture, the achievements of modern medicine, the consolations of the true religion, and so on. Undoubtedly, in some persons altruism and selfishness were present simultaneously.

But perhaps most importantly, many French, especially in high government and military positions, saw the war over Vietnam as a fight to maintain France's status as a power in the world, a status cast under a cruel and devastating light by France's sudden collapse before the German onslaught of 1940. The last French commander in chief in Vietnam, General Paul Ely, bluntly expressed the thinking of many Frenchmen: "In the Far East, like it or not, our position as a great power is at stake."[1]

To fully understand that statement, one needs to be aware that sustained conflict with the Viet Minh flared in French Vietnam hardly two years after the liberation of Paris, and less than seven years after the Fall of France. And in addition, would not a French withdrawal from Indochina immediately call into the most serious question their position in French North Africa, where one million Europeans lived (many of them French men and women who had been born there), that very North Africa, most notably French Algeria, from which, less than three years before the outbreak of war in Vietnam, General de Gaulle and his Free French had launched their return in force to their Nazi-occupied homeland? No, the loss of French North Africa, especially Algeria, would be unthinkable.[2] Therefore, Vietnam had to be held, Vietnam had to remain under the flag of France: a Gallic version of the Domino Theory.

For many Frenchmen, and even more so for many Americans, the war in French Vietnam would inexorably be subsumed into the narrative of the Cold War: a struggle between the West (NATO France aided by the U.S.) and international Communism (Ho's Viet Minh backed by the USSR and Maoist China). But that analysis would come later. When the French decided to fight in 1946, it was imperialism—*grandeur*—and not primarily anti-Communism that animated the French war effort. In a very perceptive study, John Cady wrote:

> The taproot of French imperialism in the Far East from first to last was national pride—pride of culture, reputation, prestige and influence. This was the constant factor which ran through the kaleidoscope of episodes of missionary dedication and daring, of naval coups, and of private adventures. . . . One need not discount the genuineness of the religious zeal which sustained the program of the Société des Missions Étrangères over two centuries or challenge the vitality of the liberal religious revival under Louis Philippe to see in both of them an expression of supreme confidence in the superiority of French spirit and culture. Christian missions were supported in large measure because they were French.
>
> Politically, French imperialism expressed itself most frequently in eastern Asia in terms of perennial rivalry with Great Britain. British pretensions of superiority were unendurable and therefore to be opposed, whenever and wherever possible. The basic considerations behind French policy in the Far East, from the time of Louis XIV to that of Louis Napoleon and Jules Ferry, had been more political than economic.[3]

It was thus truly for their conception of the greatness of France that De Gaulle, Leclerc, D'Argenlieu, and other French leaders who had not long before battled to end German hegemony in France, would now battle to maintain French hegemony in Vietnam. Bernard Fall was right when he observed that the Vietnamese conflict began, at least, as a war of colonial reconquest.[4]

THE COMMUNISTS IN VIETNAM

The Vietnamese Communist Party would eventually emerge as the primary opponents of the French. That Party was "a subversive movement launched from outside Vietnam by the Soviet Government as an instrument for embarrassing France."[5] Hence it differed radically from all other anti-French organizations within Vietnam. Close connection to the Soviets inspired Vietnamese Communists with the bracing conviction that they were members of a universal brotherhood whose eventual victory was guaranteed by Marxian science. More concretely, the Comintern[6] provided funds, discipline, and schooling in Moscow in the basic techniques of underground organization and survival. It was, above other factors, this Soviet patronage that provided the strategic and tactical superiority of Vietnamese Communists over Vietnamese nationalists.

The Party's supreme leader was Ho Chi Minh. He was born in 1890, in Nghe An province, which was an old-time hotbed of rebellion on the central coast. A graduate of Vietnam's most prestigious secondary school, Ho's original name was Nguyen That Than. During his career he would adopt several aliases until he was widely known as Ho Chi Minh, "he who enlightens." Ho had impeccable Communist credentials. In Moscow he took courses in Marxist theory and Leninist tactics at the University of the Toilers of the East. During a later sojourn in Moscow, he studied the arts of deception at the Comintern's famous Lenin School. Ho also spent some time with Mao Tse-tung's Eighth Route Army.[7]

One often heard the comment that Ho Chi Minh was "a nationalist first and a Communist second." But of course that is a meaningless statement: all Communist revolutionaries in colonial areas had by definition to be nationalists, because only through the expulsion of the colonial authority could they take power. Thus "Ho had two aims. The first was to achieve independence. . . . But this was not all he wanted. The second aim was that Vietnam, once independent, should be ruled by his party . . . it had to be a Communist Vietnam."[8] Ho and his fellow Communists had no wish whatsoever to be one component in a Vietnamese government; they desired an independent Vietnam only if it was completely controlled by the Party: "indeed the fight for independence was for them only a vehicle for the conquest of power."[9]

Before 1941, three major obstacles had blocked the Viet Minh's path to power: the French colonial administration, Vietnamese rival nationalist parties, and then the Japanese occupation. But soon enough, the efficient French police broke up the non-Communist nationalists (with much help from the Viet Minh), the Japanese thoroughly and irrevocably humiliated the French, and then the Allies crushed the Japanese. By the end of World War II, the Viet Minh's path ahead to full domination seemed clear.

And domination was the only outcome Ho and his cohorts would accept. In June 1948, while large-scale fighting between the Viet Minh and the French and their allies had been raging for over a year and a half, former Emperor Bao Dai, recognized as Head of the Vietnamese State by France, put his signature to a French document that began: "France solemnly recognizes the independence of Vietnam." Whatever measure of absolute independence might have been lacking, complete sovereignty would undoubtedly have followed in the foreseeable future, peacefully. But the Viet Minh had no intention of accepting such a scenario. Ho Chi Minh wanted complete independence *under the control of his party*; the ineluctable result of his insistence on total power would be many years of bloody combat. In Ho's view, a protracted and bitter anti-French conflict would in fact pay enormous dividends, because it would unite the Vietnamese and cement the control of his Communist party over them. Ho knew the Soviets (and eventually the Maoist regime in China) would assist him, and he correctly calculated that opinion in France would grow weary of a protracted conflict in a distant land. Thus he was willing to make war no matter how long it would persist and no matter how many of his countrymen would perish. Yet, when the war against the French and their Vietnamese allies finally came to a halt in 1954—a brutal eight year war, a civil war, that had destroyed so many innocent lives and consumed so much painfully accumulated wealth and wasted so much irreplaceable time and opportunity—even after all that, Ho and his followers found themselves in control of only the northern half of their country. Could such a victory have really been worth it to the Viet Minh? And after 1954 they faced an anti-Communist state in South Vietnam determined to resist them and increasingly assisted by the Americans.[10] So there would have to be yet more war, and more Vietnamese deaths.

A TRUE CIVIL WAR

The conflict that took place in Vietnam between 1946 and 1954 was by no means a simple or straightforward struggle between the French and the Viet Minh alone. On the contrary, hundreds of thousands of Vietnamese chose to side with the French, or oppose the Viet Minh (not necessarily the same choice). One of the best English-language works on the Viet Minh conflict observes that "today it is little appreciated that the war as a whole, and the [climactic] battle of Dien Bien Phu itself [discussed below], were far from being clear-cut confrontations between Europeans and Indochinese, but involved significant numbers of Vietnamese fighting under French command" or under Vietnamese nationalist command.[11] The conflict was in fact the latest in a series of Vietnamese civil wars involving foreign powers. This civil war would continue long after the French left Vietnam.[12]

One of the roots of this widespread Vietnamese hostility to the Viet Minh was the latter's violence against civilians. To repeat an essential point: the Viet Minh wanted not an independent Vietnam but an independent Vietnam controlled exclusively by them. To this end, they carried out a deliberate and systematic campaign to destroy the noncommunist nationalists, murdering real or potential rivals in great numbers or betraying them to the French police. "The elimination of their opponents," writes Joseph Buttinger, "was one of the most common means the Communists used to establish Viet Minh control over the entire nationalist movement."[13] During 1946 alone the Viet Minh massacred thousands of nationalists in Tonkin.[14] As George Modelski states, Viet Minh bloodletting "became a vice, an intoxication with violence."[15] Their "odious methods"[16] turned important groups in Vietnamese society to a stance of uncompromising hostility to the Viet Minh, not least in the regions of what would later become the state of South Vietnam.

Indeed, a powerful Communist organization with deep roots had never existed in the southern provinces of Vietnam. This was largely due to the presence in those areas of important social groups which were indifferent or hostile to the Viet Minh. The Communists had been murdering leaders and members of the popular Trotskyist party in Cochinchina since the 1930s.[17] Saigon (like Hanoi) had only a small Communist organization. This was the result both of effective police surveillance and of the indifference of its relatively sophisticated population to the Viet Minh, who were commonly viewed as bomb-throwing peasants.[18] The half-million ethnic Chinese of Cochinchina were especially unenthusiastic about the Viet Minh. One consequence of all this was that when the Japanese, who had occupied Vietnam in 1941, unexpectedly surrendered, the Viet Minh in the south, unlike their counterparts in the north, had hardly any armed units and thus could not seize control of Saigon.

But the most powerful single source of persistent Communist weakness in the south was the hostility toward them of two popular indigenous religious sects, the Cao Dai and the Hoa Hao.[19] The Viet Minh engaged in such gratuitous and destructive anti-French violence at the time of the Japanese surrender (fall, 1945) that they alienated the sects, and not only them.[20] That was an extremely debilitating circumstance for the Communists, because the Cao Dai and the Hoa Hao between them enjoyed the allegiance of what was almost certainly a majority of the inhabitants of populous Cochinchina, and each possessed its own armed militia. Serious fighting between the armed sects and the southern Communists, during which the Viet Minh assassinated sect leaders and killed great numbers of ordinary members, broke out very soon after the Japanese surrender and continued well into 1947.[21] The effects of all this Viet Minh bloodletting were predictable and profound: "Communist terror gradually drove [the sects] into the French camp."[22] The long-term consequences of this Viet Minh violence would be immense.

THE BAO DAI COALITION

Another massive stumbling block for the Viet Minh: the willingness of many to resist them was reinforced by French recognition of the independence of the State of Vietnam under former Emperor Bao Dai.[23] His government would eventually receive embassies from more than thirty countries, including Australia, Belgium, Brazil, Britain, Canada, Italy, the Netherlands, Spain, Thailand, Turkey, and the United States.[24]

An independent state must have an army. The French assisted Bao Dai in setting up the Vietnamese National Army (VNA), which by the end of 1953 enrolled 200,000 soldiers, and would grow larger. Many young VNA officers and enlisted men would in future years hold important posts in the ARVN, the Army of the Republic of [South] Vietnam.[25] In this chapter, the term CEF (for *Corps Expéditionnaire Français en Extrême-Orient*) will refer to all official, regular forces fighting in Vietnam under the French flag and in French uniform, including Frenchmen, Foreign Legionnaires, North Africans and West Africans, and also—very notably—scores of thousands of Vietnamese. In the CEF, Frenchmen were a minority, second in numbers to Vietnamese, except within the officer corps. The CEF is of course entirely distinct from those hundreds of thousands of Vietnamese serving in the VNA, the armed forces of Bao Dai's State of Vietnam. Between 1946 and 1950, the Vietnamese in the CEF and the VNA together incurred about 7,500 casualties a year; this was an extremely high rate, the equivalent of more than 75,000 annual American casualties in 2015.[26] (More statistics on these forces will follow.)

As World War II drew toward its end, the political future of Vietnam was profoundly unclear. One significant example of early uncertainty and even confusion is offered by the Vietnamese Catholic community, who comprised at least 10 percent of the total population. They were painfully aware that their adherence to their Church generated widespread suspicion that they were reflexively pro-French. Hence, many of their leaders originally wanted to avoid any confrontations with the Viet Minh, which at that time was attempting to present itself as a nationalist, not a Communist, movement. As Donald Lancaster points out, such a conciliatory approach by the leadership of the Church was fundamentally flawed and was thus bound to fail: "This desire on the part of the Vietnamese hierarchy that the Roman Catholics should redeem their unfortunate [pro-French] reputation deprived the [anti–Viet Minh] nationalist cause of the support of an important minority who were in the last resort irreconcilably opposed to the Communists."[27] But soon enough, frequent and ferocious attacks by Viet Minh militants upon Catholic villages and organizations convinced Catholic groups to undertake the formation of their own armed militias. Before the end of 1949, most Catholics, especially those in the northern provinces, where the Viet Minh were strongest and most violent, had adhered to the substantial and widening coalition around Bao Dai.[28]

The small nationalist Dai Viet party in Tonkin, as well as the VNQDD (The Vietnam Nationalist Party), along with similar groups, also gathered around Bao Dai's banner. For many members of such organizations, it was undoubtedly more patriotic—more *Vietnamese*—to prefer the traditional nationalism of Bao Dai to the Euro-Leninism of Ho Chi Minh, who had lived outside of Vietnam for most of his adult life.

Significantly, those who were coming together around Bao Dai and his State of Vietnam also included quite a few nationalists who had been early supporters of the Viet Minh but had become deeply disenchanted by its increasingly heavy-handed Communism.[29]

But most importantly by far, in 1948 the indigenous southern religious sects, the Cao Dai and the Hoa Hao, overwhelmingly concentrated in Cochinchina, pledged their support to Bao Dai; in return, the French granted the sects virtual autonomy over their regional bases, a short-sighted policy.[30] It was easy for the French and Bao Dai to win the allegiance of the sects, who after all had excellent reasons for hating the Viet Minh, as we have seen. By 1954 these sects together could field at least 40,000 armed men in the anti-Viet Minh effort.

Thus, opposition to the Viet Minh was wide, deep, and determined. All told, "there were by the spring of 1954 nearly 300,000 Vietnamese fighting against the Viet Minh" in the CEF, the VNA, and local militias, equal to the number of fighting men under the Viet Minh's military commander, General Vo Nguyen Giap. "This French capacity," writes John T. McAlister, "to mobilize substantial Vietnamese manpower for military purposes at the beginning as well as at the conclusion of the war suggests an important commentary" on the reality of the situation in Vietnam.[31] An additional way to understand this: Giap's 300,000 fighters amounted to less than 1 percent of the entire Vietnamese population.

WHY THEN DID THE FRENCH LOSE?

One often hears or reads that "the Viet Minh defeated the French." But like so many statements about Vietnam, that one is blatantly misleading. Clearly, the French were not defeated in the same sense that the Germans and the Japanese—and the French themselves—were defeated in World War II. No Viet Minh units occupied Paris or Toulon; for that matter, no Viet Minh units occupied Hanoi or Saigon or Hue until after the French had given up the conflict. It would clearly be much more precise, much more accurate, to state that in the summer of 1954 a sufficient number of politicians in Paris had become convinced that the French could not achieve their objectives in Vietnam at a price they were willing to pay, and so decided to abandon the conflict, and their Vietnamese allies.[32]

Why did that happen? This is a central, even the key, question about the Viet Minh conflict, because by any objective standard, the disparities between the French and the Viet Minh—in terms of population, productive capacity, accumulated wealth and military experience—would have pointed straight to, practically demanded, at least a serviceable approximation to a French victory. An explanation of the French failure can be divided into those factors that were mainly military and those that were mainly political. To consider the military factors first, prominent among them would be external interference in the conflict, the problem of French numbers, and the French logistical situation.

First, regarding external interference, it is essential for any counterinsurgent force to isolate the battle area from outside help to the insurgents. Two distinguished students of insurgency have recently written that "unless governments are utterly incompetent, devoid of political will, and lacking resources, insurgent organizations normally must obtain outside assistance if they are to succeed,"[33] and that "external assistance appears to be the most common enabler of insurgent success."[34] The records of such conflicts as those in the Philippines and Malaya after World War II, in South Vietnam, and in Soviet Afghanistan provide ample evidence for the validity of those views.

The French were never able to isolate their enemies from external assistance. The Japanese during and immediately after World War II offer the first instance of such help to the Viet Minh, help that was clearly vital to any serious Viet Minh effort against the French.

The Japanese and the Viet Minh

In the summer of 1940, with metropolitan France fallen before Hitler's armies, Japanese troops began the occupation of French Vietnam. Ho Chi Minh and his followers took advantage of these events to establish a front organization, the League for the Independence of Vietnam, or Viet Minh for short. Ostensibly a nationalist coalition, the Viet Minh was tightly under the control of Ho and his fellow Communists.

During most of their occupation of Vietnam, the Japanese had been satisfied with indirect rule over the country, maintaining a façade of French administration. But on March 9, 1945, apparently just two days before the French had planned to begin a major offensive against the Viet Minh guerrillas,[35] the Japanese disarmed and imprisoned all the French forces in the country within their grasp. "The psychological effect of this action was exactly as intended: the peoples of Indochina who witnessed the disarming of French soldiers concluded that French rule was at an end for all time, and with it the whole system of government and apparatus of law and order for which France had stood."[36] And as the intended climax to these events, on March 11, 1945, Emperor Bao Dai, under Japanese direction, proclaimed the independence of Vietnam (specifically Annam and Tonkin).

The Japanese troops in Vietnam, numbering perhaps 70,000, were not nearly enough to control both the cities and the countryside, and besides, the Japanese cared little about Viet Minh activities in rural areas. Thus, under the direction of Vo Nguyen Giap, the high school history teacher turned military leader, the Viet Minh's small armed units began to increase at a fairly rapid rate and to train in preparation for the day when the war would end, the Japanese would go home, and power in Vietnam would be up for grabs.[37] By the middle of 1945, Giap may have had 5,000 disciplined men at his command. He also exercised a degree of political control over close to a million peasants in provinces adjacent to the China border. Almost from the beginning of the Japanese occupation, these seven provinces in the Viet Bac, the mountainous region north of Hanoi and east of the Red River, made up the stronghold of the Viet Minh.[38] This so-called Free Zone was, George Modelski believed, "the true foundation of [the Viet Minh's] ultimate success" and "made the difference between survival and defeat."[39]

Following Japan's surrender in the summer of 1945, the Japanese in Vietnam handed over great quantities of arms and ammunition to the Viet Minh. In this manner the Viet Minh obtained, among other things, 18 tanks and 31,000 rifles.[40] Of arguably even greater importance, large numbers of Japanese military personnel, perhaps as many as forty-five hundred, decided to stay in Vietnam and join the Viet Minh in their efforts. These Japanese soldiers acted as instructors to train Giap's recruits and as supervisors for his weapons-making facilities; some directly entered his guerrilla units.[41] (Japanese troops also provided guns and training for units of the Cao Dai religious sect in Cochinchina.[42])

The Viet Minh received another tremendous windfall when Allied Commander General Douglas MacArthur forbade Allied landings in Japanese-held territory in Southeast Asia until the formal Japanese surrender took place. That prohibition included French landings in French Vietnam. The formal Japanese surrender took place in September, and in that very month, in Hanoi, under the benevolent neutrality of the Japanese occupation, Ho Chi Minh proclaimed the independence of Vietnam. Thus "this directive [of MacArthur's] had enormous consequences in Indochina, for a political vacuum [in Vietnam] was created which was happily filled by Communist leadership. That leadership is still there."[43] Even worse, the Nationalist government of Chiang Kai-shek refused to allow French forces to reenter northern Vietnam until March 1946, fully half a year after the surrender of Japan. With restrained anger, General de Gaulle wrote in his war memoirs that these actions by France's alleged allies "had fatally compromised the effect which the immediate arrival of French troops and officials and the disarmament of the Japanese by our forces might have produced."[44]

In spite of all these bitter provocations, however, "the de Gaulle government now [1944] installed in Paris was determined to restore French power over the whole country [of Vietnam]."[45]

In summary, the Japanese had all but destroyed French prestige in the eyes of Vietnamese society, supplied the Viet Minh with arms, instructors, and experienced recruits, and then allowed Ho's Communists to proclaim themselves the government of an independent Vietnamese state. It is difficult to imagine how the subsequent conflict could have lasted so long, have ended as it did, or have even begun, had the Viet Minh not received all this priceless assistance from the Japanese. A second major example of fundamental external interference on the side of the Viet Minh is provided by Communist China, especially after Maoist forces reached the Sino-Vietnamese border during 1948–1949.

The Communist Chinese and the Viet Minh

Along the chain of mountains separating northern Vietnam from China, the French possessed several well-sited and well-constructed forts. In October 1950, the high command imprudently ordered the fort at Cao Bang to be abandoned. Sixteen hundred soldiers, plus hundreds of civilians, headed slowly toward the city of Lang Son, 85 miles to the south, along a route that was more a track than a road. At the same time, 3.500 French Moroccan troops moved north to meet the column coming from Cao Bang. The Two groups linked up, but then great swarms of Viet Minh overwhelmed them, with enormous loss of life. "The disaster [south of Cao Bang] was above all a moral one. The essential fact was that French troops—considered the best— had been annihilated in open country by an army of Vietnamese peasants who had up to then been despised."[46] Thus, in Lancaster's judgment, Cao Bang constituted "the greatest defeat in the history of French colonial warfare."[47] Hard on the heels of this calamity, French military authorities, for reasons hard to understand, then decided to abandon Lang Son itself, a city of 100,000 and the main French strongpoint in the entire border region. A truly invaluable cornucopia consequently fell to the Viet Minh: 10,000 75-mm artillery shells, gasoline, medicines, and much else. To Bernard Fall, Lang Son was "France's greatest colonial defeat since Montcalm had died at Quebec."[48] In his judgment, the fall of Lang Son signified that "for the French, the war was lost then and there," because the Vietnam-China border was now wide open.[49]

Thus, these debacles along the northern frontier meant that the Viet Minh had unrestricted access to assistance from Mao Tse-tung's newly-established regime in China, including accelerated training, an accessible safe haven, and most of all, abundant military supplies.[50] And when the Korean War came to an end in 1953, "the Chinese Communists were now able to spare greatly increased quantities of materiel in the form of guns and ammunition (largely supplied by the Soviets) for use on the Indochinese battlefields. More advisers were being sent in and the Chinese were making available to the Viet Minh logistical experience that they had gained in the Korean War."[51] They also provided them with American weapons that had been captured in Korea and were often of better quality than those possessed by the CEF.[52] Chinese supplies to the Viet Minh eventually reached four thousand tons a month; this was a greater amount than the CEF was receiving from France.[53] Just for the battle of Dien Bien Phu in the spring of 1954, the Chinese provided the Viet Minh with scores of artillery pieces, 60,000 shells, and 2.4 million rounds of ammunition.[54] And between 1956 and 1963, Chinese aid to the new North Vietnamese regime included thousands of artillery pieces and 28 naval vessels. Chinese antiaircraft troops defended important sites in the North. A total of 320,000 Chinese engineers and other troops served in North Vietnam. In Chen Jian's bland assessment, "without that support, the history, even the outcome, of the Vietnam war might have been different."[55]

And "after weapons, munitions, radios and training in their use, the professional education of Vietnamese officers was China's most vital contribution to the transformation of General Giap's guerrillas into an army."[56] Forty thousand Viet Minh received training in China, and Chinese officers and instructors would make a vital contribution to the French defeat at Dien Bien Phu.[57]

With Chinese Communist power established on the northern border, and vast quantities of supplies pouring over it, Ho chose the occasion to proclaim the complete adherence of his Viet Minh to the international Communist movement led by Joseph Stalin and Mao Tse-tung, with all the consequences to the Vietnamese people which that announcement would eventually entail.

Noted authorities on the Viet Minh war, over many years and from quite different vantage points, have agreed that the availability of abundant Chinese supplies across the Tonkin border was primary and decisive for the outcome in the Franco–Viet Minh conflict. What follows are some examples of a very widespread agreement. In 1963, Bernard Fall wrote that "when Red China occupied all the provinces bordering on Tongking, late in 1949, and thus provided the Viet Minh with a 'sanctuary' where its troops could be trained and its supplies stored and replenished, the war had, for all practical purposes, become hopeless for the French."[58] One-quarter of a century after that statement, Phillip Davidson expressed his conclusion that "without a friendly China located adjacent to North[ern] Vietnam, there would have been little chance for a Viet Minh victory against the French, and later against the Americans and South Vietnamese."[59] And ten years after that, Chen Jian added his concurrence that "China's involvement in the First Indo-China War [1946–1954] was deep. Beijing provided large quantities of ammunition and military equipment to the Viet Minh, helped the Viet Minh train military commanders and troops, and Chinese advisors participated in the Vietnamese Communist leadership's decision-making processes." Thus he concludes that "it is fair to say that China's support had played a decisive role in the shaping of a series of Viet Minh victories during the war, such as those in the border campaign, the northwest campaign and, especially, the Dien Bien Phu campaign."[60]

INADEQUATE ALLIED NUMBERS

The second principal military factor affecting the efforts of the French in this conflict was their woefully insufficient numbers. A standard formula (not accepted by all commentators) states that a successful counterinsurgency requires a superiority of ten to one over the insurgents. This apparently extraordinary disparity is necessary because the counterinsurgents must attempt to maintain order, keep open lines of communication, and protect population centers, symbolic buildings, and strategic installations everywhere, all the time, whereas the insurgents are (presumably) free to engage in action only at times and places where they have the advantage of surprise and numbers. Now, by 1953 General Giap was in command of something like 300,000 armed fighting men of various levels of competence and equipment. That meant that, employing the 10:1 ratio, the French and their Vietnamese allies would have needed a total force of 3,000,000, which of course was entirely out of the question, quite unthinkable. Even a completely insufficient ratio of three-to-one would have required the allies to maintain a force of 900,000 troops.

But the actual situation on the ground was of a radically different order. In the first place, the average soldier in the French Expeditionary Corps was not French, quite the contrary: in May 1954, when the population of metropolitan France was over 40,000,000, French soldiers in the CEF numbered only

54,000, less than 30 percent of that army. There were in addition 15,000 French naval and air personnel; 30,000 colonial troops, largely North African and "Senegalese" (which meant West African); 20,000 Foreign Legionnaires; and no less than 70,000 Vietnamese wearing the uniform of France (many of them in elite paratroop battalions), 37 percent of the total. These persons were of course quite distinct from the men in Bao Dai's Vietnamese National Army.[61] And after one adds the 200,000 Vietnamese who comprised that indigenous army[62] to the total strength of the CEF, and also includes an estimated 60,000 Vietnamese serving in the sect forces and the Catholic militias, the total figure under French command or allied with it is about 450,000—a mere half of the hopelessly insufficient three-to-one ratio over Giap's forces calculated in the above paragraph. (Please note once again a fact whose tremendous importance will become manifest later in this book: in the last year of the Viet Minh conflict, the total number of Vietnamese in the CEF, in the Vietnamese National Army, and in the sect and Catholic forces outnumbered the Viet Minh troops under General Giap.) The relatively small number of soldiers from metropolitan France was a consequence of the fact that the French parliament forbade the sending of French conscripts to Vietnam; hence all French soldiers in that country were professionals or volunteers (not a bad circumstance in itself). If only 2 percent of the French male population had been conscripted and sent to Vietnam, that would have provided an additional 400,000 French troops to be added to the actual 69,000 in all branches in 1954. (And, as in every modern army, only a minority of those 400,000 would have been in actual combat units. Of the more than half a million troops whom General Westmoreland would command in Vietnam in 1968, less than 100,000 were combat soldiers.[63]) And regarding the members of the much-romanticized French Foreign Legion, who comprised close to 30 percent of the European manpower in Indochina: it is true that something like 50 percent of those Legionnaires were of German origin, but since their average age was under 23, it would be grossly mistaken to conclude or suspect that those persons were former Nazis trying to escape vengeance in Europe.[64]

Thus, although according to every empirical index, France was much stronger than the Viet Minh even—or especially—in 1954, the French efforts to suppress the insurgency would finally prove completely unsuccessful. The main explanation for that outcome is that while the Viet Minh waged total war, putting forth incredible effort and exacting staggering sacrifices from soldiers and civilians, the French fought a limited war, meaning, most importantly, no draftees to Vietnam. It is undeniably true that the Viet Minh had good leaders, and many of them in all ranks were dedicated and quite brave. Nevertheless, the main reason why the French could not achieve their aims is that they never were willing to commit sufficient forces to fight a proper counterinsurgent war. Consequently, the French were not *decisively* superior to their enemies *where the fighting was taking place.*

But even without the availability of conscripts, the French could have coped to some degree with the problem of inadequate manpower if they had possessed sufficient mobility. Perhaps the greatest military advantage of modern societies over underdeveloped ones is air power, but the weakness of their air force meant, among other results, that the French were lacking mobility; the CEF never had, for example, more than ten helicopters at one time.[65] This airpower deficiency is arguably the most important reason for the loss of Dien Bien Phu (discussed below).

Such mobility as the CEF possessed consisted mainly of its paratroops, some of the finest light infantry in the world. The conflict in Vietnam was the only war after 1945 to see numerous drops of such units. In October 1947, CEF paratroopers (a very large proportion of whom were Vietnamese) very nearly captured both Ho Chi Minh and General Giap in their Viet Bac stronghold. If they had succeeded in doing so, the war would soon have come to an end.[66] But French commanders overused their paratroops, on several occasions sacrificing whole battalions on missions far beyond their strength.

Of course, it would have greatly strengthened the allied effort if the French had properly trained and equipped the Vietnamese National Army, but as will soon be seen, France was not able to properly supply the CEF, much less build up a really effective VNA.

The French logistical situation was the third factor creating great difficulties for them. U.S. aid did not arrive in quantity in Vietnam until 1951. Before that time, CEF forces were using weapons dating from the 1930s, including some of Japanese, British, Chinese, and German make.[67] Such conditions were made even worse because the supply base of the Viet Minh was right across the Chinese border, whereas a very great proportion of the supplies of the CEF came from France. Consider that Saigon was nearly 5,500 nautical miles from Marseilles—more than 10,000 kilometers, or 6,200 land miles, two and a half times the distance between New York and San Diego. Washington, DC, is closer to Moscow than Paris is to Hanoi.

And, always in the background, but never forgotten, was the realization, with all its debilitating effects on the psychological state of the French and their allies, that in the last analysis, the French could decide to just go home.

But none of this is to insist that the French had no chance of success. Not even the fact that the CEF was a road-bound force not well prepared for counterinsurgency. General Navarre blamed the outcome of the war on the politicians in Paris who supplied him with an "inadequacy of means": he meant that Paris had not given him what he wanted. His position is not without merit. But it is the particular end sought that determines whether the means are adequate or not.[68] Before the Viet Minh conflict had begun in earnest, General Leclerc wrote with much foresight: "The ambitions [the ends] of this country in the age in which we live should correspond to available means, or else we will have catastrophe. *Better to hold half or a third of [Vietnam] solidly than the whole of it feebly.*"[69] If Leclerc's general approach had been adopted, probably the most appropriate French strategy would have been to hold the Hanoi-Haiphong region and Cochinchina in strength, properly equip and train the Vietnamese National Army, and wait for better times.[70] But choosing such a course would have required overcoming "that fundamental failing which plagued all French commanders in Indochina—a gross underestimation of Giap and the Vietminh."[71]

FRENCH POLITICAL DISARRAY

Far from the field of battle, the French war effort in Vietnam was further hampered by serious political problems inside France. The Fourth Republic (1946–1958) was a multiparty parliamentary system. Among those parties was the *Parti communiste français* (PCF), one of the largest such parties outside of the Soviet Union. In the 1951 national election, out of 19 million votes 5 million were cast for Communist candidates; in the National Assembly of 627 members, 101 were Communists.

The PCF provided a great deal of valuable intelligence to the Viet Minh and explained to it the most effective terms in which to address propaganda to French prisoners of war.[72] In addition, Communist factory workers sabotaged shipments of munitions to Vietnam, and Communist mobs abused departing troops at railway stations and stoned trains unloading wounded soldiers.[73] And, during the less than eight years of the Vietnam conflict, the politicians in Paris set up and pulled down no fewer than 16 different cabinets.[74] Under these conditions, sustained direction of and planning for the war was extremely difficult. Perhaps even more damaging to the war effort, from 1945 to 1954, French forces in Vietnam had eight different commanders in chief.[75]

DIEN BIEN PHU

Fairly or not, the siege and fall of the French fortress complex at Dien Bien Phu has long been emblematic of the entire conflict, and probably always will be.

By the end of 1953, the war had become a stalemate: the Viet Minh could not expel the French, and the CEF and its VNA allies could not suppress the Viet Minh. The French Command hoped to break the stalemate by providing General Giap an irresistible temptation to abandon guerrilla tactics and fight a conventional battle. They thus established a large garrison in a fortress complex at a place called Dien Bien Phu, close to the border of Laos and far from the center of French power. The French hoped that taking this bait, the Viet Minh commander would commit his best conventional units to attacking Dien Bien Phu, which units would of course be immediately and thoroughly chewed up by superior French competence and firepower.[76] After the battle ended, General Navarre, who was CEF commander in Vietnam at the time, testified that "we were absolutely convinced of our superiority in defensive positions; this was considered in Indochina as a dogma. . . ."[77] Other French "dogmas" maintained that the Viet Minh had little or no artillery in the general vicinity of Dien Bien Phu, and even if they had, they would find it impossible to supply their guns with sufficient shells. Accordingly, by aircraft and parachute the French Command inserted a force of 16,000 soldiers into Dien Bien Phu.

But why did General Giap accept this invitation to battle? A senior Hungarian (Communist) diplomat reported this conversation with Giap: "The battle of Dien Bien Phu, he told us, was the last desperate bid of the Viet Minh army. Its forces were on the verge of complete exhaustion. The supply of rice was running out. Apathy had spread among the populace to such an extent that it was difficult to draft new fighters. Years of jungle warfare had sent morale in the fighting units plunging to the depths."[78] And during the battle at Dien Bien Phu itself, heavy casualties, unreliable medical care, and inadequate food would further undermine Viet Minh morale.[79]

The siege of Dien Bien Phu opened on March 13, 1954—with a tremendous Viet Minh artillery bombardment. Its defenders understood immediately that they were in an almost certainly fatal trap.

At Dien Bien Phu the French had built an airstrip where supplies could be landed and by means of which the wounded could be evacuated. Quite predictably, from the first hour of the siege, Viet Minh artillery made the airstrip too dangerous to use. Thus, the only way to get even the most urgent supplies to the defenders of the fortress was by parachute—"the most ineffective delivery method in modern war."[80] The troops inside Dien Bien Phu needed a minimum of 200 tons of supplies per day. French aircraft could drop only 120 tons per day. Of those, the CEF could recover only about 100 tons, because the rest fell (literally) into the hands of the besieging forces.[81] French planes mistakenly dropped thousands of artillery shells into the Viet Minh lines. Bernard Fall wrote that "in the final days of the battle the Vietminh would have run out of [their] own 105mm ammunition [artillery shells] had it not been for the French misdrops."[82]

The battle of Dien Bien Phu, during which 16,000 CEF soldiers were under siege by 100,000 Viet Minh troops, lasted 56 days. The last strongpoint in Dien Bien Phu was overrun on May 8, 1954, the ninth anniversary of VE Day. In his final radio message to Hanoi, Dien Bien Phu's commander, Brigadier General Christian de Castries, said: "In five minutes everything will be blown up here. The Viets are only a few metres away. Good luck to everybody."[83]

In the eyes of the French military, at least, it had been the four-to-one artillery advantage enjoyed by the Viet Minh that defeated the defenders of Dien Bien Phu. Moreover, the artillery and antiaircraft capability of the Viet Minh during the battle was, in General Navarre's rather tame observation, "the principal surprise of the battle."[84] The explanation of General Ely, the last French commander in Hanoi, is notably similar: "The failure at Dien Bien Phu was due to the fact that this isolated base was attacked by an enemy with artillery and antiaircraft."[85]

In the later days of the battle, the French High Command in Hanoi had decided that an attempt to rescue Dien Bien Phu by means of troops on the ground would have been too dangerous. Had the French been able, however, to mount massive and sustained air attacks on the Viet Minh around Dien Bien Phu, and to deliver sufficient supplies to its defenders, it is as close to a certainty as such matters can ever be that the whole enterprise would have been saved, just as the U.S. Marines and South Vietnamese soldiers defending Khe Sanh would be saved in the same manner years later. But the air power available to the CEF was completely inadequate to such an operation. One serious obstacle was the weather: during the rainy season, conditions over northwestern Vietnam frequently made flying the aircraft of 1954 dangerous and sometimes impossible. In addition, the most up-to-date French planes were too big and too fast for the airfields in Vietnam, and the older types were too few. In effect, therefore, the French had air supremacy over all Indochina, but only in the sense that the Viet Minh had no air force of their own; in actual fact their control of the skies was hardly more than nominal. They never had many more than 100 modern aircraft (C-47s and C-119s) at any one time, and did not have those until 1952. And as late as 1954, the CEF possessed exactly 10 helicopters.[86] By 1953 Chinese anti-aircraft was knocking many of those planes out of the skies. And according to reliable testimony, the Viet Minh anti-aircraft fire over Dien Bien Phu proved to be more murderous than that over Nazi Germany during World War II.[87] Many of the Viet Minh anti-aircraft units had Chinese advisers with them.[88] Besides, the besiegers liked to operate at night; and "in view of the French mastery of the air, the Viet Minh made a veritable fetish out of camouflage."[89]

The defenders of Dien Bien Phu represented less than 5 percent of French and allied forces in Indochina, while Giap committed nearly 50 percent of his available combat forces to the siege.[90] By the end of the battle, 7,200 CEF troops had been killed, as compared to 20,000 Viet Minh.[91] Of the CEF troops in Dien Bien Phu, 36.3 percent were Vietnamese, 18.6 percemt were French. The rest were Foreign Legionnaires (26 percent), North Africans (17.5 percent) and West Africans (1.6 percent).[92] Many hundreds of CEF prisoners would die in captivity or be "unaccounted for"; most of the latter were Vietnamese.

The battle of Dien Bien Phu was in some ways like the Battle of Yorktown: decisive psychologically, not strategically. But however relatively small the battle was in the grand scheme of the war, the fall of Dien Bien Phu tipped the political balance inside the French National Assembly against continuing the conflict. On June 19, 1954, in Paris, Pierre Mendès-France became prime minister on the pledge that he would end the fighting in Vietnam within 30 days, or resign. Within a few months French forces would evacuate the northern half of Vietnam.

SOME COSTS OF THE WAR

The price of the war in terms of the lives of Frenchmen and their Vietnamese allies was very high. The CEF lost 92,000 killed, missing, and unaccounted-for prisoners. Of these, 40,000 (43.4 percent of the total) were Vietnamese.[93] In Bao Dai's Vietnamese National Army, total casualties may have reached 45,000. During 1952 alone, 1,860 soldiers from France were killed or missing, compared to 4,049 Legionnaires and North Africans, and no less than 7,730 Vietnamese in the CEF and the NVA; Vietnamese comprised 57 percent of total allied killed and missing for that year.[94] In all, over 14,000 Vietnamese CEF/VNA prisoners of war remained unaccounted for, equal to 63 percent of all unaccounted-for allied prisoners, and 91 percent of all Vietnamese prisoners.[95] Since the Viet Minh treated all Vietnamese in allied units as traitors, it is highly probable that all those missing prisoners were killed during or after the war.

The number of French soldiers lost in Vietnam would equal over 140,000 Americans in 2015, three times the number of battle fatalities the Americans suffered during their own later involvement in Vietnam. Relative to its population, France lost well over twice as many soldiers in Vietnam as the U.S. did in Korea. In particular, the French officer corps suffered severely: 1,300 lieutenants, four generals, and twenty-one sons of generals or marshals were lost, including Lieutenant Bernard de Lattre, son of the famous World War II military hero and one-time commander in Vietnam.[96] By 1953, more French officers were dying in Vietnam than were being graduated from the national military academy at St. Cyr.[97] Of the more than two thousand women who served with the French forces in Vietnam, one hundred and fifty were killed.[98] In summary, "The numbers suggest that the French troops fought hard in Indochina."[99]

The number of Viet Minh who died in combat will never be known, in part because great efforts were made to remove the dead and wounded from the battlefield in order to thwart French intelligence. Estimates of those dead run from 250,000 to 400,000.

As to innocent civilians, the death toll can only be estimated. It may well have been close to two million.[100] The fundamental cause of these deaths was the insistence on the part of Ho Chi Minh and his Communist Party that an independent Vietnam had to be under their totalitarian control, no matter what the cost.

THE GENEVA AGREEMENTS

For many years Hanoi propaganda insisted that the American involvement in the Vietnam conflict was rooted in Ngo Dinh Diem's refusal to let the people of South Vietnam participate in an honest election on the future of their country as required by the "agreements" at Geneva. This view achieved a great public relations victory for the Communist side in the United States of the 1960s and is widely repeated even today. But such an understanding of the outcome of Geneva is entirely, profoundly false. What is the actual story of the Geneva Agreements?

In the spring of 1954, a conference including representatives from the UK, France, the USSR and China, with a Viet Minh delegation under Chinese "sponsorship," convened in Geneva. French military commanders and the Viet Minh signed the so-called Geneva Agreements, which partitioned Vietnam into a Communist north and a non-Communist south roughly along the seventeenth parallel. The U.S. government silently acquiesced in this action as the least objectionable option in a bad situation.

At the time of Geneva, more than thirty countries, including France, the U.S. and the UK, recognized the government of Bao Dai as the legitimate government of *all of Vietnam.* Bao Dai and his prime minister Ngo Dinh Diem declared, unremarkably, that France had no right to give away any part of Vietnam to anybody. Thus the Bao Dai government could not agree to elections to "reunify" Vietnam since in its view that country had not been lawfully divided. Concerning the actions of the French at Geneva, Arthur J. Dommen's magisterial study of the war asks, "Who had ever heard of the commander [Ely] of an allied [French] army in time of war authorizing the signing of an armistice agreement—much less one that gave away half an ally's territory to the enemy—without so much as consulting the ally? No one, because it had never been done before."[101]

Only representatives of the French army and the Viet Minh—no one from Bao Dai's government or the United States or anybody else at all—signed the Geneva agreement to end the fighting. As to the so-called "Final Declaration," the locus of the famous call for "free general elections" to be held by 1956 at the latest to settle the future of Vietnam, the English text of the

Geneva Agreements has less than one hundred and fifty words regarding such elections, and says nothing at all about the manner of conducting them: who could vote, in what places and under whose supervision, and who would count these votes, among other absolutely essential questions. And no one at all—*nobody*—signed this "Final Declaration."[102]

Therefore, it is really difficult to understand why it should have come as a surprise to anyone when Ngo Dinh Diem, who had been constitutionally appointed by Bao Dai as prime minister of the State of Vietnam, rejected from the outset these Geneva "agreements" to which he and his government were vehemently opposed, and when he especially and unmistakably rejected the idea of holding elections regarding the question of unification of the two Vietnamese jurisdictions. He and his supporters in Saigon, as well as prominent political figures in Washington, dismissed out of hand the idea that there could be a free election in a North Vietnam under a Communist regime. To say the least, a great deal of real-life experience undergirded this position. Many, many years of "elections" in Communist countries gave the Bao Dai government every reason to expect that the Communist rulers in Hanoi would proclaim that at least 98 percent of the vote in their section of Vietnam had been cast in favor of "reunification." North Vietnam had a considerably larger population than the South. Even, therefore, if a clear, a quite substantial, majority of southern voters should reject unification under the Viet Minh—and this was a completely predictable outcome in light of all the groups in the south that had opposed the Viet Minh, including the Cao Dai, the Hoa Hao, members and veterans of the CEF and the VNA and their families, Catholics, non-Communist nationalists, the Saigon middle class, the substantial Chinese and other ethnic minorities, and, not least, nearly one million refugees from the Communist North—even then, the millions of Vietnamese in the south would be consigned against their will to the rule of the northern Stalinist party-state, with its long memory and its taste for vengeance.

But in addition, according to the authors of the *Pentagon Papers,* erecting two geographical jurisdictions in Vietnam made reunification elections exceedingly improbable.[103] Many scholarly authorities agreed with that view.[104] And Robert F. Randle observes that in light of "the very profound ambiguities in the relevant Geneva documents" and the "ambiguities and incompleteness of the final declaration, it does no justice to the complexities of the Vietnamese situation, either in fact or in legal theory, to speak glibly of 'violations' of the 'Geneva Accords.'"[105]

The world at large agreed with that assessment. The Eisenhower Administration, which had signed absolutely nothing at Geneva, supported Diem's position, in which stance it enjoyed bipartisan backing: for example, the junior senator from Massachusetts, John F. Kennedy, who would become the next President of the United States, declared that "neither the United States nor Free [South] Vietnam is ever going to be a party to an election obviously stacked and subverted in advance."[106] Significantly, after the partition France continued its diplomatic relations with the Diem government but did not fully recognize the regime in Hanoi until 1973. When the member states of the Colombo Plan (then including Australia, Canada, Ceylon, India, New Zealand, and Pakistan) had to choose the site of their 1957 conference, they selected President Diem's Saigon. And what of the Communist Powers? The last possible day to schedule any North-South elections passed in the summer of 1956. The Soviet bloc reacted to this milestone with notable insouciance. The USSR, in fact, soon thereafter proposed that the United Nations admit to membership *both* North and South Vietnam. Apparently the wide world (except for some American professors) knew that attacks upon Diem and the South Vietnamese government because of their refusal to hold the "free elections" that had been "agreed upon" at Geneva were nothing but Communist propaganda, of which even the Communists had soon grown tired.

NOTES

1. George Kelly, *Lost Soldiers: The French Army and Empire in Crisis* (Cambridge, MA: The MIT Press, 1965), p. 63. "To many Frenchmen it seemed that if France did not stand firm in one part of the empire, she might lose it all"; Ellen J. Hammer, *The Struggle for Indochina 1940–1955* (Stanford, CA: Stanford University Press, 1966), p. 209. See John Cady, *The Roots of French Imperialism in Eastern Asia* (Ithaca, NY: Cornell University Press, 1954).

2. The resolution of the Algerian question would tear the Fourth Republic, and its army, to pieces.

3. Cady, *Roots of French Imperialism,* pp. 294–295.

4. Bernard Fall, *Street without Joy* (Mechanicsburg, PA: Stackpole, 1994 [orig. 1961]), p. 16.

5. Dennis J. Duncanson, *Government and Revolution in Vietnam* (New York: Oxford University Press, 1968), p. 140.

6. Comintern: short for The Communist International, a Moscow-based organization for providing guidance to and discipline over Communist parties outside the Soviet Union. Succeeded in 1947 by the Cominform (Communist Information Bureau).

7. For background on Ho and his party, see Ho Chi Minh, "The Path Which Led Me to Leninism," in *On Revolution,* by Ho Chi Minh, ed. Bernard Fall (New York: Praeger, 1967); William Duiker, *The Communist Road to Power in Vietnam* (Boulder, CO: Westview, 1981); Duncanson, *Government and Revolution;* Bui Tin, *Following Ho Chi Minh: Memoirs of a North Vietnamese Colonel* (Honolulu, HI: University of Hawaii Press, 1995).

8. Joseph Buttinger, *Vietnam: A Dragon Embattled,* vol. 1, *From Colonialism to the Viet Minh* (New York: Praeger, 1967), p. 379.

9. Buttinger, *Dragon Embattled,* vol. 1, p. 399.

10. George Modelski, "The Viet Minh Complex," in *Communism and Revolution: The Strategic Uses of Political Violence,* ed. Cyril Black and Thomas P. Thornton (Princeton, NJ: Princeton University Press, 1964), p. 202.

11. Martin Windrow, *The Last Valley: Dien Bien Phu and the French Defeat in Vietnam* (Cambridge, MA: Da Capo, 2004), p. 188. General Navarre wrote that 300,000 Vietnamese were fighting against the Viet Minh and 400,000 for it; Navarre, *Agonie de l'Indochine* (Paris: Plon, 1956), p. 46. General Navarre was very ungenerous in his remarks about the quality of the VNA, most of whose principal deficiencies were the fault of the French themselves.

12. "The Vietnamese civil war and the East-West conflict were merely suspended"; Ives Gras, *Histoire de la Guerre d'Indochine* (Paris: Denoel, 1992), p. 583.

13. Buttinger, *Dragon Embattled*, vol. 1, p. 408; see David G. Marr, *Vietnam 1945: The Quest for Power* (Berkeley, CA: University of California Press, 1995), p. 519.

14. Dommen, *The Indochinese Experience*, p. 154.

15. Modelski, "Complex," p. 210. Compare Simon Schama describing "a central truth of the French Revolution: its dependence on organized killing to accomplish political ends"; *Citizens: A Chronicle of the French Revolution* (New York: Alfred Knopf, 1989), p. 637.

16. Buttinger, *Dragon Embattled*, vol. 1, p. 435.

17. The Trotskyists had been winning 80 percent of the vote in Cochinchinese elections before the Pacific War.

18. Duiker, *Communist Road*, p. 152.

19. On the Cao Dai, see Jayne Susan Werner, *Peasant Politics and Religious Sectarianism: Peasant and Priest in the Cao Dai in Vietnam* (New Haven, CT: Yale Southeast Asian Studies, 1981); on the Hoa Hao, see Hue Tam Ho Tai, *Millenarianism and Peasant Politics in Vietnam* (Cambridge, MA: Harvard University Press, 1983).

20. Donald Lancaster, *The Emancipation of French Indochina* (London: Oxford University Press, 1961), pp. 136–137.

21. Bernard Fall, *The Two Vietnams: A Political and Military Analysis.* 2d ed. revised (New York: Praeger, 1967), p. 101.

22. Buttinger, *Dragon Embattled*, vol. 1, p. 410; for French negotiations with the Hoa Hao and also the Binh Xuyen, see Dommen, *Indochinese Experience*, pp. 194–195, and Gilbert Bodinier, ed., *La Guerre d'Indochine, 1945–1954: Le retour de la France en Indochine. Textes et documents* (Vincennes: Service historique de l'Armée de Terre, 1987), vol. 2, pp. 463–467.

23. Bao Dai has not been treated well by history, but Douglas Pike called him "an underrated man" in his *Viet Cong: The Organization and Techniques of the National Liberation Front of South Vietnam* (Cambridge, MA: MIT Press, 1967), p. 48. For other positive evaluations of Bao Dai, see Lancaster, *Emancipation,* p. 182, and Dommen, *Indochinese Experience,* p. 184. See also Bao Dai's instructive autobiography, *Le Dragon d'Annam* (Paris: Plon, 1980).

24. Hammer, *Struggle*, p. 321; see the full list of states in Dommen, *Indochinese Experience*, p. 1036n.

25. Hammer, *Struggle,* p. 287. By the beginning of 1954, the Vietnamese National Army counted 200,000, with another 50,000 special contract soldiers; close to 80,000 belonged to local militia and police forces; an additional 100,000 Vietnamese were in the French forces. *FRUS, 1952–1954*, vol. 25, part 1, p. 908.

26. Michael Carver, *War Since 1945* (New York: Putnam, 1981), p. 112.

27. Lancaster, *Emancipation*, p. 196. Bernard Fall, *The Viet Minh Regime: Government and Administration in the Democratic Republic of Vietnam* (New York: Institute of Pacific Relations, 1956), pp. 69–72.

28. Lancaster, *Emancipation*, p. 196.

29. See Bui Diem, *In the Jaws of History* (Boston: Houghton Mifflin, 1987). Lancaster writes that "many who had been inspired to join the Viet Minh were now dismayed to discover that their desire for national independence was being exploited in order to impose upon the country an alien Communist regime, which was likely to prove more destructive of the national heritage than had been the case with the short-lived French protectorate"; Lancaster, *Emancipation*, p. 175.

30. Duncanson, *Government and Revolution*, p. 189; Bodinier, *La guerre d'Indochine*, vol. 2, pp. 463–66.

31. John T. McAlister, *Vietnam: The Origins of Revolution* (Garden City, NY: Doubleday Anchor, 1971), p. 281; and see Henri Navarre, *Agonie de l'Indochine* (Paris: Plon, 1956), p. 46.

32. On this very important question, see the groundbreaking essay by Andrew Mack, "Why Big Nations Lose Small Wars: The Politics of Asymmetric Conflict," *World Politics*, vol. 27 (1975); but see also Jeffrey Record, *Beating Goliath: Why Insurgencies Win* (Washington, D.C.: Potomac Books, 2007), a slender volume bristling with provocative insights. Other studies of this particular subject are Ivan Arreguin-Toft, *How the Weak Win Wars: A Theory of Asymmetric Conflict* (New York: Cambridge University Press, 2005), and Gil Merom, *How*

Democracies Lose Small Wars: State, Society, and the Failures of France in Algeria, Israel in Lebanon, and the United States in Vietnam (New York: Cambridge University Press, 2003); both of these last two studies are erudite and vigorous, but offer very controversial conclusions.

33. Bard O'Neill, *Insurgency and Terrorism: From Revolution to Apocalypse* (Washington, DC: Potomac, 2005), p. 111.

34. Jeffrey Record, "External Assistance: Enabler of Insurgent Success," *Parameters* 36 (Autumn 2006).

35. Peter M. Dunn, *The First Vietnam War* (New York: St. Martin's, 1985), p. 67.

36. Duncanson, *Government and Revolution*, p. 155.

37. Lancaster, *Emancipation*, p. 116.

38. The provinces of Cao Bang, Ha Giang, Tuyen Quang, Bac Kan, Tai Nguyen, Bac Giang and Lang Son.

39. Modelski, "Viet Minh Complex," pp. 194 and 208.

40. Fall, *Two Viet-Nams*, p. 65; see also Joyce Lebra, *Japanese-Trained Armies in Southeast Asia* (New York: Columbia University Press, 1977), and Edgar O'Ballance, *Indo-China War*, p. 55.

41. O'Ballance, *Indo-China War*, p. 56; McAlister, *Vietnam*, p. 233.

42. Lancaster, *Emancipation*, p. 88.

43. Dunn, *First Vietnam War*, p. 112.

44. Charles de Gaulle, *The War Memoirs*, vol. 3, *Salvation,* trans. Richard Howard (New York: Simon and Schuster, 1960), p. 260. In the same volume, de Gaulle writes of "the hostility of the Allies—particularly the Americans—in regard to our Far Eastern position," p. 187.

45. Windrow, *The Last Valley*, p. 84.

46. Gras, *Histoire de la guerre*, p. 354.

47. Lancaster, *Emancipation*, p. 218.

48. Fall, *Street Without Joy*, p. 30.

49. Fall, *Two Vietnams*, p. 111.

50. During the war China supplied scores of thousands of rifles along with great quantities of mortars and machine guns. See, among others, Gras, *Histoire de la guerre*, p. 315. Dean Rusk reported that 30,000 Viet Minh were training in China; *FRUS,* 1950 vol. 6, p. 878.

51. Dwight D. Eisenhower, *The White House Years: Mandate for Change, 1953–1956* (Garden City, NY: Doubleday, 1963), p. 338.

52. O'Ballance, *Indo-China War*, p. 162.

53. O'Ballance, *Indo-China War*, p. 262.

54. Chen Jian, "China and the First Indochina War, 1950–1954," *China Quarterly*, no. 133 (March 1993).

55. Chen Jian, "China's Involvement in the Vietnam War, 1964–1969," *China Quarterly*, no. 142 (June 1995), p. 380.

56. Windrow, *Last Valley*, p. 157.

57. Duncanson, *Government and Revolution*, p. 177.

58. Fall, *Two Viet-Nams*, p. 108.

59. Phillip B. Davidson, *Vietnam at War: The History, 1946–1975* (Novato, CA: Presidio, 1988), pp. 35–36; see also pp. 59–60, and 71.

60. Chen Jian, "China and the Vietnam Wars," in *The Vietnam War*, ed. Peter Lowe (New York: St. Martins, 1998), p. 158. See also Chen Jian, "China and the First Indochina War, 1950–1954," *China Quarterly*, no. 133 (1993), and Qiang Zhai, *China and the Vietnam Wars, 1950–1975* (Chapel Hill, NC: University of North Carolina Press, 2000).

61. John Pimlott, "Ho Chi Minh's Triumph," in Ashley Brown and Sam Elder, eds., *War in Peace* (London: Orbis, 1981), p. 67. O'Ballance presents similar figures; *Indo-China War*, p. 174. These figures approximate those presented in Navarre, *Agonie,* p. 22. The French relied heavily on their Vietnamese troops, who were not at all difficult to recruit; David W. P. Elliott, *The Vietnamese War: Revolution and Social Change in the Mekong Delta, 1930–1975,* vol. 1, (Armonk, NY: M.E. Sharpe, 2003), pp. 133 and 147.

62. Hammer, *Struggle*, p. 287. O'Ballance gives a figure of only 100,000 actually participating in the VNA, but this number is uniquely low; *The Indo-China War*, pp. 195–96.

63. Robert Thompson, *No Exit from Vietnam* (New York: David McKay, 1969), p. 53; Andrew Krepinevich, Jr., *The Army and Vietnam* (Baltimore, MD: Johns Hopkins University Press, 1986), p. 197.

64. Windrow, *Last Valley*, p. 198.

65. Fall, *Street without Joy*, p. 242.

66. Davidson, *Vietnam at War*, p. 49; George K. Tanham, *Communist Revolutionary Warfare: From the Viet Minh to the Viet Cong* (New York: Praeger, 1967), p. 9; Lucien Bodard, *The Quicksand War: Prelude to Vietnam* (Boston: Little, Brown, 1967), p. 13.

67. Windrow, *Last Valley*, p. 179.

68. "We know of no example in military history of a soldier who went into battle with all the means he thought he needed. The great military leader is the one who knows how to win with the means at his disposal"; Roger Trinquier, *Modern Warfare: A French View of Counterinsurgency* (Westport, CT: Praeger, 2006), p. 74.

69. Jacques Dinfreville, *L'opération Indochine* (Paris: Editions internationales, 1953), quoted in Kelly, *Lost Soldiers*, p. 33n. Leclerc had never believed in the possibility of a strictly military French reconquest of all of Vietnam; see Adrien Dansette, *Leclerc* (Paris: Flammarion, 1952).

70. See Davidson, *Vietnam at War*, p. 275.

71. Davidson, *Vietnam at War*, p. 172. "The supercilious rejection by the [French] general staff of unpopular facts reported to them by the fighting men in the field was to remain a constant factor in the Vietnamese situation"; Bernard Fall, *Hell in a Very Small Place* (Philadelphia, PA: Lippincott, 1967), p. 50.

72. Kelly, *Lost Soldiers*, p. 89.

73. Lancaster, *Emancipation*, p. 267; Fall, *Street without Joy*, p. 257.

74. For disunity, lack of direction, and domination of foreign policy by domestic and tactical-electoral concerns, see Philip M. Williams, *Crisis and Compromise: Politics in the Fourth Republic* (London: Longmans, 1964*)*.

75. The following are French sources that have been useful, and sometimes provocative: Michel Bodin, *La France et ses soldats: Indochine, 1945–1954*, vol. 1, *Le retour de la France en Indochine 1945–1946* (Vincennes, France: Service Historique de l'Armée de Terre, 1987); Gilbert Bodinier, ed., *La Guerre d'Indochine, 1945–1954: Le retour de la France en Indochine: Textes et documents* (Vincennes, France: Service historique de l'Armée de Terre, 1987); Pierre Boyer de La Tour, *Le martyre de l'armée française: De l'Indochine à l'Algérie* (Paris: Presses du Mail, 1962); Pierre Carles, *Des Millions De Soldats Inconnus: La Vie De Tous Les Jours Dans Les armées de la IVeme république* (Paris: Lavauzelle, 1982); Jacques Dalloz, *La guerre d'Indochine 1945–1954* (Paris: Editions de Seuil, 1987); Jacques Dinfreville, *L'Opération Indochine* (Paris: Editions Internationales, 1953); Cristopher E. Goscha, "'La guerre par d'autres moyens': Réflexions sur la guerre du Viet Minh dans le Sud-Vietnam de 1945 à 1951" in *Guerres Mondiales et Conflits Contemporains*, n. 206 (2000); Christopher E. Goscha, *Vietnam: Un état né de la guerre, 1945–1954* (Paris: Armand Colin, 2011); Daniel Grandclement, *Bao Dai ou les derniers jours de l'empire d'Annam* (Paris: Lattes, 1997); Ives Gras, *Histoire de la Guerra d'Indochine* (Paris: Denoel, 1992); Joseph Laniel, *Le drame Indochinois* (Paris: Plon, 1957); Jose Maigre, "Le general Nguyen Van Hinh et la création de l'armée vietnamienne," *Revue historique des armées*, no. 194 (January 1994); Henri Marc and Pierre Cony, *Indochine français* (Paris: Editions France-Empire, 1946); Jean Marchand, *L'Indochine en guerre* (Paris: Pouzet, 1955); Paul Mus, *Viet-Nam: Sociologie d'une guerre* (Paris: Editions du Seuil, 1952); Guy Pedroncini and Philippe Duplay, eds., *Leclerc et l'Indochine 1945–1947* (Paris: Albin Michel, 1992); Pierre Pellissier, *Dien Bien Phu* (Paris: Perrin, 2004); Charles-Henri de Pirey, *La Route Morte: RC41950* (Paris: Indo Éditions, 2002); Jean Pouget, *Nous étions à Dien Bien Phu* (Paris: Presses de la Cité, 1964); Pierre Rocolle, *Pourquoi Dien Bien Phu?* (Paris: Flammarion, 1968); Jean Sainteny, *Histoire d'une paix manqué: Indochine, 1945–1947* (Paris: Amiot-Dumont, 1953); Raoul Salan, *Mémoires: Fin d'un empire, vol. 2: Le Viet-minh mon adversaire* (Paris: Presses de la Cité, 1971); Frédéric Turpin, *De Gaulle, les gaullistes et l'Indochine 1940–1956* (Paris: Les Indes savantes, 2005).

76. Later, General Navarre defended the idea of viewing Dien Bien Phu as a means of protecting Laos from invasion by Giap's forces, and stated that he did not envision a battle to "smash" the Viet Minh; Navarre, *Agonie,* pp. 199–200. See also Pierre Rocolle, *Pourquoi Dien Bien Phu?* (Paris: Flammarion, 1968).

77. Windrow, *Last Valley,* p. 222.

78. Janos Radvanyi, *Delusions and Reality: Gambits, Hoaxes and Diplomatic One-upmanship in Vietnam* (South Bend, IN: Gateway, 1978), p. 8.

79. Fall, *Hell in a Very Small Place,* pp. 237–238.

80. Davidson, *Vietnam at War,* p. 237.

81. Davidson, *Vietnam at War,* p. 219. Quite aside from the crucial problem of supplying the soldiers inside Dien Bien Phu with tolerably sufficient *quantities* of food was the question of *kinds* of food. The defenders of Dien Bien Phu came from many nations and cultures. Six different types of food rations were required: European, North African, West African, Vietnamese, T'ai, and "prisoners of war." Muslims of course could not eat the standard canned pork of the French (actually, of the Americans); Europeans could not subsist mainly on rice for very long, but all the Vietnamese wanted rice with every meal. And of course French aircraft parachuted 50,000 gallons of wine and 7,000 gallons of "wine concentrate" into the besieged fortress.

82. Fall, *Hell in a Very Small Place,* p. 473n.

83. Windrow, *Last Valley,* p. 616.

84. Navarre, *Agonie,* 218–219.

85. Paul Ely, *Lessons of the War in Indochina* (Santa Monica, CA: RAND, 1967), vol. 2, p. 154.

86. Fall, *Street without Joy,* p. 242.

87. Fall, *Hell in a Very Small Place,* p. 237.

88. Fall, *Hell in a Very Small Place,* p. 266. The Chinese provided one hundred artillery pieces, 60,000 shells, and 2.4 million rounds of ammunition for the battle at Dien Bien Phu; Chen Jian, "China and the First Indochina War," 1950–1954," *China Quarterly,* no. 133 (March 1993). Further, from 1956 to 1963, Chinese aid to North Vietnam included ten thousand artillery pieces and 28 naval vessels. Chinese antiaircraft troops defended important sites in the North. A total of 320,000 Chinese engineers and other troops served in North Vietnam. "Without that support, the history, even the outcome, of the Vietnam war might have been different"; Chen Jian, "China's Involvement in the Vietnam War, 1964–1969," *China Quarterly,* no. 142 (June 1995), quotation on p. 380.

89. Fall, *Street without Joy,* p. 65.

90. Fall, *Hell in a Very Small Place,* p. 225.

91. Pimlott, "Ho Chi Minh's Triumph," p. 77.

92. Windrow, *Last Valley,* p. 647; O'Ballance, *Indo-China War,* p. 237. And see figures in Fall, *Hell in a Very Small Place,* p. 481.

93. Windrow, *Last Valley,* p. 694n. Numbers of course vary. O'Ballance wrote that 23,000 Vietnamese in CEF units were never accounted for; *Indo-China War,* p. 249. See Fall, *Street without Joy;* Thomas C. Thayer, *War without Fronts: The American Experience in Vietnam* (Boulder, CO: Westview, 1985), p. 9; Pike, *Viet Cong,* p. 49n. See also Anthony Clayton, *The Wars of French Decolonization* (New York: Longmans, 1994).

94. Lancaster, *Emancipation,* pp. 281 and 251n.

95. Windrow, *Last Valley,* p. 648.

96. Fall, *Street without Joy,* p. 45.

97. National Intelligence Estimate, December 29, 1950, in *FRUS,* 1950, v. 6, p. 959.

98. Fall, *Street without Joy,* p. 136.

99. Thayer, *War without Fronts,* p. 9.

100. See *Agence France Press,* April 3, 1995. "The war had cost the French Expeditionary Corps 59,745 dead and missing in action, of which 26,923 were [Vietnamese] serving in the Corps. The Vietnamese National Army had lost 58,877 dead and missing in action. But the main casualties had been the civilians . . . of which an estimated 100,000 to 150,000 *had been assassinated by the Viet Minh*"; Dommen, *Indochinese Experience,* p. 252, my emphasis.

101. Dommen, *Indochinese Experience,* p. 248.

102. See the relevant Geneva documents in Robert F. Randle, *Geneva 1954: The Settlement of the Indochinese War* (Princeton, NJ: Princeton University Press, 1969), pp. 569–607, and in Robert F. Turner, *Vietnamese Communism: Its Origins and Development* (Stanford, CA: Hoover Institution Press, 1975), pp. 365–381.

103. *Pentagon Papers*, vol. 1, pp. 161–166.

104. See Victor Bator, *Vietnam: A Diplomatic Tragedy: The Origins of U.S. Involvement* (London: Faber and Faber, 1965); McAlister, *Vietnam*, esp. pp. 325–326; R. B. Smith, *An International History of the Vietnam War*, vol. 1, *Revolution versus Containment, 1955–1961* (New York: St. Martin's, 1983), esp. pp. 20, 30; and Buttinger, *Vietnam at War*, p. 843.

105. Randle, *Geneva 1954*, pp. 444–445.

106. Wesley Fishel, ed., *Vietnam: Anatomy of a Conflict* (Itasca, IL: Peacock, 1968), p. 147; *Pentagon Papers*, vol. 1, p. 245.

Chapter Two

The Coming of Ngo Dinh Diem

Although only dimly remembered today, for over a decade the most notable Vietnamese figure in the struggle to avoid a complete Communist takeover of Vietnam was Ngo Dinh Diem. Who was he?

William Duiker, a distinguished American student of Vietnam, has written that "Ho Chi Minh recognized [Diem] as a formidable opponent who possessed a substantial constituency of fervent supporters in the RVN [Republic of Vietnam, i.e., South Vietnam]."[1] For the noted French authority on Vietnamese affairs Paul Mus, "only one man could ever hope to challenge Ho Chi Minh for leadership—Ngo Dinh Diem. Because he alone had the same reputation for virtue and austerity as Ho."[2] To Joseph Buttinger, Diem "was the only outstanding leader in the anti-communist camp."[3] That same author later wrote:

> Ngo Dinh Diem was the leader whose record and talents made him most fit for the task of building a new state out of chaos before anti-Communist nationalism completely expired. His untainted integrity, his tenacious refusal to compromise with colonialism, and his profound insight into the political nature of his enemies was topped only by the courage he displayed toward friend and foe in creating the truly independent and strictly unified administration that his country needed then more than food and arms.[4]

Moreover, Arthur J. Dommen, one of the premier English-language students of the Vietnam conflicts, wrote that "in the testimony of defectors from the [Communist] Viet Minh, Diem ranked as the only nationalist Vietnamese the Communists were worried about."[5] Some have caricatured Diem as an outdated mandarin, but a powerful case can be made that not only was he a leader of austerity, intellect, and rectitude, but in fact a forward-looking, nationalistic, conservative modernizer.

But this Diem, the constitutional leader of the Republic of Vietnam and recognized as such by literally dozens of countries, became the victim of betrayal and assassination in which the United States government and the American media played key roles. Years later, CIA Director William Colby identified U.S. complicity in the killing of President Diem as America's first great mistake in Vietnam. Many agree with him.[6] One very recent study suggests that "in the historiography of the Viet Nam War, no figure is more desperately in need of revision than Ngo Dinh Diem."[7] Another work wisely urges us "to analyze the Diem regime on its own terms and in the context of modern Vietnamese history, not just the history of U.S. foreign relations."[8] In this and the subsequent chapter, we will at least attempt to accomplish such an analysis.

Diem was born in 1901 in the old capital city of Hue. The son of a mandarin who held a high position in the Imperial court at Hue, he was a Christian like his fellow Asian nationalists Chiang Kai-shek of China and Syngman Rhee of Korea, and indeed a member of one of the oldest Roman Catholic families in Vietnam. Having accepted Catholicism centuries before, the Ngo family had because of this to endure persecution and even execution for generations, a legacy of stubborn resistance that deeply influenced Diem.

Declining a scholarship to study in Paris, Diem instead attended the French-run School of Law in Hanoi, from which he graduated first in his class.[9] Convinced that an independent Vietnam would need trained administrators, Diem decided to enter the governmental structure. Consequently, in 1925 Emperor Bao Dai appointed him, at a remarkably young age, to be governor of Bin Thuan province (northeast of Saigon), and in 1933 made him minister of the interior (an office held previously by a relative of Diem). Diem's responsibilities included carrying out certain administrative reforms Bao Dai had promised the previous year. Diem got into trouble with the French colonialists from the start, because he asserted that Vietnam needed and deserved some real powers of self-government. In later years he would insist that the Communists could be fought successfully only through a program of social reform and convincing steps toward substantial Vietnamese independence.

Diem's nationalism so antagonized the French that he had to resign. As one authority has written, "His earlier government career had stamped him as an able administrator, his resignation in 1933 gave him credentials as a principled nationalist, and his subsequent behavior emphasized that he was a man who would not compromise his principles for political gain."[10] He preserved this reputation for rectitude even during the Japanese occupation, when many other Vietnamese nationalists drank from the poisoned cup of collaboration with the conquerors of the French. In March 1945, immediately after they had taken over complete control of Vietnam, the Japanese (and others) advised Bao Dai to offer the premiership to Diem, which he did not once but twice.[11] Suspicious of the true motives of the Japanese, and skeptical of their ability to withstand the Americans, Diem made no reply.

Ho Chi Minh also recognized Diem's prestige as a highminded nationalist. At a meeting at Ho's headquarters in February 1946, Ho offered Diem the post of minister of the interior in his new revolutionary Viet Minh government.[12] Diem, however, was deeply mistrustful of the Viet Minh's real aims; besides, the Communists had murdered one of his brothers in 1945. The two men could reach no understanding and Ho allowed Diem to depart unmolested from his headquarters.[13] In the following years, as the Viet Minh war reached it height, Emperor Bao Dai three more times asked Diem to return and take over the premiership. Diem insisted each time that the war against the Viet Minh should be run by the Vietnamese, not by the French. Long distrusting Diem for his alleged Francophobia, the French would agree to nothing of this nature. Soon the Viet Minh put a price on Diem's head. Informed by the unfriendly French authorities that they could not guarantee his safety, Diem left Vietnam in 1950, traveling first to Rome and later to the United States, Belgium, and France.

From his resignation as interior minister in 1933 to his final acceptance of the premiership in the summer of 1954, Diem's mature career had been one long refusal to be anybody's instrument, even at the price of exile both inside and outside Vietnam. Many essentially decent persons throughout history have been unable to resist the offer of political power from the hands of those whom they opposed or despised, on the grounds that such power would enable them to accomplish some good or at least fend off some greater evil. But Diem distinguished himself from other nationalists because prior to 1954 he had declined attractive offers to collaborate with the French colonialists, the Japanese conquerors, the Viet Minh, or Bao Dai. By refusing time and again to accept high office at the price of becoming, or appearing to become, a puppet, Diem had demonstrated his "perfect integrity, competence, and intelligence to all Vietnamese nationalists."[14] His intransigent nationalism, "born of a profound, of an immense nostalgia for the Vietnam of the past, of a desperate filial respect for the society of ancient Annam,"[15] his self-conscious rootedness in Vietnamese history, along with his paradoxical but devout adherence to a minority religion—at different times these characteristics would be sources of both strength and weakness to him; but they all marked him out as a man who could not be deflected from his chosen course by the temptations of office or even by physical threats.

By means of two agreements initialed in June 1954, the French recognized the complete independence of the State of Vietnam under Bao Dai. Only the territory south of the 17th parallel, however, and not even all of that, was under his control. On June 18, 1954, the day Pierre Mendès-France took the oath as prime minister of France, Diem announced (in Paris) that he had accepted Bao Dai's offer to become prime minister of Vietnam. Perhaps Bao

Dai made his final and successful offer of the premiership to Diem because he believed Diem could get the backing of the Americans, among whom Diem had some important contacts. Or perhaps he hoped that the assumption of high office in such troubled times would finish off Diem politically.[16] Nobody can be sure. At any rate, before accepting the appointment, Diem had demanded full emergency powers, civil and military. Bao Dai granted them, since nobody else of any stature in Vietnam wanted the thankless job of being prime minister of a war-weary country that was being cut into two parts by the French and the Viet Minh. Thus the man and the hour came together.

A recent study of Diem's career urges us to keep two very important points in mind. First, "contrary to what many authors have suggested, Diem was neither plucked from obscurity nor installed in office by the United States in 1954. Rather, he was a prominent and active figure in Indochinese politics who successfully engineered his own appointment as premier." And second, "Diem's thinking about politics and society was defined above all by his determination to fashion a new vision of how Vietnam might become a modern state."[17]

DIEM'S FIRST DAYS IN POWER

"The overriding need in South Vietnam," states one study of those early days, "was to establish a governmental authority independent of the French and superior to the many centrifugal forces."[18] To undertake that task was truly daunting. Starting from the bottom, Ho Chi Min had spent twenty years building up the party-army organization through which he now ruled half of Vietnam. In his capital at Hanoi, Ho was the legatee both of the coup d'état called the August Revolution (1945) and the victory at Dien Bien Phu (1954). Diem, in contrast, was starting out to build a new state from the top down; he had few resources outside of his own reputation and determination.

While Ho's Democratic Republic of Vietnam had emerged from the war with a large and experienced army, South Vietnam's long borders with North Vietnam, Laos, and Cambodia were largely defenseless. Inside South Vietnam, moreover, the Viet Minh possessed a good network of fighters, assassins, and informants. In Diem's first days as prime minister, as he looked out of his office window at Saigon, then one of the loveliest cities in all Southeast Asia, he knew that his real authority did not extend even as far as his eye could see. The French civil administration was pulling out and taking everything movable, even the telephones; yet 40,000 French troops would remain, menacingly, in South Vietnam until the end of 1955.[19] The gangster society Binh Xuyen was in control of the police force in Saigon. The armed followers of one powerful religious sect (the Cao Dai) controlled the province west of Saigon, while the troops of another sect (the Hoa Hao) ruled in the southern Delta area. The Diem government's link with formal legitimacy, Emperor Bao Dai, was sullenly hostile to his new prime minister. The Communist regime in Hanoi glared down upon him. And an inundation of refugees was about to descend from the north. Wesley Fishel commented: "I would say without hesitation that historians will rank the mess inherited from [Diem's] predecessors and the French with the worst since God knows when."[20]

If Diem were to become the successful rival to Ho Chi Minh as the champion of the Vietnamese people and their aspirations, he first had to extricate himself from the debris of the French imperial system and put an end to all vestiges of French control in the south.[21] But the French intended to maintain a "presence" south of the 17th parallel (and perhaps north of it as well); they were therefore determined that Diem had to go. The French had readily at hand an apparently perfect instrument for their policy: General Nguyen Van Hinh, who was not only the Chief of Staff of Bao Dai's army, but also a French citizen and an officer in the French Air Force. Hinh spoke openly of leading a coup against Diem. In November 1954, General J. Lawton Collins, President Eisenhower's new special envoy to Saigon, made it clear to Hinh that U.S. aid for the South Vietnamese armed forces would be cut off if Diem were removed by force.[22] Hinh at length ignored these warnings and in April 1955 made a bungled armed assault against Diem, which failed, ending Hinh's career in Vietnamese politics. But the French had not yet played their last anti-Diem card.

Since General Hinh was not the only high-ranking Vietnamese who would conspire against Diem, the prime minister had to try to fill civil offices and military commands with men who were not only competent but trustworthy as well. This presented a major challenge. In the first place, hardly anyone expected Diem's government to last more than a few months at best. Even more important, under the French colonial administration, Vietnamese had generally been prevented from obtaining any experience of governmental work at the higher levels. Diem also needed persons who were anti-Communist but not tainted by collaboration with the French, whom Diem distrusted and who were openly plotting against him. Later the problem of finding enough competent leaders would be aggravated by the Communist policy of assassinating local government figures who were too good at their jobs.

All these factors help explain why Diem, from the earliest days of his prime ministership, employed the traditional Vietnamese expedient of filling his administration with family members, close personal friends, and proven loyalists. Thus Diem's brother Can was in effect the political boss of central Vietnam. Another brother, Thuc, became Archbishop of Hue. Brother Nhu founded and ran the regime's major political vehicle, the Revolutionary Workers Party. Brother Luyen was made ambassador to London, and brother

Nhu's father-in-law filled the sensitive post of ambassador to Washington. Two other Nhu in-laws were made chief justice and foreign minister, respectively. (In 1963, John F. Kennedy was President of the United States, his brother Robert was the U.S. Attorney General, and another brother, Teddy, was U.S. Senator from Massachusetts.)

In addition to his relatives, Diem forged his government through "personal ties with key lieutenants selected on the basis of individual loyalty to him and his brothers."[23] Diem's closest associates were often men of northern birth and/or Catholic religion. Roman Catholicism had traditionally been stronger in Tonkin (in the north) than in Cochinchina (the Mekong Delta-Saigon area), where the numerous French colonialists were often anti-clerical or aggressively atheist. In the months after the 1954 partition, close to a million Tonkinese, mainly Catholics, streamed into South Vietnam. Once the Hanoi regime had pretty well cut off this flow of refugees, native and immigrant Catholics composed roughly 10 percent of the South's population of about 17 million; in the capital city of Saigon, Catholics may have been as many as one in seven.[24]

Naturally, Diem looked upon the northerners who fled the Viet Minh regime as the most reliably anti-Communist elements in the population, and more and more made them his political base.[25] Northerners, especially Catholics, seem to have constituted a majority of the Civil Guard, South Vietnam's first militia.[26] Not only were northern Catholics a reliable bulwark of an independent South Vietnam, but they were also the major source of personnel with western-style education.[27] Understandably, then, the Diem administration began to fill up with northern and often Catholic appointees, even at the local level, where they had no personal ties and spoke with a regional accent that southerners often found irritating. Equally understandably, this northernization caused wide resentment and even hostility in a society characterized by intense regionalism (especially in view of the fact that Diem and his family, while not northern, had their roots outside of Cochinchina, and were demonstratively Catholic).

SOUTH VIETNAMESE SOCIETY

At the Geneva Conference, the southern part of Vietnam had escaped being handed over to Ho and his Communists mainly because of the relative weakness of the Viet Minh movement there. Ho had often noticed and complained about the individualism of southerners, especially Cochinchinese, their distaste for collectivism, and their orientation to entrepreneurism.[28] Other, equally powerful, reasons why Communism was weak in the southern provinces of Vietnam have been discussed earlier (see chapter 1). This infertility of southern soil for the implantation of Communism is substantiated by the membership figures for the Communist party in the late 1940s, when the Viet Minh war was reaching its height: out of 180,000 party members, only 23,000 were to be found in Cochinchina.[29] In northern Vietnam, due to police repression and Communist assassinations, there had in the end existed no plausible alternative between the French and the Viet Minh; later opposition there to Ho's regime was largely unorganized, and would manifest itself only in emigration or sporadic armed peasant revolts. But in the south, the weakness of the Communist party was in large part a consequence of the presence of well-organized and popular groups that had resisted the Viet Minh during the war.

One of these groups, identified earlier, was the religious sect known as the Hoa Hao. Founded in 1939, it soon developed into a sort of mutual protective association; its cooperatives offered the peasant some shelter from the demands of landlords, and membership in the growing organization meant a measure of protection from crime in the unsettled "wild west" atmosphere of western Cochinchina.[30] Non-Communist and anti-French, the Hoa Hao enjoyed the favor of the Japanese during World War II, and thus had been able to obtain many weapons from them. Numerous southern Trotskyists sought refuge within the sect when the Viet Minh set out to eliminate them in 1945. Two years later, Communists openly murdered the sect's revered founder, Huynh Phu So.

The most powerful organization in the south, however, was probably the Cao Dai, whose founders had consciously modeled their new indigenous religion on the Roman Catholic Church. Many Cao Dai leaders were well educated and had worked for the French administration. They were thus in a position to offer relief to peasants hard pressed by landlords. The sect also developed elaborate insurance and welfare systems for its members. Culturally nationalist, Cao Dai's leaders had been on bad terms with the colonial authorities before World War II, but they came to fear the Viet Minh more than they resented the French, and had sided with the latter by 1947. In the years before the partition of Vietnam, Cao Dai held seats in all cabinets, and under Bao Dai and the French the sect had attained a large measure of territorial autonomy. By the end of the Viet Minh war, Cao Dai was the largest political grouping in Cochinchina, deploying from 15,000 to 20,000 armed men and ruling an extensive area north and west of Saigon.

Besides being home to the powerful Cao Dai and Hoa Hao sects, as well as a native Roman Catholic element, and several middle-class nationalist parties, South Vietnam also contained ethnic minorities in the mountains and perhaps a million resident ethnic Chinese (half of them in Saigon) who were notably unenthusiastic about Ho and his Communists. Peasants not belonging to one or another of these groups usually displayed distrust of all political entanglements. Add to this mixture the fact that southern Vietnam was relatively far from the Communist China border, and it is easy to see why the

Viet Minh in that region had not reached an organizational and military level comparable to that in the north. And of course, soon after partition a flood of anti-Communist refugees arrived. But if the presence of disparate groups and powerful organizations were an obstacle to the domination of southern society by the Communists, they would also prove a barrier to the effective unification of South Vietnam, a unification essential if the Diem government was successfully to confront the looming threats of internal subversion and external aggression.[31]

U.S. ASSISTANCE

Faced as they were by so many difficulties and threats, Diem and his southern state were clearly not going to survive without help from the outside. Such assistance was on its way. Colonel Edward G. Lansdale, USAF, had served in the O.S.S. (a forerunner of the CIA) during World War II, and had then become special adviser and close friend to Philippine President Ramon Magsaysay in the successful struggle against the Communist Huk guerrillas. Washington would eventually retire him in his fifties (at the rank of Major General) for being too outspoken. But in 1954, he arrived in Saigon to help Diem. Lansdale found that Diem's headquarters in Saigon's Independence Palace were so wide open that gunmen might have simply walked in off the streets and killed Diem and his ministers. Colonel Napoleon Valeriano, commander of the Presidential Guard Battalion in Manila, soon came to help Lansdale set up security for Diem; in short order a lightly-armed but alert guards unit was established next to Independence Palace.[32]

Lansdale was only the harbinger of assistance from the United States, which would eventually reach enormous proportions. U.S. policy toward Indochina since partition had been to "seek an independent non-Communist South Vietnam."[33] According to the thinking of the Eisenhower administration and its successors, if South Vietnam fell to the Communists, so would Laos and Cambodia; Burma would be lost to non-Communist influence, Malaysia might be taken over by Indonesia, which was itself on the verge of going Communist, the Philippines would become "shaky," and threats to Australia, New Zealand and Japan would "increase."[34] Hence the United States would support South Vietnam, provided it could locate a reliable leader. After some initial hesitation, the Americans decided that Ngo Dinh Diem was that leader. His unimpeachable personal integrity, his long and clean record as an uncompromising nationalist, his anti-Communism and *presumed* pro-Americanism were all very attractive to Washington. He clearly had the backing of the northern refugees, and besides, the opposition to Diem within South Vietnam was so fragmented that there was no plausible alternative.[35] Thus the United States helped Diem take over control of the army from the Bao Dai–appointed and mutinous General Hinh.

But it was not only in the Eisenhower administration that Diem found backing. His brother Bishop Thuc interested the influential Archbishop of New York, Francis Cardinal Spellman, in the cause, and Spellman in turn introduced Diem to Congressman Walter Judd and Senators Mike Mansfield and John F. Kennedy, all of whom became his admirers. In October 1954, Mansfield (eventually Democratic floor leader in the Senate) had become convinced that support for Diem was much in the interest of the United States, and later he wrote that "in the jungle of colonial decay, corruption and military defeat which characterized Saigon in 1954, Diem assumed the [leadership] with few assets other than his nationalism, his personal incorruptibility, and his idealistic determination."[36] In May 1955 Minnesota Senator Hubert Humphrey declared that "Premier Diem is the best hope that we have in South Vietnam; he is the leader of his people."[37] A year later Senator John F. Kennedy maintained that South Vietnam was the "cornerstone of the Free World in Southeast Asia" and "an inspiration to those seeking to obtain and maintain their liberty in all parts of Asia—and indeed the world."[38] And in 1957 an influential officer of the Council on Foreign Relations wrote in the prestigious journal *Foreign Affairs* that "history may yet adjudge Diem as one of the great figures of twentieth century Asia."[39]

CONFRONTING THE BINH XUYEN

One of the tactics employed by the French in fighting the Viet Minh, especially in the south, had been to arm the southern sects and local warlords, conceding to each group what amounted to autonomy within its particular territory. As a consequence of this French policy, Diem faced in his first days in office an absence of orderly administration in the countryside, indeed something close to politico-military anarchy. The most immediate threat came from a criminal society known as the Binh Xuyen. Evolving out of a river gang called the Black Flag Pirates, the Binh Xuyen by 1954 controlled most of the prostitution, drug, and gambling activities in Saigon. Its members had received training and arms during World War II from the Kempeitai, the notorious Japanese military police, and from time to time had worked closely with the Communists. But the Binh Xuyen had also supported Bao Dai in his maneuverings with the French, and in turn Bao Dai, immediately before he left Vietnam in 1954, sold (yes, sold) control of the Saigon police force to the Binh Xuyen.[40] This control, plus their private army and the enormous profits they made from vice operations in Saigon, gave the Binh Xuyen leaders something close to absolute authority over most sections of the capital.[41] Now, from his self-imposed exile, Bao Dai was encouraging the Binh Xuyen to unite with the sects against Diem.[42] But in September 1954, Diem gave the Cao Dai and the Hoa Hao seats in his cabinet; he also used some of the money he was getting from the United States to win key sect leaders to his side. Having thus divided the sects from the Binh Xuyen, Diem was ready for a confrontation with the latter.

Colonel Lansdale has reported that he convinced the Binh Xuyen leader, one Bay Vien, to approach Diem with a compromise; the Binh Xuyen would recognize Diem's authority in return for his permitting certain of their more lucrative activities to continue. Diem did not trust Bay Vien and spurned the offer.[43] Binh Xuyen forces thereupon attacked the presidential palace on March 29, 1955. Bao Dai sought to intervene from afar and save the Binh Xuyen. The French authorities still on the scene interfered with fuel supplies for Diem's forces;[44] then, seeing that the fight was going against the Binh Xuyen, the French High Command arranged a truce. New fighting broke out on April 28, and within a week Diem's troops drove the Binh Xuyen from Saigon. Surviving elements of this group found their way into the jungles and eventually joined the Communist guerrillas (a small but interesting sidelight on the nature of the Viet Cong).

Some Americans in later years criticized Diem for the time and energy he spent cleaning out the Binh Xuyen, and for spilling blood on the streets of Saigon. The episode allegedly revealed his preference for intransigent authoritarianism over prudent compromise. But, as Diem asked, would Charles de Gaulle, entering liberated Paris in 1944, have shared authority with an organized criminal group that had collaborated with the German occupation? Besides, fighting the Binh Xuyen gained Diem the loyalty of many army officers, the respect of foreign governments, and the gratitude of numerous ordinary Vietnamese who had long suffered exploitation by the Binh Xuyen and their French colonial accomplices.[45] The defeat of the Binh Xuyen also convinced Cao Dai and Hoa Hao leaders that they should cooperate with Diem, and their armed forces were at least nominally incorporated into the government's Civil Guard militia.

DIEM'S EARLY ACCOMPLISHMENTS

In the aftermath of Geneva, few were predicting the emergence of a stable regime in Saigon. When Diem took over on his first day as prime minister, he actually controlled only a few square blocks of downtown Saigon, and was confronted by the simultaneous hostility of Bao Dai, the military high command, the French, the armed sects, the Binh Xuyen, the southern Communists, the Hanoi regime, and indeed the whole Communist world. Yet by the first anniversary of the notorious Geneva Agreements, the shy, ascetic, uncharismatic Diem had defied Bao Dai's efforts to remove him, thwarted an army coup, defeated the Binh Xuyen, brought the army, the police, and the entire city of Saigon under his control, incorporated the sects into his security apparatus, abolished the French-run Bank of Indochina so that South Vietnam would have full control over its own currency and foreign exchange, and obtained the promise of the French to evacuate their remaining troops.[46] He had also directed the successful settling of almost a million refugees, a tremendous accomplishment when one considers that the influx of northerners into South Vietnam would have been the equivalent of 18,000,000 new arrivals into today's United States in one year's time.

These triumphs would not have been possible without U.S. aid, but they also reflected Diem's devotion to hard work; he usually put in 16- and even 18-hour days, giving up his favorite hobbies of shooting and photography.[47] As his government entered into a period of relative tranquility Diem sought to enhance the links between the peasantry and the government by touring the countryside; from mid-1957 to mid-1958, he took 33 separate trips covering 14,000 miles.[48] These visits to the peasantry appear to have been genuinely well received.[49]

The domestic social and economic picture began to improve significantly. Between 1955 and 1961 the number of South Vietnamese in primary schools doubled, the number of university students increased five-fold, and secondary students increased nine-fold.[50] Economically the partition was hard on South Vietnam; the country had no important natural resources; in the pre-partition economic system, the south sent rice to the north, from which came chemicals, coal, glass, textiles, and other manufactured items.[51] In 1955, out of perhaps 17,800,000 inhabitants, the south had only 50,000 industrial workers. But there was plenty of rice, abundant fishing, the remains of the French rubber industry, and Saigon's light manufacturing establishments and good seaport. The government inaugurated a small-scale land-reform program, built roads to connect the highlands with the coastal cities and the delta, and attacked malaria, the principal cause of illness in the country.[52] South Vietnamese economic progress under Diem was not negligible, particularly if one compares it with the North, and keeps in mind that soon after the beginning of his administration Diem was faced with a Hanoi-inspired guerrilla insurgency.[53] By the fall of 1955, with the most pressing crises solved or contained, with his government recognized by 36 other countries,[54] Diem was ready to rectify the anomalous situation in which he was, in constitutional terms, merely the chief minister of the absent and hostile Bao Dai. In a plebiscite on October 23, 1955, a massive turnout of voters—despite Viet Minh Radio in Hanoi urging voters to stay home—overwhelmingly agreed that South Vietnam should be a republic, with Diem as first president. The U.S. Embassy in Saigon stated that the vote figures were "reasonably accurate," and Australian, British, and French representatives in Saigon agreed:

"The secrecy of the ballot was everywhere respected, and no evidence was found of fraud or direct intimidation."[55]

Regarding the parliamentary elections of 1956 and 1959, Robert Scalapino of the University of California wrote that "in general, it appears that the voting was carried out in fairness and secrecy and that the ballots were honestly counted." [56] In 1961, the *New York Times* attributed President Diem's reelection that year not to coercion or fraud but to growing prosperity and widespread anti-Communism.[57] (Two years earlier, an editorial in the *New York Times* proclaimed that "a five-year miracle, not a 'plan,' has been carried out. [South] Viet Nam is free and is becoming stronger in defense of its freedom and of ours. There is reason today to salute President Ngo Dinh Diem."[58] On the 1966 elections for the Constituent Assembly Sir Robert G. K. Thompson, one of the architects of the defeat of the Communist insurgency in Malaya,[59] wrote that:

> the turnout and the percentages were about normal for most western countries but, with the disruption of war and with the Vietcong instructing voters to boycott the election and using terror to intimidate them, the turnout was remarkably high, and demonstrated the outstanding feature of all the elections— the determination of the South Vietnamese people not to be deterred, whatever the threat, from having a say in their own future.[60]

In the Lower House elections of August 1971, 1,239 candidates competed for 159 seats. "The honesty of this election was never questioned, but received little attention."[61] Thompson's final tart judgment on this topic: "anyone who brushes elections in South Vietnam aside as being corrupt and worthless is only doing so because the results do not suit his political view."[62]

In any case, following the 1955 constitutional plebiscite, an 11-member commission, including well-known French-educated legal scholars, along with Filipino and American advisers, set to work to draw up a constitution for the new republic. The document that emerged from this commission in 1956 foreshadowed to a remarkable degree the one Charles de Gaulle promulgated for the French Fifth Republic a couple of years later. It laid down separation of powers, with a dominant executive, a subordinate legislature, and a judiciary with vague authority. The president and the members of the National Assembly were elected to five-year terms by universal suffrage: the president of South Vietnam (unlike the president of the French Fifth Republic) did not have the power to dissolve the National Assembly, nor could the Assembly dismiss cabinets. In emergencies, the president could rule by decree in the absence of the Assembly and suspend the law in any part of the country. Diem now had the firm legal footing to consolidate and expand the power of the new state that had so unexpectedly emerged from the wreckage left by the collapse of French colonialism.[63]

In Douglas Pike's view, Diem's regime "was as good as most Asian governments at the time and better than some."[64] For the authors of *The Pentagon Papers*, certainly no admirers of Diem, "at its worst, the Government of South Vietnam compared favorably with other Asian regimes with respect to its degree of repressiveness."[65] It could certainly stand comparison with those of Indonesia's Sukarno or North Korea's Kim Il-sung, not to speak of Cambodia's Pol Pot. Mao Tse-tung's insane "Great Leap Forward" resulted in the premature deaths of at least 20 million Chinese.[66] Ho Chi Minh presided over the killing of literally thousands of peasants, men and women, during compulsory land collectivization in North Vietnam after 1954, and would insist that all of Vietnam had to be forcibly united under Communist rule even at the cost of countless Vietnamese dead.[67] And as Sir Robert Thompson famously observed, "[Diem] has certainly not been as ruthless as we [British] were in Malaya under both Labour and Conservative Governments."[68]

THE VIET CONG

Up until 1963, the most serious threat facing the Diem government came from the Communist-led insurgents generally known as the Viet Cong (VC). A guerrilla movement that developed in South Vietnam after 1956, it had a number of diverse roots, but the timing of the outbreak, as well as its power and durability, can be explained in terms of only one factor: a decision by Hanoi. Distinguished students of this insurgency agree that, far from being a spontaneous uprising by an exasperated population, the two-decade struggle for South Vietnam "began by deliberate Communist design."[69] North Vietnamese efforts to depict the southern insurgency as autonomous were effective but "patently false,"[70] because from its beginnings the movement was "organized and directed from the North."[71] Hanoi's decision to take over South Vietnam by force derived partly from awareness that the Communists could never win a free election in South Vietnam and partly from fear that non-Communist Asia could not fail to draw conclusions from both the Hanoi regime's assaults on the northern peasantry and the emerging higher standard of living in South Vietnam.[72]

The VC insurgency was fueled by former Viet Minh who had gone to Communist North Vietnam in 1954 and now infiltrated back into the South.[73] But many indigenous persons eventually joined (or in later years were coerced into joining) the insurgency. In an arresting passage, Eric Bergerud stated that:

> [The Viet Cong] offered an avenue of social advancement more exciting than anything the [Saigon] government could propose. The insurgents would after all become the leaders of the new Vietnam. The Party offered young men and

women a powerful vision of the future. In return, it asked absolute political
dedication, obedience, and a willingness to face the very real prospect of
death. . . . *So it did not really matter whether or not [the insurgency] had the
support of a majority of the peasantry.* . . . [T]he Party had what it needed, the
support of the most politically aware and most determined segment of the
peasantry.[74]

Once a person became, by whatever route, a member of a VC unit, the
leadership devoted a great deal of time and energy to indoctrinating him. Viet
Cong pronouncements constantly stressed the inevitability of final victory.
They also provided a convenient vocabulary of political heroism to those
who originally had joined for more selfish motives. Moreover, Douglas Blaufarb emphasizes that joining the Party often meant breaking ties with one's
family, village and clan; thus, for one's psychological and social survival,
dedication to the Party and its aims had to become total.[75]

The Viet Cong were never able to expand their following from the countryside into the cities; on the other hand, Diem freely distributed arms to
hundreds of thousands of peasants through the Self-Defense Corps. Diem
was easily reelected president in 1961, and in December of that year President Kennedy assured Diem of U.S. support for his government, with South
Vietnam receiving highest priority in terms of increased aid.[76] By 1963 no
fewer than eighty countries maintained diplomatic relations with Diem's
government. As R. B. Smith observed,

> Grievances and "contradictions" were undoubtedly present in South Vietna-
> mese society and were especially acute under a regime more preoccupied with
> security than with social welfare. But the fact that it was necessary for the
> Communist side to resume the armed struggle at all in 1959–60 suggests that
> the purely political struggle had not been sufficient to translate the "contradic-
> tions" into successful revolution. From that point on the critical factor was the
> developing armed struggle itself and the American failure to deal with it in
> time.[77]

Despite the manifest and varied challenges facing his government, Diem had
been able to keep the South Vietnamese state on an even keel in part because
of the open support of the Americans and because so many in the South knew
a great deal about life in North Vietnam.[78] Yet before 1963 had concluded,
Diem would be murdered, his administration ruined, and South Vietnam
hurled into an apparently irreversible crisis, from which it could be extricat-
ed, if at all, only by the massive intervention of U.S. military power. How
could such a calamity have occurred?

NOTES

1. William J. Duiker, *Ho Chi Minh* (New York: Hyperion, 2000), p. 533.
2. Quoted in Ellen J. Hammer, *The Struggle for Indochina, 1940–1955: Viet Nam and the French Experience* (Stanford, CA: Stanford University Press, 1966), p. 47.
3. Joseph Buttinger, *Vietnam: A Dragon Embattled*, Vol. 2, *Vietnam at War* (New York: Praeger, 1967), p. 1009.
4. Joseph Buttinger, quoted in Marguerite Higgins, *Our Vietnam Nightmare* (New York: Harper and Row, 1965), p. 12.
5. Arthur Dommen, *The Indochinese Experience of the French and the Americans: Nationalism and Communism in Cambodia, Laos and Vietnam* (Bloomington, IN: Indiana University, 2001), p. 263; confer *FRUS* 1952–1954, vol. 13, part 2, p. 2371, Dec. 14, 1954.
6. William Colby, *Lost Victory: A Firsthand Account of America's Sixteen-Year Involvement in Vietnam* (Chicago, IL: Contemporary, 1989). General Westmoreland wrote that "Diem's downfall was a major factor in prolonging the war"; *A Soldier Reports*, p. 62. For Lyndon Johnson, "the worst mistake we ever made was getting rid of Diem"; quoted in Henry F. Graff, *The Tuesday Cabinet: Deliberation and Decision on Peace and War under Lyndon B. Johnson* (Englewood Cliff, NJ: Prentice-Hall, 1970).
7. Edward Miller, *Misalliance: Ngo Dinh Diem, The United States, and the Fate of South Vietnam* (Cambridge, MA: Harvard University Press, 2013).
8. Philip Catton, *Diem's Final Failure: Prelude to America's War in Vietnam* (Lawrence, KS: University Press of Kansas, 2003), p. 3. Despite the title, this book is not hostile to Diem.
9. See details on Diem in Buttinger, *Dragon Embattled*, vol. 2, pp. 1253–1257.
10. Robert Scigliano, *South Vietnam: Nation under Stress* (Boston: Houghton Mifflin, 1964), p. 17.
11. Philippe Devillers, *Histoire du Vietnam de 1940 à 1952*, 3d ed. (Paris: Editions du Seuil, 1952), p. 126.
12. Bernard Fall, *The Two Vietnams: A Political and Military Analysis*, 2d ed. revised (New York: Praeger, 1967), p. 240.
13. Robert Shaplen, *The Lost Revolution: The U.S. in Vietnam, 1946–1966* (New York: Harper and Row, 1966), p. 110.
14. Fall, *Two Vietnams*, p. 240. The quotation is from Devillers, *Histoire du Vietnam*, p. 63. See also Scigliano, *South Vietnam*, p. 16.
15. Jean Lacouture and Philippe Devillers, *La fin d'une guerre: Indochine 1954* (Paris: Seuil, 1960), quoted in Scigliano, *South Vietnam*, p. 64.
16. Scigliano, *South Vietnam*, p. 17. And see Edward Miller, "Vision, Power and Agency: The Ascent of Ngo Dinh Diem, 1945–1954," *Journal of Southeast Asian Studies*, 35 (Oct. 2004), pp. 433–458.
17. Miller, *Misalliance*, pp. 20–21.
18. Roy Jumper and Marjorie Weiner Normand, "Vietnam," in George McTurnan Kahin, ed., *Government and Politics in Southeast Asia* (Ithaca, NY: Cornell University Press, 1964), p. 399.
19. Ronald Spector, *Advice and Support: The Early Years of the U.S. Army in Vietnam* (New York: Free Press, 1985), p. 238.
20. Catton, *Diem's Final Failure*, p. 9.
21. Scigliano, *South Vietnam*, p. 183; William Henderson, in Wesley Fishel, ed., *Problems of Freedom: South Vietnam since Independence* (New York: Free Press, 1961), p. 187.
22. Scigliano, *South Vietnam*, p. 18.
23. Jumper and Normand, "Vietnam," p. 431.
24. Jumper and Normand, "Vietnam"; but Scigliano thinks the Catholic population was only 7 percent; *South Vietnam*, p. 53.
25. Scigliano, *South Vietnam*, p. 53.
26. Spector, *Advice and Support*, pp. 321–322.
27. Douglas Pike, *Viet Cong* (Cambridge, MA: MIT Press, 1966), p. 59.
28. Samuel L. Popkin, *The Rational Peasant* (Berkeley, CA: University of California Press, 1979), p. 240.

29. Popkin, *Rational Peasant,* p. 242
30. Popkin, *Rational Peasant,* p. 211.
31. Hue Tam Ho Tai, *Millenarianism and Peasant Politics in Vietnam* (Cambridge, MA: Harvard University Press, 1963); Jayne Susan Werner, *Peasant Politics and Religious Sectarianism: Peasant and Priest in the Cao Dai in Vietnam* (New Haven, CT: Yale University Southeast Asian Studies, 1981).
32. Edward G. Lansdale, *In the Midst of Wars: An American's Mission to Southeast Asia* (New York: Harper and Row, 1972), p. 178.
33. National Security Action Memorandum, "U.S. Objectives in South Vietnam," March 16, 1964, in *The Pentagon Papers*, Gravel Edition (Boston, MA: Beacon Press, 1971), vol. 3, p. 499.
34. Ibid., p. 500.
35. Hammer, *Struggle*, p. 356; Jumper and Normand, "Vietnam," p. 400.
36. Senator Mike Mansfield in *Harper's Magazine*, January 1956, p. 348.
37. *Pentagon Papers*, vol. 1, p. 297.
38. *Vital Speeches*, vol. 22 (August 1, 1956), p. 618.
39. William Henderson, "South Vietnam Finds Itself," *Foreign Affairs*, January 1957; quoted in Fishel, *Problems of Freedom*, p. 183.
40. Denis Warner, *Certain Victory: How Hanoi Won the War* (Kansas City: Sneed, Andrews and McMeel, 1978), p. 88. By 1954 the Binh Xuyen "was operating 'Grande Monde,' a gambling slum in Cholon; 'Cloche d'Or,' Saigon's preeminent gambling establishment; the 'Noveautes Catinat,' Saigon's best department store; a hundred smaller shops, a fleet of riverboats, and a brothel, spectacular even by Asian standards"; *Pentagon Papers*, vol. 1, p. 293.
41. *Pentagon Papers*, vol. I, p. 293.
42. Lansdale, *In the Midst of Wars*, p. 258.
43. Ibid., p. 177.
44. Scigliano, *South Vietnam*, p. 22.
45. See Senator Mike Mansfield, "Reprieve in Viet Nam," *Harper's*, January 1956.
46. Jumper and Normand, "Vietnam," p. 401.
47. Denis Warner, *The Last Confucian*, p. 73.
48. Scigliano, *South Vietnam*, p. 57.
49. Tran Van Don, *Our Endless War* (San Rafael, CA: Presidio, 1978), p. 62.
50. Fall, *Two Vietnams*, p. 314.
51. Scigliano, *South Vietnam*, p. 101.
52. Scigliano, *South Vietnam*, p. 105–106. For a very positive assessment of Diem's land-reform efforts, see Wolf Ladejinsky, "Agrarian Reform in the Republic of Vietnam," in *Problems of Freedom: South Vietnam since Independence*, ed. Wesley Fishel (New York: Free Press, 1961).
53. Fall, *Two Vietnams*, p. 315.
54. The Japanese government, for example, paid reparations only to Diem's government, not to Hanoi.
55. *FRUS 1955–1957: Vietnam*, pp. 591–593.
56. "The Electoral Process in South Vietnam: Politics in an Underdeveloped State," *Midwest Journal of Political Science*, vol. 4, no. 2 (May 1960), p. 151.
57. *New York Times*, April 10, 1961. In early November 1960 some army officers attempted a coup against President Diem that quickly came to nothing. "The coup attempt that broke out in Saigon in the early hours of November 11, 1960, had nothing to do with democratic rule [but] was the work of mid-level career officers who were dissatisfied with the state of affairs [promotions] within the military"; Dommen, *Indochinese Experience*, p. 418.
58. *New York Times*, July 7, 1959.
59. There are many excellent studies of the Malayan conflict. Among them: Sir Robert Thompson, *Defeating Communist Insurgency: The Lessons of Malaya and Vietnam* (New York: Praeger, 1966); Anthony Short, *The Communist Insurrection in Malaya, 1948–1960* (London: Frederick Muller, 1975); Lucian Pye, *Guerrilla Communism in Malaya* (Princeton, NJ: Princeton University Press, 1956); Richard Stubbs, *Hearts and Minds: The Malayan Emergency of 1948–1960* (Singapore: OUP, 1989); John Cloake, *Templer, Tiger of Malaya* (Lon-

---

don: Harrap, 1985). See also Thompson's *Make for the Hills: Memories of Far Eastern Wars* (London: L. Cooper 1989).

60. Thompson, *Peace Is Not at Hand*, p. 10.

61. Thompson, *Peace Is Not at Hand*, p. 13.

62. Thompson, *Peace Is Not at Hand*, p. 15; and see Howard R. Penniman, *Elections in South Vietnam* (Washington, DC: American Enterprise Institute, 1972).

63. J. A. C. Grant, "The Vietnamese Constitution of 1956," *American Political Science Review* 52 (June 1958).

64. Pike, *Viet Cong*, p. 57.

65. *Pentagon Papers*, vol. 1, p. 325.

66. John K. Fairbank, *The Great Chinese Revolution, 1800–1985* (New York: Harper and Row, 1986), p. 296; Richard Madsen, "The Countryside under Communism," in *The Cambridge History of China*, volume 15, *The People's Republic*, part 2, *Revolutions within the Chinese Revolution* (New York: Cambridge University Press, 1992), 642; Lucian Pye, *China,* 4th ed. (New York: HarperCollins, 1991), p. 250. Mao caused the deaths of more persons than Stalin and Hitler combined; Phillip Short, *Mao: A Life* (New York: Holt, 2000), p. 631.

67. Fall, *Two Vietnams,* pp. 155–156; P. J. Honey, ed., *North Vietnam Today: Profile of a Communist Satellite* (New York: Praeger, 1962), p. 8; Hoang Van Chi, *From Colonialism to Communism: A Case Study of North Vietnam* (New York: Praeger, 1964), p. 72.

68. Sir Robert Thompson, quoted in Mark Moyar, *Triumph Forsaken: The Vietnam War, 1954–1965* (New York: Cambridge University Press, 2006), p. 245. Regarding British coercive methods during the Malayan insurgency, see David French, *The British Way in Counterinsurgency 1945–1967* (Oxford, England: Oxford University Press, 2011).

69. Fall, *Two Vietnams*, p. 316.

70. Timothy Lomperis, *The War Everyone Lost—and Won: America's Intervention in Vietnam's Twin Struggles* (Baton Rouge, LA: Louisiana State University Press, 1984), p. 57.

71. William Duiker, *The Communist Road to Power in Vietnam*, 2d ed. (Boulder, CO: Westview, 1996), p. 199; see also Douglas Pike in Peter Braestrup, ed., *Vietnam as History* (Washington, DC: University Press of America, 1984), p. 73; Guenter Lewy, *America in Vietnam* (New York: Oxford University Press, 1978), p. 40 and passim; Turner, *Vietnamese Communism*, pp. 229–232; Jeffrey Race, *War Comes to Long An: Revolutionary Conflict in a Vietnamese Province* (Berkeley, CA: University of California Press, 1972), pp. 104–107; "Vietnam: We Lied to You," *Economist,* February 26, 1983; R. B. Smith, *An International History*, vol. 1, pp. 16–17. After its conquest of the South, Hanoi did not try any more to hide its instigation and direction of the war; see, inter alia, General Van Tien Dung, *Our Great Spring Victory* (New York: Monthly Review Press, 1977), p. 206 and passim; and Bui Tin, *Following Ho Chi Minh: Memoirs of a North Vietnamese Colonel* (Honolulu: University of Hawaii Press, 1995), p. 41.

72. Wolf Ladejinsky in Michigan State University Social Science Research Bureau, *Problems of Freedom* (Glencoe, IL: Free Press, 1961), p. 175; Ellen Hammer, "South Vietnam: The Limits of Political Action," *Pacific Affairs*, vol. 35, no. 1 (Spring 1962); Lansdale, *In the Midst of Wars*, also believes that Hanoi made the decision for forcible reunification on the basis of its unwillingness to be compared to the South.

73. Catton, *Diem's Final Failure*, p. 74; Spector, *Advice and Support*, p. 330; Truong Nhu Tang, *Viet Cong Memoir*, p. 240.

74. Eric M. Bergerud, *The Dynamics of Defeat: The Vietnam War in Hau Nghia Province* (Boulder, CO: Westview, 1991), pp. 23 and 326. "No matter how hard a government village chief worked, he could never hope to become more than a village chief, whereas a poor peasant [in the VC] could hope to become the village secretary, the district secretary, or even higher—his lack of education and his inability to speak flawless French would not weigh against him. In fact, they would be in his favor"; Jeffrey Race, *War Comes to Long An: Revolutionary Conflict in a Vietnamese Province* (Berkeley, CA: University of California Press, 1972), p. 170.

75. Douglas Blaufarb, *The Counterinsurgency Era: U.S. Doctrine and Performance* (New York: Free Press, 1977), p. 8.

76. James Lawton Collins, *The Development and Training of the South Vietnamese Army, 1950–1972* (Washington, DC: U.S. Army Center of Military History, 1975), pp. 23–24.

77. Smith, *International History*, vol. 1, p. 233.
78. Scigliano, *South Vietnam*, p. 189.

Chapter Three

The Murder of President Diem

"And a man's enemies shall be those of his own house."—Matthew 10:36

By early 1963, President Ngo Dinh Diem had become highly displeasing to certain U.S. policymakers.[1] This situation had been developing for several years. For one example of negative attitudes toward Diem, after visiting Saigon for exactly two and a half days in November 1961, John Kenneth Galbraith, President Kennedy's ambassador to India, wrote to him that a military government would be more vigorous than Diem's in fighting the VC.[2] "Probably nowhere in American diplomatic history," writes Arthur Dommen, "is there an example of an influential envoy reaching such a sweeping judgment about the politics of a country in so short a time and with the economy of not even meeting its leader."[3] But Galbraith went further: "It is a cliché that there is no alternative to Diem's regime . . . [but] *nothing succeeds like successors*."[4] And Chester Bowles, another Kennedy ambassador to India, actually wrote these words:

> Nor am I convinced by the familiar argument that "there is no available successor." It is not too much to say that almost any articulate, courageous, anti-Communist Vietnamese with a good reputation who puts himself at the head of a group to overthrow Diem, and who outlines a policy of continued vigorous anti-communism combined with anti-favoritism, better government administration and land reform, would find himself a national hero in a matter of weeks.[5]

This insouciance about who or what would or might follow the removal of Diem is one of the most absolutely astonishing characteristics of the intellectuals, real and pseudo, who played such a prominent role in the Kennedy Administration.

47

While by the summer of 1963 the Buddhist excitement (which we shall soon examine) was uppermost in the Kennedy Administration's view, certain trends within the inner circle of the Saigon government had long been arousing Washington's anxiety. Diem's fervent nationalism occasionally expressed itself in a display of mild irritation toward American officials who thought they knew more about his country than he did: "Unaccountably, in Washington's eyes, Diem felt that as a Vietnamese he had a better grasp of the political significance of Buddhism than the two Americans primarily responsible for East Asian affairs, Averell Harriman [recently defeated for reelection as Governor of New York] and Roger Hilsman."[6] Diem also had serious doubts about the reliability of the Americans in a protracted conflict. In any case, Diem had made it clear that he did not wish his country to be flooded with American military personnel, fearing that the arrival of large numbers of foreign troops would play right into the hands of Communist propagandists, as well as further disrupt South Vietnam's already troubled society.[7] He sometimes openly bridled at what one scholar describes as "the neocolonialism that never lay very far from the surface of the U.S. approach to the patron-client relationship with South Vietnam," the U.S. version of *la mission civilisatrice*.[8] In essence, Diem believed, with good reason, that failure to separate himself from the French had deeply undermined Bao Dai. Diem was determined not to make that same mistake with the Americans.

Even more irritating to Washington was Ngo Dinh Nhu, Diem's brother and closest adviser. A graduate of the prestigious Ecole des Chartes in Paris, Nhu was "the regime's leading skeptic of American intentions in South Vietnam."[9] Nhu "was dangerous because he was working for independence for Vietnam—even from the American ally who had given the Vietnamese so much."[10] In April 1963, Nhu requested a reduction in the ever-burgeoning number of U.S. military advisers (the 1,000 U.S. military personnel in South Vietnam in 1960 had grown to 11,000 at the end of 1962).[11] "These huge increases," writes Edward Miller:

> were uncomfortably reminiscent of the era of French colonial rule. In [the brothers'] view, the main problem with the growing American presence was not simply that it appeared to lend credence to Communist allegations about the regime's subordinate relationship to Washington. The brothers were more concerned that too many South Vietnamese—including many of their own officials and military officers—continued to display a "colonial mentality" that would facilitate American efforts to transform the country into a U.S. protectorate.[12]

Diem told one visitor: "I wish to increase [ARVN's size]; the United States refuses to supply weapons and other means; the United States only wants to send more [American] troops into Vietnam."[13]

In the opinion of French Ambassador Roger Lalouette, this reluctance on the part of the president and his brother to be engulfed by the Americans "was the main reason for the American decision to overthrow Diem. That, and the growing pro-French orientation of the Saigon government."[14] In the eyes of some key Washington policymakers, "if the Ngos [President Diem and his brother Nhu] did not allow [Americans] the freedom of action they wanted, they could always find Vietnamese more amenable to American wishes."[15]

But most damaging of all, perhaps, rumors surfaced concerning tentative contacts between Nhu and Hanoi. Diem had always employed a number of ex-Communists in his government, and the gossip was that Diem, through his brother, was seeking negotiations with Ho for a loose federation of North and South, thus freeing each of them from Chinese and American dictation, respectively.[16] President de Gaulle publicly stated his desire to see all of Southeast Asia "neutralized." These rumors of a possible peace in Vietnam negotiated behind Washington's back heavily tipped the Administration scales against the Diem government.[17]

It was in this complicated context that a series of events occurred that would provide the occasion—and the excuse—for elements in the Kennedy Administration to overthrow Diem: the so-called Buddhist Crisis.

THE BUDDHIST TROUBLES

The Buddhist Crisis that began in the spring of 1963 was a big surprise to everyone in South Vietnam.[18] Throughout the nine years of Diem's leadership there had been no hint of anti-regime animosity on the part of any of the numerous Buddhist tendencies or factions. The affair had its beginnings in April 1963, when Monsignor Ngo Dinh Thuc, archbishop of Hue and brother of the president, celebrated the jubilee of his ordination to the priesthood. For a week, bunting hung from churches in the old capital, the white-and-yellow papal flag flew everywhere, and schoolchildren received a holiday, as if this anniversary were some sort of national fete. Buddha's birthday fell on May 8. Monks in Hue urged their followers, in imitation of the recent Catholic celebration, to display Buddhist flags. On May 6, local officials incomprehensibly decided to enforce an old law prohibiting the flying of any flag unless the national flag was also displayed. A delegation of monks protested to the province chief, a Catholic. The minister of the interior, also a Catholic, happened to be in Hue at that time. He gave his permission for the flying of Buddhist flags, and the monks expressed satisfaction. Nevertheless, the Hue events had aroused long-simmering resentments and ambitions. A Buddhist figure named Tri Quang and his monk accomplices, at least some of whom were certainly in league with the Viet Cong, were determined to bring down the Diem government.[19] An increasingly effective manipulation of the U.S. visual media would be one of their principal weapons.[20]

On May 8, a crowd in Hue instigated by some monks and Viet Cong agents attempted to seize a local radio station in order to broadcast an attack on the government. A riot was developing when explosions of uncertain origin occurred, producing a stampede that resulted in several deaths.[21] Years later the authors of the *Pentagon Papers* wrote that "Government troops fire[d] on a Buddhist protest demonstration killing nine and wounding fourteen."[22] That is completely incorrect.[23] And others besides Buddhists were hurt in the affair.[24]

Learning of the incident, Diem dismissed the Hue province chief and received a delegation of monks from Hue, with whom he exchanged peaceable sentiments. Still, the pseudo-monk Tri Quang declared that he would not rest until Diem had been overthrown. On June 11 occurred the first immolation of a monk: in a downtown plaza in Saigon (hundreds of miles from Hue) an elderly Buddhist monk was doused with gasoline by his assistants, who then set him on fire. The foreign press was standing by, having been duly alerted for a sensational incident. Grisly pictures of the suicide appeared all over the world the next day, including on President Kennedy's Oval Office desk. The newspapers advised the American public that the persecution of the Buddhists by the Catholic Diem regime must be savage indeed if despairing and anguished monks were willing to take their own lives in protest. (This, of course, was a grossly ethnocentric distortion of reality. Buddhist attitudes regarding death are quite different from those of most Westerners, and religious self-immolations were not uncommon in Vietnam, without any necessarily political implications.) The U.S. media further explained to the Americans that since everybody in Southeast Asia had a religion, and since Catholics were less than a fifth of the South Vietnamese population, then the Buddhists must be at least four-fifths, and therefore Diem had clearly aroused the overwhelming majority of the population against himself.

If these notions about a great and inflamed Buddhist majority in the population (and by extension in the army) were correct, this was a very serious problem indeed. But Marguerite Higgins (the first woman to receive a Pulitzer Prize for international reporting) wrote at the time that only about 4.5 million of South Vietnam's 17 million population (in 1963) were Buddhist.[25] According to the General Association of Buddhists, 30 percent of the population of South Vietnam were Buddhists.[26] The CIA estimated South Vietnam's population at about 16 million, of whom only 3–4 million were more than nominally Buddhist, and that the followers of the anti-government militant monks amounted to perhaps one million, almost all townsmen.[27] Some calculated that the radical monks represented only 400,000 Buddhists.[28] (Notably, government relations with monks in rural areas remained amicable throughout the period of sensationalized self-immolations.)

Yet Roger Hilsman, President Kennedy's assistant secretary of state for Far Eastern affairs (no less), insisted as late as 1992 that the population of South Vietnam had been 98 percent Buddhist.[29] Decades after these events, Dean Rusk would still write that "Diem had to reconcile with the Buddhists, who amounted to 95 percent of the population."[30] Didn't any of these people even *hear* of the Hoa Hao and the Cao Dai? (The Department of State actually knew astonishingly little about the Vietnamese.[31]) With equally impressive disinclination (or inability) to perform the most elemental research, the authors of the *Pentagon Papers* informed President Johnson that under President Diem "Northern Catholics came to fill almost all important civilian and military positions."[32] But in fact Diem's cabinet in 1963 contained five Catholics, five Confucians, and eight Buddhists, the latter including the vice president and the minister of foreign affairs; in the military high command were three Catholics and 16 Confucians or Buddhists.[33]

As the number of monks' suicides increased, they were condemned by the very highest Buddhist authorities.[34] At the same time, Roger Lalouette, the French ambassador in Saigon, told the new U.S. Ambassador Henry Cabot Lodge that "in the days of the French administration [of Vietnam] suicides of Buddhists were very common and had no effect whatever on the population. They create much more excitement abroad than in Vietnam."[35] (Recall that the French had no reason to make excuses for Diem.)

The President's sister-in-law, invariably referred to in the U.S. media as "Madame Nhu," an outspoken feminist leader and a member of the South Vietnamese parliament, made some astoundingly impolitic remarks about the suicides. But later, in Paris, referring to American journalists in Saigon who waited eagerly for the next exciting opportunity to film burning human flesh, she asked what would happen if a Frenchwoman were about to hurl herself from a high window and journalists merely waited at the scene prepared to capture the event on film. The answer was that in France, it would have been a serious criminal offense not to go to the aid of someone in danger of death.[36]

(Now, let us suppose that a Catholic priest announced his intention to sit down in front of the White House and commit suicide by fire to protest some governmental policy. Would he not be taken immediately to an institution where he could be restrained, perhaps indefinitely?)

Some anti-government demonstrations occurred in Saigon through the early summer, but Secretary of State Rusk noted that "in fact, GVN [Government of Vietnam] has gone most of the way to meet [militant Buddhist demands]."[37] The following month the CIA reported that spokesmen for the Buddhist militants "convey the unmistakable impression that even if the government can satisfactorily refute these charges [of discrimination], the Buddhists will raise new charges and the militant wing indicate they intend to keep up the pressure until the Diem regime is overthrown."[38] Besides, on

June 3, the CIA stated that "there has been no formal suppression of religious freedom in South Vietnam."[39]

On May 31, the U.S. Embassy noted that political oppositionists were taking control of the allegedly Buddhist protests, thus complicating what sort of response Diem could offer.[40] The CIA reported on July 8 that "if [Diem] makes the gestures of further conciliation toward the Buddhists currently being pressed on him, he has no assurance that these will satisfy them and no guarantee that such gestures, which could be interpreted as additional signs of weakness, would not merely whet the appetite of his antagonists for further unsustainable concessions."[41] And both the Embassy and the CIA expected that Tri Quang would turn to the VC in his determination to oust Diem.

If Diem really had been the ruthless dictator some American journalists portrayed him to be, he would have tossed Tri Quang and his immediate henchmen into prison, at a minimum. Indeed, if South Vietnam had been like North Vietnam, neither Buddhist demonstrations nor the later Tet Offensive would have been possible. Compared to North Vietnam, Diem and his successors allowed a great deal of personal liberty. Somehow these disparities always escaped the attention of most American reporters, and quite a few American legislators and academics as well, and to this day.

By August, ARVN generals told Diem that they believed the protests had gone on too long. They further believed that Tri Quang's followers were storing weapons in certain pagodas in the capital. The senior generals of ARVN agreed that these pagodas had to be taken over, and Tri Quang's monks, who came from rural areas, must be sent home.[42] Accordingly, on August 20 Diem proclaimed martial law. On August 21, ARVN units entered 12 pagodas (of the 4,766 pagodas in South Vietnam).[43] Most of the generals in charge of the pagoda seizures were Buddhists, including General Ton That Dinh, son of a Buddhist nun (about whom more later). Gordon Cox, the Canadian representative in Saigon of the International Control Commission which supposedly supervised the peace arranged in 1954 at Geneva, informed the U.S. government that the raids were "fully warranted by the warlike preparations being made in the pagodas and the evident intention of Tri Quang and his followers to overthrow the government."[44] Reports about murdered monks were widely circulated after the pagoda takeovers,[45] but when a UN investigating commission arrived on October 24, the allegedly murdered monks—all four of them—were indeed alive and thriving.[46] Besides, Diem had for years been doing much to make friends with rural Buddhists, constructing or refurbishing many pagodas and winning wide approval.[47]

It is very interesting to note also that before the Hue incident of May 8, there were no mentions of any "Buddhist problem" in innumerable and lengthy reports coming into Washington from various U.S. agencies in Saigon.[48] Nevertheless, in the view of the compilers of the *Pentagon Papers*, "for better or worse, the August 21 pagoda raids decided the issue for us [the U.S]";[49] that is, to participate in a military coup against the constitutional president of an allied state.

LODGE

In August 1963, President Kennedy replaced Frederick Nolting as U.S. ambassador to Saigon with Henry Cabot Lodge, former senator from Massachusetts. The Joint Chiefs of Staff were at first happy with the appointment, believing Lodge would see through the "tendentious" newspaper stories about events in Vietnam.[50] But in fact, Lodge's actions in Saigon, and the encouragement he received from key second-rank members of the Kennedy Administration, reveal some of the very worst aspects of U.S. foreign policy-making in those days, a volatile combination of breathless naiveté, Olympian arrogance, grotesque ethnocentrism, and bald ignorance. The Lodge episode suggests President Kennedy's "equation of diplomacy with public relations," to the extent that "the risky wager on a coup evidently seemed to Kennedy less fraught with danger than continuing to support Diem in the face of almost daily cries of outrage in the [American] press."[51]

Lodge had been defeated for reelection to the Senate, by John Kennedy no less, in 1952. In the following years he had achieved a certain celebrity as President Eisenhower's ambassador to the United Nations, and was Richard Nixon's running mate in 1960 (the ticket that Kennedy–Johnson defeated). Some have suggested that President Kennedy wanted Lodge in Saigon "because the idea of getting Lodge [a prominent Republican] mixed up in such a hopeless mess as Vietnam was irresistible."[52]

The events that would transpire in 1963 illustrate how President Kennedy often bypassed the National Security Council, "a body that had been designed precisely to prevent the kind of improvisation in foreign policy in which Kennedy was about to indulge."[53] This was indeed a perilous path because, in Ellen Hammer's analysis, "the policy makers of the Kennedy era, priding themselves on their tough-mindedness, were impatient with high-sounding protestations of respect for the independence of South Vietnam as an ally and sovereign nation. In the name of the struggle against the Viet Cong, they claimed the right to intervene in Vietnamese affairs as they chose."[54] According to the *Pentagon Papers*, "the administration hewed to the belief that if the U.S. be but willing to exercise its power, it could ultimately always have its way in world affairs."[55]

Arriving in Saigon on August 22, 1963, "Lodge had only a sketchy knowledge of Buddhism and little information on the South Vietnamese culture to which he was heading."[56] One of his first official acts was to give shelter in the U.S. Embassy to the agitator Tri Quang, even though the South Vietnamese authorities were seeking him on charges of trying to overthrow the government. (Now, suppose the Russian Embassy in Washington sheltered persons sought by the FBI on charges of terrorism?)

It is clear, writes Anne Blair, "that Lodge was out of his depth in Vietnam. He quickly became exasperated with the sophistication and multilayered loyalties of the Vietnamese with whom he was called upon to work. Drawing swift rather than well-substantiated conclusions, he oversimplified the political picture in South Vietnam and came to throw up his hands at the difficulty of getting anything done in 'the orient.' His cables by early 1964 take on the color of the colonizer's attitude toward 'the natives'; the Vietnamese become lazy, unpredictable, insensible to good advice, and required to be addressed slowly, and with much repetition."[57]

Lodge rarely left Saigon and did not of course speak Vietnamese. But he ignored reports from the U.S. army and the CIA, both of which had large numbers of people in the field, away from the lugubrious atmosphere of Saigon café/barroom society. At a conference with President Kennedy and principal cabinet members, CIA Director John McCone baldly observed that Lodge had been in South Vietnam only a short time, and needed to get out of Saigon and see more of the country.[58]

As Arthur Dommen wrote: "Diem was the elected president of a constitutional government and was incorruptible."[59] Eighty countries maintained diplomatic relations with his government; "in 1963, the United States was dealing with a friendly government in South Vietnam, not an enemy."[60] Nevertheless, irritated by hesitations in Washington about giving the green light for an army coup against President Diem, Lodge actually wrote this message: "Whenever we thwart attempts at a coup, as we have done in the past, we are incurring very long lasting resentments, we are assuming an undue responsibility for keeping the incumbents in office, and in general we are setting ourselves in judgment over the affairs of Vietnam."[61] And—of course, what else?—after the murder of President Diem that had occurred with his blessing, Lodge assured Kennedy's National Security Advisor McGeorge Bundy that "the next government would not bungle and stumble as much as the present one."[62] For Lodge, bungling and stumbling apparently justified, or even required, the overthrow of a friendly government and the inevitable assassination of its head. (The CIA in Saigon had warned that any coup against President Diem would end in his assassination.)[63]

Many South Vietnamese, including several ARVN generals, assumed the U.S. press was like the South Vietnamese press; that is, that the *New York Times*, by now bitterly and loudly and relentlessly hostile toward President Diem, was the organ of the Kennedy Administration, and that therefore the American government wanted Diem removed. Then in August that administration announced cuts in its aid to South Vietnam. "The cuts," said General

Duong Van ("Big") Minh, "erased all our doubts."[64] As Arthur Dommen points out, "the coup of 1963 had nothing to do with democratizing the regime."[65] General Tran Thien Khiem, later South Vietnam's ambassador to Washington, said that "the revolt was staged to please the United States. We thought that was what the Kennedy Administration wanted."[66] The die was cast. General Minh would take charge of the coup and (presumably) be named president of the republic. Michael Forrestal, a member of the National Security staff and a protégé of Harriman, stated as late as 1987 that the choice of General Minh as Diem's successor had been an appropriate one because "he was tall, a good tennis player, and spoke English."[67] That such a judgment could be made about a man who had betrayed and murdered his constitutional president is one more chilling revelation of the utter fatuity that linked the Saigon Embassy and the White House.

ADMINISTRATION OPPONENTS OF THE COUP

Nevertheless, an impressive, diverse and articulate panoply of members of the Kennedy Administration expressed, from the first moves to the last day, their deep opposition to any U.S. participation in or encouragement of a coup against President Diem. This group included Vice President Johnson, Attorney General Robert Kennedy, Director of CIA John McCone, the chief of the CIA's Far East Division William Colby, Kennedy's former Ambassador to Saigon Frederick Nolting, the Chairman of the Joint Chiefs of Staff General Maxwell Taylor, Commander of the U.S. military mission in Vietnam General Paul Harkins, the U.S. Marine Corps counterinsurgency expert General Victor Krulak, and—not least—Secretary of Defense Robert McNamara.

General Taylor, Secretary McNamara, and DCI McCone had been circumvented, and President Kennedy deceived, by Harriman, Hilsman and company, who on August 24 sent on their own totally inadequate authority this (later notorious) message to Lodge in Saigon:

> If, in spite of all your efforts, Diem remains obdurate . . . then we must face the possibility that Diem himself cannot be preserved. . . . Ambassador and country team should urgently examine all possible alternative leadership and make detailed plans as to how we might bring about Diem's replacement. . . . You may also tell appropriate military commanders we will give them direct support in any interim period of breakdown of central government mechanism.[68]

Neither the Secretary of State nor the Secretary of Defense had seen this message, but each had been told that the other had approved it. ("Had McNamara, McCone, or Taylor been contacted," writes Mark Moyar, "there is little doubt that the cable [quoted above] would never have left Washington, given the respect [they] had for Diem and the fury with which they subsequently reacted to this trickery."[69]) General Taylor ascribed what he called the "end-run message" to "the well-known compulsion of Hilsman and [Michael] Forrestal to depose Diem."[70]

Harriman was visibly (and understandably) upset when on September 17 President Kennedy sent Secretary of Defense McNamara and General Taylor to Saigon.[71] Harriman's dislike of Diem was "both personal and unforgiving," according to Robert Kennedy; his attitude toward Diem "became an emotional matter . . . and in fact his advice was wrong. In fact, it started us down a road which was quite dangerous."[72]

At the National Security Council meeting of August 31, Vice President Johnson spoke forcefully against the idea of a coup.[73] (The first man Johnson fired when he became president was Roger Hilsman, one of the conspirators in the affair of the August 24 telegram.[74]) In early September General Krulak, the Special Assistant for Counterinsurgency Activities to the Joint Chiefs, journeyed to South Vietnam. After speaking with 87 U.S. advisers and 22 ARVN officers, he reported that the war against the Viet Cong was going well and that he had found no sentiment among ARVN officers to remove Diem.[75] Along the very same line, on October 2, Chairman of the Joint Chiefs Taylor, having returned from his visit to South Vietnam, told the President: that "I am convinced that the Viet Cong insurgency in the north and center can be reduced to little more than sporadic incidents by the end of 1964."[76] CIA Director McCone told the Kennedy brothers that he could see no possible successor doing a better job than Diem.[77] He also told the U.S. Senate Foreign Relations Committee that "we have not seen a successor government in the wings that we could say positively would be an improvement over Diem."[78] Ambassador Nolting cabled Harriman that he opposed any effort to remove "the legitimate [Diem] government which happens also, in my opinion, to be the best available at the present time."[79] Nolting also vigorously denied press stories reports that President Diem discriminated in favor of Catholics.[80] As one eminent authority has written, Diem's enemies in Washington "feared Nolting more than any other American because he had shown up their arguments for the coup to be a patchwork of lies that wouldn't hold water."[81] So Nolting was called home, to be replaced by Lodge. (The Nolting case raises the disturbing question of what President Kennedy thought he had U.S. ambassadors in foreign capitals for anyway.) General Harkins, the ranking U.S. military commander in Vietnam, disagreed with the view of Henry Cabot Lodge all along the line, and in October he especially contradicted Lodge's estimate of the military situation.[82] Up to the last days, he sent messages to General Taylor very skeptical about the advisability of a coup.[83]

Almost on the eve of the move against Diem, General Taylor and DCI McCone warned President Kennedy that even if a U.S.-backed coup were successful, it would hurt the war effort. When Kennedy said that he did not understand why that would be so, they had to explain to him the painfully obvious facts that a coup would trigger a purge of administrators and commanders high and low by the coup plotters in order to get rid of numerous Diem loyalists.[84] And only hours before the move against Diem, Kennedy's National Security Adviser Bundy cabled his misgivings about the coup to Lodge.[85] (President Kennedy was trying to make up his mind about letting a cabal of South Vietnamese generals overthrow President Diem at the same time as his administration was refusing to recognize Latin American regimes that had achieved power through military coups.)[86]

THE MEDIA AND DIEM

The U.S. media were major actors in these fateful events. Some inexperienced members of the American press corps in Saigon noisily detested Diem, seeing no connection between his problems and the long and complex history of Vietnam. In their eyes, everything was Diem's fault; the United States would lose South Vietnam to the Communists if something drastic were not done about Diem and his family. U.S. Ambassador Nolting reported that the dislike of some of the American newsmen in Saigon for President Diem "verges on neurotic."[87]

One of the veteran, and hence more careful, American reporters in Vietnam was Keyes Beech of the *Chicago Daily News;* he had received a Pulitzer Prize for his Korean War reporting. Beech described Saigon as "a sophisticated snakepit of intrigue and rumor where American and Vietnamese officials are currently spending most of their waking hours figuring out ways to slit one another's throats."[88] Alas, few Americans in South Vietnam, especially the journalists most critical of Diem, ever spent any time outside of this "sophisticated snakepit" except for an occasional daytrip, not that more trips away from Saigon would have been very enlightening, since they spoke no Vietnamese and very little French. They thus had to limit their "sources" to Vietnamese who spoke English, or in a very few cases, French; how they imagined that such persons were representative of the South Vietnamese population, especially the peasantry, remains a profound mystery. As it turned out, two of the media's prime sources were in fact Communist agents, Pham Ngoc Tao and Pham Xuan An, the latter attached to North Vietnamese Army intelligence.[89] It was mainly from those two poisonous sources that the anti-Diem journalists got their stories about alleged dissension in the ARVN officer corps. They criticized Diem for not introducing Western-style democratic practices, which existed nowhere in East Asia except Japan and the Philippines (and only precariously there), in a Vietnam which was besieged from within and without by Communist forces, and where, in the manner of the Viet Minh two decades previously, the Viet Cong systematically assassi-

nated schoolteachers, health workers, and local officials; by 1965 the number
of civilians assassinated by the Viet Cong approached 25,000. The effects of
this massive campaign of terror on the population in the countryside was
devastating.[90] And the destruction of personal safety in the villages of course
had a tremendous negative impact on state activities.[91] The government's
anti-malaria campaign ground to a halt; many schoolrooms in guerrilla-in-
fested areas were closed.[92] It would be difficult above all to overestimate the
psychological impact of the constant terror. Through the most truly heinous
attacks on innocent civilians, the Viet Cong effectively taught the peasantry
the dangers of associating with the government or resisting the insurgents.[93]
The Viet Cong boasted of their terror tactics; when, for example, in 1966,
they opened fire with mortars on the main market center of Saigon, killing
and maiming many, the Viet Cong radio called the attack "a resounding
exploit."[94] Sometimes the Viet Cong would murder the entire family of an
official or schoolteacher just to make their point more effectively;[95] the mass
murder of 17 persons in Chau Doc in July1957 was one of the most grisly
examples of these tactics.

This was but one of the conditions in South Vietnam with which Diem
had to contend. But all that made little impression on those reporters who
blamed President Diem for everything. His principal press antagonist was
David Halberstam of the *New York Times*. According to Anne Blair, he "had
taken up the story of a developing dispute between Diem and various Buddhist groups as a vehicle for writing about the political situation in South
Vietnam with the quite conscious motive of promoting a coup against
Diem."[96] In his reporting about the occupation of the pagodas, Halberstam
told his readers that many monks and nuns were beaten or bayonetted or fired
upon, that "the main pagodas in Vietnam" had been pillaged, and that "Catholic" and "Buddhist" army units had fired upon one another. All these statements were completely, grotesquely false, but would nevertheless get Halberstam a Pulitzer Prize, and help to severely distort elite opinion in the U.S.
about Diem.[97] Moreover, as Francis X. Winters observes,

> in the course of his 1963 anti-Diem campaign, Halberstam did not hesitate to
> reiterate misrepresentations of easily verifiable facts. For example, during the
> spring and summer Buddhist crisis in several cities (but not in the country-
> side), Halberstam "explained" the religious makeup of the South Vietnamese
> government. On June 17, July 17 and July 20 his front-page articles repeated:
> "The President [Diem] and most government officials are Roman Catholic."[98]

Such statements were not only grossly incorrect and highly inflammatory,
but could have been checked and corrected with the expenditure of very little
time and effort. (In fact, as might have been expected by anybody familiar
with the politics of South Vietnam, it was ex-northerners, not Catholics, who
were the dominant group in Diem's government.[99])

Concerning the manner in which some American journalists reported the Buddhist immolations, Ellen Hammer delivered this damning indictment: "Never in all that time did these reporters who were so dedicated to the truth stop to inquire whether such deaths by fire had ever before occurred in Vietnam. Yet there was no secret about it; they had only to talk with knowledgeable people, Vietnamese and others, and consult old books and newspapers."[100] (But how do you do that if you are familiar with neither the Vietnamese or even the French language?)

The inexperience of American journalists in Saigon, and their tendency to stay inside the capital, were critically noted by many. Ambassador Nolting reported that "older, more experienced correspondents are not stationed here because editors apparently cannot persuade such men to live in Saigon, and in fact often have difficulty finding anyone at all who will agree to come."[101] "[Army Chief of Staff] General Wheeler stated that 'perhaps it would be better to try to get the press to send especially experienced men out, individually.'"[102] In July 1963, Major General Victor Krulak reported that notable advances were being made in the campaign against the Viet Cong.[103] He further suggested that "what is needed is a few venturesome newsmen who are willing to forego the comforts of the city and endure a little mud and discomfort. Those so inclined would be rewarded with a picture of resolution and progress [in the anti-VC war] which they would not quickly forget."[104] In fact, several seasoned journalists, including Keyes Beech, Marguerite Higgins, and Joseph Alsop, were vigorously refuting what Halberstam wrote.[105] Nevertheless, the historian Mark Moyar has maintained that "Halberstam was twenty-eight when he came to Vietnam. Before he left, fifteen months later, he would do more harm to the interests of the United States than any other journalist in American history."[106] And Arthur Dommen stated that Halberstam wrote some of "the most hypocritical passages in American letters."[107]

President Kennedy himself became aware "that Mr. Halberstam of the *New York Times* is actually running a political campaign; that he is wholly unobjective, reminiscent of Mr. Matthews in the Castro days.[108] [The President] stated that it was essential that we not permit Halberstam to unduly influence our actions."[109] But President Kennedy would fail to follow his own good advice.

President Kennedy's press chief, Pierre Salinger, later testified to the hostility of certain American correspondents toward Diem. General (and later Ambassador) Taylor wrote of their "full-scale vendetta" against the South Vietnamese president; "To me, it was a sobering spectacle of the power of a few relatively young and inexperienced newsmen who, openly committed to 'getting' Diem, . . . were not satisfied to report the events of foreign policy but undertook to shape them."[110] Ambassador Nolting wrote that "our media and our government were incredibly gullible" during the

Buddhist crisis and that "I have no doubt that the American media played a major role in undermining U.S. confidence in the Diem government."[111] The anxiety that the likes of Halberstam aroused within certain Washington circles was illustrated by a communication from Michael Forrestal of the National Security Council staff to President Kennedy, stating that he and Averell Harriman would make "a rapid and vigorous effort to improve press relations in Saigon *even at some cost to our relationship with the Diem government.*"[112]

In July 1963 Assistant Secretary of State Robert Manning complained in a long message to President Kennedy of the "bitterness and contempt displayed by American correspondents for President Diem." He went on to note that "they unanimously maintain that the Vietnamese program cannot succeed unless the Diem regime is replaced"; they are "convinced that their own assessment represents a more authoritative and realistic picture than is being given to Washington by its own representatives [that is, the Central Intelligence Agency, the U.S. Embassy, and the U.S. military]"; and "one element in the present hostility between the press and the [U.S.] Embassy is wounded ego on the part of the correspondents who have a highly developed sense of [their own] importance." In summary, the correspondents are too inbred . . . [and] have convinced themselves that they are the only ones who know or will recognize the truth about the situation in Vietnam."[113]

And from Saigon, National Security Council staffer Michael Forrestal informed the President that "the American press representatives are bitter and will seize on anything that goes wrong and blow it up as much as possible."[114] At about the same time, General Krulak wrote a memorandum of his conversation with Clement Zablocki, a Democratic member of the House of Representatives (1949–1983) from Wisconsin; the Congressman told him that "the conduct of the resident U.S. press is a grave reflection upon their entire profession. They are arrogant, emotional, unobjective, and ill-informed. The case against them is best expressed by their having been repudiated by much of the responsible U.S. press."[115]

Television news was not much better. For example, CBS cut its famous 1963 interview of President Kennedy by Walter Cronkite from one half hour to only 12 minutes. Many of the President's words of understanding and sympathy for Diem were suppressed in order to provide more time for commercial messages.[116]

"It seems probable," wrote Marguerite Higgins, "that the American public would have been less hostile to Diem if it had realized that he was not repressing anybody because of their religion but trying to put down a political rebellion led by some extremist Buddhists aimed at overthrowing his government. Nobody in the State Department at that time had the courage or sense of fair play to correct what they knew to be a distorted image of Vietnam."[117] Her judgment of the State Department may be too gentle:

Under Secretary of State George Ball actually told President Kennedy that "you get more by talking to the correspondents than the U.S. Embassy, the CIA, or the U.S. Military."[118] Ball habitually informed the Saigon Embassy—from his office in Washington—what "the Vietnamese people" were thinking.[119] "And thus is history recast," wrote Higgins:

> All those Vietnamese-speaking Americans circling the countryside for the purpose of testing Vietnamese opinion; all those American officers gauging the morale of the troops; all those CIA agents tapping their sources (hopefully) everywhere; all those dispatches from Ambassador Nolting—an army of data-collectors in reasonable agreement had been downgraded in favor of press dispatches stating opposite conclusions. It was the first time I began to comprehend, in depth and some sorrow, what was meant by the *power* of the press.[120]

This deeply disquieting phenomenon—Washington insiders discounting reports from the U.S. Embassy in Saigon, the CIA, and the U.S. military in favor of sensational media reports filed by inexperienced writers or film-makers—would reappear again and again, most notably during the Tet Offensive of 1968, to be discussed later on. In any event, writes John O'Donnell, "Henry Cabot Lodge gave the go-ahead for the military coup against President Diem. I believe to this day that this decision was one of the two most serious mistakes that the United States made in South Vietnam."[121]

THE COUP

During the preparations for the coup, the conspirators arrested officers known to be loyal to President Diem, including the commanders of the Air Force, the Marines, the elite Airborne Division, the territorial militia, and the police force, and deliberately murdered at least one, the chief of naval operations.[122] All over South Vietnam, half of the ARVN division commanders remained loyal to Diem, but could not come to his aid because the plotters had taken care to block key transportation routes to Saigon.[123] Hence loyal units did not arrive to rescue Diem during the siege of the Presidential Palace. These events would play a very important role in all the post-coup bitterness and conflicts within ARVN.

The outcome of the coup was never a sure thing. The key to a successful coup would be, of course, the ARVN units inside Saigon. President Diem had appointed 37-year-old Ton That Dinh, the youngest of ARVN's generals and a man he trusted, to command ARVN forces around the capital. But Dinh secretly nursed a grievance against the president for failing to give him an additional star and other rewards. The plotters easily seduced him into their circle, but apparently never trusted this vain and disloyal young man.[124]

The attack on the Presidential Palace began in the early morning of November 1. One of the leaders in the assault was Colonel Nguyen Van Thieu, a
convert to Catholicism, eventually to be elected President of the Republic.

Inside the Palace, Special Forces officers recommended to Diem a vigorous assault on the coupmakers' center of command, the Joint General Staff
Headquarters. Diem declined this advice because the Joint General Staff
embodied to him the authority of the armed forces. [125]

From the Presidential Palace, Diem called the U.S. Embassy and spoke to
Lodge, who revealed a "chilling indifference to the fate of Diem." [126] Afterward, Diem and Nhu simply walked out of the palace and entered a car,
contrary to some American press reports about their use of a secret tunnel. [127]

The two brothers found temporary haven in a church in the Chinese
suburb of Cholon. Diem called the Palace to instruct his loyal defenders there
to lay down their arms and avoid more bloodshed, but his call was traced and
the brothers were soon arrested. General Don has written "without equivoca-
tion" that General Minh gave the order for the murder of the two brothers, an
accusation also leveled at Minh by other authoritative sources. [128] Tran Van
Huong, a prominent critic of Diem, said: "The generals knew very well that,
having no talent, no moral virtues, no political support whatsoever, they
could not prevent a spectacular comeback of the President and Mr. Nhu [the
president's brother] if they were alive." [129] When Ngo Dinh Can heard of the
murder of his brothers, he appealed to the American consul in Hue for sanctuary. Alas, different rules applied to him than to Tri Quang, the agitator who
found shelter in Lodge's Embassy. The Americans handed Can over to the
generals, who promptly shot him. [130]

AFTERWARD

The murder of President Diem—what Marguerite Higgins called "this unprecedented betrayal of an ally"—predictably evoked diverse responses. [131]

From Cambridge, Massachusetts, Galbraith, fatuous sycophant to the end,
wrote to Harriman: "Dear Averell, The South Vietnam coup *is another great
feather in your cap.* Do get me a list of all the people who told us there was
no alternative to Diem." [132]

As a wartime austerity measure, Diem had closed the Saigon nightclubs.
They reopened after his death. "Young interior minister General Dinh had
been persuaded by some Western photographers to go to a night club and do
the twist [dance] to show that he was 'liberal and in touch with the people,'
as one US caption proclaimed. (An interesting insight into Occidental val-
ues.)" [133]

To the Viet Cong and Hanoi, the murder of Diem was "heaven-sent." [134]
Tran Nam Trung, chief of the Viet Cong military committee, said: "They'll

never find anyone more effective than Diem."[135] Indeed, for Arthur Dommen, "the overthrow of President Ngo Dinh Diem was the greatest Communist victory since Dien Bien Phu."[136]

The authors of the *Pentagon Papers* wrote: "Thus, the nine-year rule of Ngo Dinh Diem came to a sudden, bloody and permanent end, and U.S. policy in Vietnam plunged into the unknown, our complicity in the coup only heightening our responsibilities and our commitments in this struggling, leaderless land. We could be certain only that whatever new leadership emerged would be fragile, untried and untested."[137] But if "we could be certain" of that, then why had Diem been removed in the first place?

"I was appalled," wrote Henry Kissinger, one day to be U.S. Secretary of State, "by the direct role the United States had evidently played in the overthrow of South Vietnam's President Ngo Dinh Diem, which led to his assassination. . . . [I]n the purge following, the country was bereft of almost its entire civil administration. For us to be seen to connive in the overthrow of a friendly government was bound to shake the confidence of other allies in Southeast Asia."[138] And not only there.

Before the coup, the Viet Cong controlled approximately 30 percent of South Vietnam's territory. Within 6 months of it, they held 40–45 percent.[139] Less than three months after the coup, Director of Central Intelligence McCone informed President Johnson that "there is no organized government in South Vietnam at this time."[140]

In January 1964, another coup overthrew General Minh and his gang (they were lucky: nobody murdered *them*). In March 1964, Secretary of Defense McNamara wrote to President Johnson:

> The political control structure extending from Saigon down into the hamlets disappeared following the November [anti-Diem] coup. Of the 41 incumbent province chiefs on November 1, 35 have been replaced (nine provinces had three province chiefs in three months; one province had four.) Scores of lesser official were replaced. Almost all major military commands have changed hands twice since the November coup. The faith of the peasants has been shaken by the disruptions in experienced leadership and the loss of physical security.[141]

A month afterward, Averell Harriman, a principal enabler of the coup/murder, actually said that "as you look back on it, Diem was better than the chaotic condition we have now."[142]

The coups and purges continued. "That entire period [October 1964–June 1965] had been marked by riots, coups and attempted coups."[143] Even before that, in September 1964, an alarmed General Westmoreland had stated that

> the officers of [ARVN] must be protected against purges solely [because of their] religious or political affiliation. . . . The Officer Corps must be assured

that its members will not be punished or expelled from the armed forces if they faithfully execute the orders of constituted authority in connection with the maintenance of law and order. They must be assured that their superiors will not accede to the arbitrary demands of pressure groups whose interest it is to destroy the discipline of the armed forces and to render ineffective the forces of law and order. [144]

(Now, to which "pressure groups" could Westmoreland possibly have been referring?) Meanwhile, the self-immolation of Buddhists, which had been Washington's miserable excuse for removing Diem, did not stop with his overthrow and murder. Quite to the contrary, *during the four months after the coup more monks and alleged monks had killed themselves than during the entire nine years of Diem's regime.* "Of course nobody writes about them anymore," Robert Kennedy said in April 1964. Previously, the self-immolations were "used to show that Diem was so bad, but . . . I don't know what they prove now." [145] Former Ambassador Nolting testified that "I believe now, however, that the [so-called Buddhist] crisis was a Viet Cong conspiracy." [146] Indeed, in 1966 Tri Quang tried to launch a full-scale Buddhist uprising, during which eleven more immolations took place. The Saigon government, with the approval of the U.S. embassy, sent troops against them and killed hundreds. [147] By May 1966, Ambassador Lodge "viewed the Buddhists as equivalent to card-carrying Communists." [148]

The influential columnist Joseph Alsop wrote this: "I came to revise my assessment of Diem and, indeed, felt some measure of guilt for having turned against him"; the assassination of Diem "can now be judged as a grim and perhaps decisive turning point for the worse in the Vietnam war." [149]

In any event, as the situation in post-Diem South Vietnam continued to deteriorate, the first Marine battalions landed at Da Nang on March 8, 1965. The following month the Honolulu Conference approved a plan for 80,000 American, Korean, and Australian troops to go to South Vietnam. That was just the beginning. [150]

And in those chaotic days, wrote General Maxwell Taylor, "there was the memory of Diem to haunt those of us who were aware of the circumstances of his downfall. By our complicity we Americans were responsible for the plight in which the South Vietnamese found themselves." [151]

Much of what passes for truth about Ngo Dinh Diem comes from the self-exculpating efforts of those who murdered him, or who urged his overthrow, and from the hagiographers of the Kennedy Administration. For all these persons, it was necessary to smear Diem's reputation, to assassinate him again and again. In the United States, "the truth" is very often what is sufficiently repeated by the chattering classes. But as one distinguished scholar noted years ago, "Diem was the embodiment of his country's soul, for good no less than for ill." [152] Washington's rejection of Diem had been rooted in his skepticism of American omniscience, or, as Blair states, "Diem was overthrown because he would not be a puppet."[153] And to Patrick Lloyd Hatcher, this rejection of Diem, and the easy assumption of superiority that preceded it, "more than any other aspect of the American intervention in Vietnam, was responsible for the disastrous end of the war."[154]

In the same vein, William Colby, Director of the Central Intelligence Agency from 1973 to 1976, writes: "The coup against Diem, then, must be assigned the stigma of America's primary (and perhaps worst) error in Vietnam. The two later ones—fighting the wrong war, refusing help to an ally at the critical moment—stemmed inexorably from it."[155]

On November 2, 1971—the eighth anniversary of the murders—a memorial service for Diem took place at his grave in Saigon. A Buddhist monk offered prayers. The eulogist, an ARVN general, said that President Diem died because he resisted the domination of foreigners and their schemes to bring great numbers of troops to Vietnam and widen the war that was going to destroy North and South.[156]

The authors of the *Pentagon Papers*, no great cheerleaders for Diem, wrote after his murder that:

> [Diem's] regime compared favorably with other Asian governments of the same period in its respect for the person and property of citizens. There is much that can be offered in mitigation of Diem's authoritarianism. He began as the most singularly disadvantaged head of state of his era. His political [inheritance] was endemic violence and virulent anticolonialism. He took office at a time when the government of Vietnam controlled only a few blocks of downtown Saigon; the rest of the capital was the feudal fief of the Binh Xuyen gangster fraternity. Beyond the environs of Saigon South Vietnam lay divided among the Viet Minh enclaves and the theocratic dominions of the Cao Dai and the Hoa Hao sects. All these powers would have opposed any Saigon government, whatever its composition.[157]

And as it turned out, Diem had been correct on all the fundamentals: (1) correct about seeking to guard himself from a coup by ambitious generals; the error lay not in his trying to do this but in his not doing it ruthlessly; (2) correct about believing that the conflict with Hanoi and the Viet Cong could not, and did not have to, be won on some kind of schedule, or even be "won" at all; and (3) correct about not wanting to have hundreds of thousands of U.S. troops in Vietnam. In the event, those massive troop numbers brought untold suffering to the Vietnamese, North and South, and helped destroy the presidencies of Lyndon Johnson and Richard Nixon.

One student of the overthrow of President Diem has observed that "there may be lessons for other, especially less powerful, nations who are contemplating alliance with the United States. Armed with such sobering historical understanding, potential allies may move more cautiously in the rapids of American alliance politics."[158]

And even if one took seriously all the most extravagant and ignorant criticisms of President Diem, did that justify, or even partly excuse, the American orchestration of a military coup against an allied government, a coup that predictably would end in murder, as well as the breakdown of the entire machinery of an allied state? Here is another way to look at the American involvement in the murder of Diem: Imagine if several all-powerful, all-ignorant staffers of the Kennedy Administration and some twenty-something reporters of the *New York Times* had concluded that President de Gaulle's sabotage of NATO was jeopardizing Western victory or even security in the Cold war to an intolerable degree. Suppose it came to the surface that those staffers and the U.S. ambassador to Paris had entered into secret negotiations with leaders of the French Army to remove President de Gaulle, and that these negotiations had been discussed several times in the presence of the President of the United States. What then?

NOTES

1. Anne Blair, *Lodge in Vietnam: A Patriot Abroad* (New Haven, CT: Yale University Press, 1995), p. 9.
2. Francis X. Winters, *The Year of the Hare: America in Vietnam, January 25, 1963–February 15, 1964* (Athens, GA: University of Georgia Press, 1999), p. 42.
3. Arthur J. Dommen, *The Indochinese Experience of the French and the Americans: Nationalism and Communism in Cambodia, Laos and Vietnam* (Bloomington, IN: Indiana University Press, 2001), p. 504.
4. *Pentagon Papers* (Boston: Beacon Press, 1971), vol. 2, p. 124.
5. "Letter from the Ambassador in India (Bowles) to the President's Special Assistant for National Security Affairs (Bundy)," *FRUS* 1961–1963, vol. 3, p. 519.
6. Winters, *Year of the Hare*, p. 30. Cecil Currey wrote: "Diem had one top American official after another coming into Saigon, telling him what he had to do. Each was supremely self-confident that he had all the technically correct information to back up his position. . . . Such experts often commented grandly on issues which they hardly understood, which must have given Diem a constant sinking feeling. He would then patiently try to correct their errors by providing broad background material. Of course this bored [these Americans] stiff and many didn't bother to hide the fact. A number of highly placed Americans regularly sounded off with their negative opinions about Diem." Cecil B. Currey, *Edward Lansdale: The Unquiet American* (Washington, D.C.: Brassey's, 1998), p. 153.
7. Ellen J. Hammer, *A Death in November: America in Vietnam, 1963* (New York: Dutton, 1987), p. 269; "The presence of U.S. troops virtually destroyed South Vietnamese society. American politicians, economists and sociologists never bothered to consider the effect half a million foreign troops would have on an underdeveloped country that had existed under feudalism for a long, long time. American PXs, bars and brothels, the smuggling dens and marijuana and opium joints, and the western and gangster films soon changed South Vietnam beyond recognition. They ravaged the ethical foundations of that society, turning it into a mad and pragmatic society of consumption, causing the downfall of innumerable young people (males and females alike). . . ." Bui Tin, *From Enemy to Friend: A North Vietnamese Perspective on the War* (Annapolis, MD: Naval Institute Press, 2002), p. 156. In April 1963, Diem told Ambassador Nolting that having too many Americans in South Vietnam would create the

image of an American protectorate and play into the hands of the Communists; *FRUS* 1961–1963, vol. 3, pp. 207–211.

8. Philip Catton, *Diem's Final Failure: Prelude to America's War in Vietnam* (Lawrence, KS: University Press of Kansas, 2003), p. 211.

9. Edward Miller, *Misalliance: Ngo Dinh Diem, the United States, and the Fate of South Vietnam* (Cambridge, MA: Harvard University Press, 2013), p. 231.

10. Hammer, *Death in November*, p. 203.

11. Dommen, *Indochinese Experience*, pp. 531–532.

12. Miller, *Misalliance*, p. 253.

13. Hammer, *Death in November*, pp. 151 and 269.

14. Hammer, *Death in November*, p. 232; see also Marianna P. Sullivan, *France's Vietnam Policy: A Study in French-American Relations* (Westport, CT: Greenwood, 1978).

15. Hammer, *Death in November*, p. 124 and pp. 222–224.

16. *FRUS*, 1961–1963, vol. 4: 55, 68–72, 89, 184; Mieczyslaw Maneli, *War of the Vanquished* (New York: Harper and Row, 1971), pp. 112–131. Dommen, *Indochinese Experience*, pp. 530–531; Winters, *Year of the Hare*, p. 12. And see Catton, *Diem's Final Failure*, pp. 194–198.

17. For suspicions that Nhu was in contact with leading VC figures, see for example *FRUS*, 1961–1963, vol. 3, p. 327, and Miller, *Misalliance*, pp. 302–311.

18. It was "a crisis that took almost everyone in South Vietnam by surprise." Miller, *Misalliance*, p. 268.

19. "It was so easy for Communist agents to disguise themselves as monks"; Marguerite Higgins, *Our Vietnam Nightmare* (New York: Harper and Row, 1965), p. 22. For Communist involvement in these Buddhist troubles, and for Tri Quang's extensive and interesting associations with the Communists north and south, see especially Mark Moyar, *Triumph Forsaken: The Vietnam War, 1954–1965* (New York: Cambridge University Press, 2006), pp. 217–218; Dommen, *Indochinese Experience*, p. 511; and Allan E. Goodman, *Politics in War: The Bases of Political Community in South Vietnam* (Cambridge, MA: Harvard University Press, 1973), p. 43.

20. Dennis J. Duncanson, *Government and Revolution in Vietnam* (New York: Oxford University Press, 1968), p. 330.

21. Winters, *Year of the Hare*, p. 29; Hammer, *Death in November*, pp. 113–116; Dommen, *Indochinese Experience*, 509–513; see telegrams to State from Hue Consulate, *FRUS*, 1961–1963, v. 3, pp. 277–278, 284–286.

22. *Pentagon Papers*, vol. 2, p. 207.

23. See footnote 21, above.

24. *FRUS*, 1961–1963, vol. 3, p. 310.

25. Higgins, *Nightmare*, p. 47.

26. Winters, *Year of the Hare*, p. 25.

27. Duncanson, *Government and Revolution*, p. 335; *Pentagon Papers*, vol. 2, p. 226. "The number of Buddhists in the country was between ten and twenty-seven percent of the population, depending on whether non-practicing Buddhists were counted"; Moyar, *Triumph Forsaken*, p. 215.

28. Winters, *Year of the Hare*, p. 34.

29. Winters, *Year of the Hare*, p. 32.

30. Dean Rusk, *As I Saw It: A Secretary of State's Memoirs* (London: Tauris, 1991), p 379. Even later, a youthful historian inexplicably referred to South Vietnam as "a country 90 percent Buddhist"; Seth Jacobs, *America's Miracle Man in Vietnam: Ngo Dinh Diem, Religion, Race, and U.S. Intervention in Southeast Asia, 1950–1957* (Durham, NC: Duke University Press, 2004), p. 5.

31. "There were a couple of Vietnamese linguists in the [U.S.] foreign service, but courses in Vietnamese language or history were not taught anywhere in the United States at this time. It was not until 1954 that the first American State Department officer was sent to Vietnam to study the language. One or two a year followed, until a training programme was begun which produced two specialists in 1957, two in 1958, two in 1959, two in 1960. In 1962, for reasons

unknown, the course was ended"; Denis Warner, *Not with Guns Alone* (Richmond, Victoria: Hutchinson of Australia, 1977), p. 107.

32. *Pentagon Papers*, vol. 2, p. 226.

33. Winters, *Year of the Hare*, p. 178. See Nolting, *From Trust to Tragedy*, p. 107; "The primary cause of Catholic over-representation . . . was not discrimination but the higher proportion of educated persons in the Vietnamese Catholic population, a legacy of the colonial era"; Moyar, *Triumph Forsaken*, p. 216.

34. Jean Lacouture, *Vietnam Between Two Truces* (New York: Random House, 1966), pp. 109–110; Winters, *Year of the Hare*, pp. 52 and 53.

35. See the cable from Lodge to President Kennedy, *FRUS*, 1961–1963, vol. 4, p. 58.

36. Hammer, *Death in November*, p. 350.

37. Rusk to Lodge, June 11, 1963; *FRUS*, 1961–1963, vol. 3, p. 382.

38. July 8, 1963; *FRUS*, 1961–1963, vol. 3, p. 476.

39. "Current Intelligence Memorandum Prepared by the Office of Current Intelligence, Central Intelligence Agency," *FRUS*, 1961–1963, vol. 3, June 3, 1963, p. 345.

40. *FRUS*, 1961–1963, vol. 3, pp. 337–338; see also June 1, p. 341 and June 3, p. 345.

41. *FRUS*, 1961–1963, vol. 3, p. 478.

42. Hammer, *Death in November*, p. 282. Both the U.S. Embassy in Saigon and the Central Intelligence Agency reported that ARVN generals told Diem he must crack down on Buddhist agitation; *FRUS*, 1961–1963, pp. 595 and 616. President Diem gave specific instructions that no bonzes were to be hurt; ibid., p. 616.

43. Higgins, *Nightmare*, p. 189.

44. Winters, *Year of the Hare*, p. 53.

45. The *Pentagon Papers* incorrectly refer to "repressions against the Buddhist clergy" after the lifting of martial law on September 16. *Pentagon Papers*, vol. 2, p. 252.

46. Hammer, *Death in November*, p. 168; see also Miller, *Misalliance*, p. 275.

47. Winters, *Year of the Hare*, p. 25.

48. See, for example: "Current Intelligence memorandum prepared in the Office of Current Intelligence, Central Intelligence Agency, January 11, 1963; *FRUS*, 1961–1963, vol. 3, pp. 19–23; "Memorandum from the Commander in Chief, Pacific (Felt), to the Joint Chiefs of Staff," January 25, 1963, ibid., pp. 35–37; "Memorandum from the Commander, Military Assistance Command, Vietnam (Harkins), to the Commander in Chief, Pacific (Felt)," January 19, 1963, ibid., pp. 37–49; "Memorandum from the Director of the Bureau of Intelligence and Research (Hilsman) and Michael V. Forrestal of the National Security Council to the President," January 25, 1963 pp. 49–63; "Telegram from the Department of State to the Embassy in Vietnam," February 25, 1963, ibid., pp. 122–123"; Memorandum from the Joint Chiefs of Staff to the Secretary of Defense (McNamara)," March 7, 1963, ibid., pp. 133–136; "Airgram from the Department of State to the Embassy in Vietnam," March 22, 1963, ibid., pp. 173–178; "Memorandum of a Conversation, Department of State," April 1, 1963, ibid., pp. 193–195; "Memorandum of a Conversation, White House, Washington," April 4, 1963, ibid., pp. 198–201.

49. *Pentagon Papers*, vol. 2, p. 203.

50. Hammer, *Death in November*, p. 170.

51. Winters, *Year of the Hare*, pp. 169, 10.

52. Kenneth P. O'Donnell, *Johnny, We Hardly Knew Ye* (Boston, MA: Little Brown, 1972), p. 16.

53. Blair, *Lodge*, p. 16.

54. Hammer, *Death in November*, p. 211.

55. *Pentagon Papers*, vol. 2, p. 204.

56. Blair, *Lodge*, p. 34.

57. Blair, *Lodge*, p. 158.

58. September 11, 1963; *FRUS* 1961–1963, vol. 4, p. 191.

59. Dommen, *Indochinese Experience*, p. 481.

60. Hammer, *Death in November*, p. 245.

61. October 25, 1963; *FRUS*, vol. 4, p. 436.

62. *Pentagon Papers*, vol. 2, p. 781 (October 25, 1963).

63. "Memorandum from the Deputy Director for Plans, Central Intelligence Agency (Helms), to the Assistant Secretary of State for Far Eastern Affairs (Hilsman)," August 16, 1963; *FRUS*, 1961–1963, vol. 3, p. 583.

64. Higgins, *Nightmare*, p. 208.

65. Dommen, *Indochinese Experience* p. 538.

66. Higgins, *Nightmare*, p. 208.

67. Winters, *Year of the Hare*, p. 32.

68. *Pentagon Papers*, vol. 2, p. 734; *FRUS*, 1961–1963, vol. 3, p. 629; Hammer, *Death in November*, pp. 179–180.

69. Moyar, *Triumph Forsaken*, p. 238; see also Winters, *Year of the Hare*, pp. 56–57.

70. General Krulak, "Memorandum for the Record"; *FRUS*, 1961–1963, vol. 3, p. 631. See Hammer, *Death in November*, pp. 179–180. "Washington insiders considered Hilsman abrasive, arrogant, and supremely confident in his own judgment"; Miller, *Misalliance*, p. 220.

71. *FRUS*, 1961–1963, vol. 4, p. 251.

72. Hammer, *Death in November*, p. 32

73. *FRUS*, vol. 4, p. 74. Johnson held onto his view of the coup through the years of his Presidency: "In my judgment this decision [to support a coup against Diem] was a serious blunder that launched a period of deep political confusion in Saigon that lasted almost two years"; Lyndon Johnson, *The Vantage Point* (Holt, Rinehart and Winston, 1971), p. 61.

74. Hammer, *Death in November*, p. 314.

75. September 10, 1963; *FRUS*, 1961–1963, vol. 4, pp. 153–160.

76. *Pentagon Papers*, vol. 2, p. 249.

77. Hammer, *Death in November*, p. 243.

78. Harold P. Ford, *CIA and the Vietnam Policy Makers*, p. 36.

79. Nolting to Harriman, February 27; *FRUS*, 1961–1963, vol. 3, p. 128.

80. *FRUS*, 1961–1963, vol. 3, p. 466.

81. Dommen, *Indochinese Experience*, p. 521.

82. Hammer, *Death in November*, p. 276; *FRUS*, 1961–1963, vol. 4, pp. 479–500.

83. October 28–30, 1963; *FRUS*, 1961–1963, vol. 4.

84. October 29, 1963; *FRUS*, 1961–1963, vol. 4, p. 470.

85. October 30, 1963; *FRUS*, 1961–1963, vol. 4, p. 500.

86. See Theodore James Maher, "The Kennedy and Johnson Responses to Latin American Coups d'Etat," *World Affairs*. Vol. 131, no. 3 (Fall 1968).

87. *FRUS*, 1961–1963, vol. 3, p. 100.

88. Higgins, *Nightmare*, p. 121.

89. Thomas A. Bass, *The Spy Who Loved Us: The Vietnam War and Pham Xuan An's Dangerous Game* (New York: Public Affairs, 2009). See also Olivier Todd, *Cruel April: The Fall of Saigon* (New York: Norton, 1990).

90. On Viet Cong murder of civilians, see Stuart A. Herrington, *Silence Was a Weapon: The Vietnam War in the Villages* (Novato, CA: Presidio, 1982), p. 137; Fall, *The Two Vietnams*, p. 281; Race, *War Comes to Long An*, p. 83; Duiker, *Communist Road to Power*, p. 180; Eric M. Bergerud, *The Dynamics of Defeat: The Vietnam War in Hau Nghia Province* (Boulder, CO: Westview, 1991), pp. 67–68; Scigliano, *South Vietnam*, p. 140; Robert Thompson, *Defeating Communist Insurgency: The Lessons of Malaya and Vietnam* (New York: Praeger, 1966), p. 27; Stephen T. Hosmer, *Viet Cong Repression and Its Implications for the Future* (Santa Monica, CA: RAND, 1970).

91. Duncanson, *Government and Revolution*, p. 261.

92. Scigliano, *South Vietnam*, p. 117. "A pattern of politically motivated terror began to emerge, directed against the representatives of the Saigon government. . . . The terror was directed not only against officials, but against all whose operations were essential to the functioning of organized political society: school teachers, health workers, agricultural officials, etc"; George A. Carver, "The Faceless Viet Cong," *Foreign Affairs,* vol. 44, no. 3 (April 1966), p. 10.

93. Thompson, *Defeating Communist Insurgency*, p. 39.

94. Duncanson, *Government and Revolution*, p. 14.

95. William R. Andrews, *The Village War: Vietnamese Communist Revolutionary Activities in Dinh Tuong Province, 1960–1964* (Columbia, MO: University of Missouri Press, 1973), pp. 59–60.

96. Blair, *Lodge,* p. 13.

97. See Halberstam's stunningly erroneous articles in *The New York Times*, August 22, 23, 24, and 25, 1963. On August 24 he actually used the expression "the sacking of the country's main pagodas." His equally error-filled piece on August 15 was characterized by Major General Kulak as "disingenuous"; *FRUS*, 1961–1963, vol. 3, p. 584.

98. Winters, *Year of the Hare*, p. 177.

99. *Pentagon Papers*, vol. 1, p. 248.

100. Hammer, *Death in November*, p. 146.

101. "Telegram from the Embassy in Vietnam to the Department of State," February 5, 1963, *FRUS*, 1961–1963, vol. 3, pp. 98–102.

102. "Memorandum of a Conversation between the Assistant Secretary of State for Far Eastern Affairs (Harriman) and the Chief of Staff, United States Army (Wheeler), Department of State, Washington, February 9, 1963, *FRUS*, 1961–1963, vol. 3, pp. 112–113.

103. *FRUS*, 1961–1963, vol. 3, p. 456.

104. *FRUS*, 1961–1963, vol. 3, p. 465.

105. William Prochnau, *Once Upon a Distant War* (New York: Times Books, 1995), pp. 397–398.

106. Moyar, *Triumph Forsaken*, p. 170.

107. Dommen, *Indochinese Experience*, p. 566.

108. Matthews, also of the *New York Times*, visited Fidel Castro's guerrilla base in the Sierra Maestra in 1957, and informed the world that far from being a Communist, Castro was decidedly anti-Communist.

109. August 26, 1963; *FRUS*, 1961–1963, vol. 3, p. 638.

110. Maxwell D. Taylor, *Swords and Plowshares* (New York: W. W. Norton, 1972), p. 300.

111. Nolting, *From Trust to Tragedy*, p. 86 and p. 116.

112. "Memorandum from Michael V. Forrestal of the National Security Council Staff to the President," February 4, 1963, *FRUS*, 1961–1963, vol. 3, pp. 97–98. My italics.

113. Assistant Secretary of State Robert Manning, "Report on the Saigon Press Situation," *FRUS*, 1961–1963, vol. 3, pp. 532, 533, 535, 537, 543.

114. *Pentagon Papers*, vol. 2, p. 724.

115. October 28, 1963; *FRUS*, 1961–1963, vol. 4.

116. Hammer, *Death in November*, p. 199.

117. Higgins, *Nightmare*, p. 83.

118. Gerald Strober and Deborah Strober, *"Let Us Begin Anew": An Oral History of the Kennedy Presidency* (New York: Perennial, 1994), p. 410, quoted in Moyar, *Triumph Forsaken*, p. 237.

119. See, for example, *FRUS*, 1961–1963, vol. 3, p. 558.

120. Higgins, *Nightmare,* p. 125; emphasis in original.

121. Harvey Neese and John O'Donnell, eds., *Prelude to Tragedy: Vietnam, 1960–1965* (Annapolis, MD: Naval Institute Press, 2001), pp. 227–228.

122. Moyar, *Triumph Forsaken,* p. 266; *Pentagon Papers*, vol. 1, p. 267.

123. Nguyen Cao Ky, *Buddha's Child: My Fight to Save Vietnam* (New York: St. Martin's, 2002), p. 96.

124. See the account of Dinh's convoluted maneuverings in *The Pentagon Papers*, vol. 1, pp. 265–267.

125. Moyar, *Triumph Forsaken*, pp. 268–269.

126. Hammer, *Death in November*, p. 297; see a partial transcript of this Lodge-Diem conversation in *Pentagon Papers*, vol. 2, p. 268.

127. Hammer, *Death in November*, p. 293, and Miller, *Misalliance*, p. 323, have it right. *The Pentagon Papers* actually (and incorrectly) referred to "one of the secret underground exits connected to the sewer system"; see vol. 2, p. 269, and also pp. 207 and 221.

128. Tran Van Don, *Our Endless War* (San Rafael, CA: Presidio, 1978), p. 112; Denis Warner, *Certain Victory: How Hanoi Won the War* (Kansas City, KS: Sheed, Andrews and McMeel, 1978), p. 129; Hammer, *Death in November*, pp. 298–299.

129. Hammer, *Death in November*, p. 300.

130. Duncanson, *Government and Revolution*, p. 341; Hammer, *Death in November*, p. 306.

131. Higgins, *Nightmare,* p. 132.

132. Winters, *Year of the Hare*, p. 111. My italics.

133. Higgins, *Nightmare*, p. 236.

134. See Hammer, *Death in November*, p. 309; William Colby, *Lost Victory: A Firsthand Account of America's Sixteen-Year Involvement in Vietnam* (Chicago, IL: Contemporary Books, 1989), p. 158.

135. Truong Vinh-Le, *Vietnam: Ou est la vérité* (Paris: Lavauzelle, 1989), p. 111.

136. Dommen, *Indochinese Experience,* p. 572.

137. *Pentagon Papers*, vol. 2, p. 270.

138. Henry Kissinger, *White House Years* (Boston: Little, Brown, 1979), p. 231.

139. William J. Duiker, *Sacred War: Nationalism and Revolution in a Divided Vietnam* (Boston: McGraw-Hill, 1995), pp. 164–165.

140. *FRUS*, 1961–1963, vol. 4, p. 736. "Only one thing is sure: the murder of Diem and Nhu brought about a period of instability that lasted until the day of the final collapse of South Vietnam"; Bui Tin, *From Enemy to Friend*, p. 155.

141. *Pentagon Papers*, vol. 2, p. 312.

142. Winters, *Year of the Hare*, p. 120.

143. *Pentagon Papers*, vol. 2, p. 362.

144. *Pentagon Papers*, vol. 2, p. 337.

145. Hammer, *Death in November*, p. 314.

146. Nolting, *From Trust to Tragedy,* p. 115.

147. Hammer, *Death in November*, p. 315.

148. *Pentagon Papers*, vol. 2, p. 376.

149. Joseph Alsop, *"I've Seen the Best of It":Memoirs* (New York: Norton, 1992), pp. 462–463.

150. *Pentagon Papers*, vol. 2, p. 355.

151. Maxwell Taylor, *Swords and Plowshares* (New York: Norton, 1972), p. 407.

152. Duncanson, *Government and Revolution*, p. xi.

153. Blair, *Lodge*, p. 158.

154. Patrick Lloyd Hatcher, *Suicide of an Elite: American Internationalists and Vietnam* (Stanford, CA: Stanford University Press, 1990), p. 317. William Colby agrees with this judgment; see his *Lost Victory*, p. 366. So did Edward Lansdale; see Cecil B. Currey, *Edward Lansdale: The Unquiet American* (Boston: Houghton Mifflin, 1988).

155. Colby, *Lost Victory*, p. 366.

156. Hammer, *Death in November*, p. 317; see also Robert Shaplen, "The Cult of Diem," *New York Times Magazine*, May 14, 1972.

157. *Pentagon Papers*, vol. 1, p. 253.

158. Winters, *Year of the Hare*, p. 4.

Chapter Four

The South Vietnamese Army

"The foundation of states is a good military organization."—Machiavelli, *The Discourses*, XX

The disdain heaped upon ARVN—the South Vietnamese Army—by American reporters and academics, throughout the war and for decades after, is equaled only by their unfamiliarity with that army's record. ARVN was certainly far from being a perfect military institution, especially at its very highest level, but Americans are not free from responsibility for that situation. In the end, abandoned and disparaged by its U.S. ally, ARVN went down fighting.

ORIGINS OF THE SOUTH VIETNAMESE ARMY

By 1948, the French faced both an urgent need for troops to fight the Viet Minh, and a rising opposition to any proposal to send conscripts from metropolitan France to Vietnam. The response of the French government was to greatly increase the number of Vietnamese serving either in the regular French forces (the CEF—*Corps expéditionnaire français*) or in the national army of the Vietnamese state (VNA) under Bao Dai. By 1953 these indigenous allies of the French numbered 300,000 men, and by the end of the Viet Minh War in July 1954 something approaching 400,000 Vietnamese were serving either in the CEF or the Vietnamese National Army. Only about 1 percent of these Vietnamese in uniform were officers.[1] It was primarily from these two military streams that the army of the future South Vietnamese state, eventually known as ARVN—the Army of the Republic of Vietnam— would emerge; nevertheless, ARVN would also include a significant number of soldiers, even officers, who had once fought in the ranks of the Viet Minh, and even of the Viet Cong.

A general staff of the Vietnamese National Army began operating in 1952. Nguyen Van Hinh, a lieutenant colonel in the regular French Air Force and a son of the prime minister of Vietnam at the time, became chief of staff, with the rank of major general. Development of this Vietnamese army (as opposed to simple increase in its size) had not made much progress by the time the Viet Minh war ended; in 1954 there was, besides General Hinh himself, a very small general staff, no artillery, no heavy armor, no engineering or communications capability, and most of the officers, especially above the rank of lieutenant, were French. For a time after partition, training of what was soon to become ARVN was in the hands of both French officers and the Americans of MAAG-V—Military Assistance Advisory Group Vietnam. When the CEF left South Vietnam for good in 1956, the Americans remained to train the expanding Southern army.

The army of independent India did not reject its British antecedents and traditions—quite the contrary—nor did the army of the Philippine Republic reject its American ones. The departing French were therefore surprised and offended when ARVN shed the uniforms and insignia of the French army to adopt those of the Americans.[2] But it casts a revealing light in the pragmatic motivation of many Vietnamese who had fought on the side of the French against the Viet Minh (not so much pro-French as anti-Viet Minh) that ARVN dated its foundation not from 1948 (the recognition of Vietnam's independence by France), but from 1955, the inauguration of the Republic of Vietnam under President Ngo Dinh Diem.

THE ARVN OFFICER CORPS

ARVN never had enough officers (especially aggressive ones), and the training of many of them was sketchy at best.[3] In the 1950s even some South Vietnamese generals were only recently elevated from the ranks of noncommissioned officers. The French founded the Vietnamese National Military Academy in 1948 at Hue, and then moved it to Dalat; in the beginning, the course of training was about two years, later extended to four. Dalat did not graduate its first four-year class until 1969. Several hundred ARVN officers attended various courses at American military schools in the Philippines, Japan, and the United States, but language could be a barrier for even the most conscientious, and of course sightseeing and shopping consumed a great deal of time.[4]

Most ARVN officers entered the service right after graduation from high school or university. Many of those with civilian work experience before joining ARVN had been teachers.[5] The commissioning system for ARVN officers placed exceedingly heavy stress on formal education. In the CEF one could not usually become an officer unless one possessed a secondary-school diploma. The army of independent Vietnam, being unwilling to have lower educational standards for its officers than the French did, retained that requirement. One result of such an emphasis on schooling was that ARVN had one of the most degree-laden officer corps in the world: in the mid-1960s, 5 percent of its generals, over 13 percent of its colonels, and nearly 15 percent of all its field-grade officers held doctoral degrees.[6] Another consequence of the stress on formal schooling was that, since Western-style education was available almost exclusively in cities, and mainly for the middle classes, ARVN possessed an officer corps largely unfamiliar with the country's peasant majority, among whom and over whom the war was being fought.[7] Beginning in 1966, steps were taken to open up the officer corps for those without the standard educational credentials, including promotion of NCOs, commissions for leadership skills or battlefield heroism, and the establishment of training schools for enlisted officer-candidates.[8] But no one will ever be able to calculate the amount of injury ARVN inflicted on its own cause by years of restrictive officer-recruitment policies; not only did these restrictions create severe difficulties in winning over or even understanding the peasantry, but very often those who had leadership ambitions and natural abilities but lacked the formal schooling necessary for advancement in ARVN joined the Viet Cong, an organization much more receptive (by sheer necessity as well as ideology) to the upwardly mobile.[9]

Largely limiting officer recruitment to the urban middle classes was not the only, nor the worst, problem afflicting the ARVN officer corps; in too many cases, assignments and promotions depended more on political considerations than on military competence. In the words of one observer, "political loyalty, rather than battlefield performance, has long dominated the promotion system in the officer corps, with the result that there is often an inverse relationship between rank and military skill."[10] This regrettable situation had deep roots in the nature of the South Vietnamese state, as well as general Southeast Asian cultural norms. In particular, President Diem's experience with the attempted coup against him by General Hinh in 1955 understandably taught him to value political loyalty above all other virtues, and he took an active personal role in officer promotions with that consideration in mind. Diem was especially partial to fellow Catholics and to Vietnamese of northern origins. There were, of course, sound reasons for those preferences: Catholic officers were much more likely than others to have attended European-type schools, and Diem considered northerners to be more energetic (with some justice), and both groups to be more fervently anti-Communist, than other Vietnamese. Even after Diem's departure, these patterns of promotion remained quite salient: in 1967, out of 25,000 ARVN officers, fully one-fourth had been born in the north, and the Catholic proportion was nearly twice that of the nation as a whole—19.4 percent of officers as compared with 10.4 percent of all South Vietnamese. (Of course many officers were both Catholic and of northern origin.) Buddhists made up an indeterminable proportion of the general population—estimates vary from 20 to 59 percent—and over 60 percent of the officer corps.[11] Many of those who were both northern and Catholic seemed to march along a smooth path to preferment and higher rank. Of course one cannot automatically assume that Catholic and/or northern-born officers were not qualified for the posts they held, but the known preference of the Diem government for members of those categories was annoying to non-Catholic and/or southern-born officers, and it must have been most especially galling in instances, probably quite numerous, where northerners and Catholics were in fact clearly of superior competence.

The politicization of the South Vietnamese Army was not the responsibility of President Diem alone, as the 1955 conspiracy of General Hinh showed. In many Far Eastern armies, superiors were historically hesitant to inflict loss of face through reprimands to subordinates.[12] Within ARVN, this tendency to overlook less than adequate performance was magnified because commanders were often reluctant to punish subordinates who had political connections.[13] (It was mainly to avoid such political complications that the highly efficient pre–World War II Japanese Imperial Navy insisted on strict adherence to seniority alone as the basis for promotion.[14]) And of course the Hanoi-orchestrated insurgency in the South allowed very little time or space for training a more thoroughly professional officer corps.

These deficiencies within the officer corps did not end with the death of President Diem—far from it. Under his eventual successor as president, General Nguyen Van Thieu, family or political ties often interfered with the disciplining or removal of officers who did not perform adequately.[15] This was a very serious shortcoming, since most ARVN commanders, inexperienced and poorly trained as they often were, pursued very conservative battlefield tactics in order not to be singled out for criticism later.[16] As a general statement with notable exceptions, good field commanders and the thousands of dedicated younger ARVN officers who were without influential patrons were the least favored for promotion.[17]

Precisely for these reasons, some American critics of U.S. involvement in the war insisted that it would have been much better to have had a unified command of ARVN and U.S. forces under an American officer, as in the Korean conflict. Under that system, General Matthew Ridgway's staff rooted out incompetent Korean commanders as soon as they discovered them, replacing them with the best men to be found, neither knowing nor caring who anybody's relatives or friends might be.[18] But predictably, "the South Vietnamese, recalling their experience with the French, rebuffed American efforts to place the ARVN under American command."[19] (Aside from but related to this issue, it is at least arguable that the supreme U.S. military commander in Vietnam should have been a Marine, for reasons to be discussed later.)

BUILDING ARVN IN THE U.S. IMAGE

In the 1950s, Col. Edward Lansdale, USAF, a close personal adviser to President Diem, argued that since armed opponents of the South Vietnamese state were few in number at that time, ARVN should be a light-infantry force well trained in anti-guerrilla tactics. Small, elite, self-confident, and highly mobile units would pursue the scattered guerrilla bands, while paramilitary elements maintained security in the cities and villages.[20] The U.S. role would have consisted primarily in supplying these forces, backing them up with air and naval power where appropriate, and shielding the South from a conventional invasion across the Demilitarized Zone.[21] A U.S.-backed ARVN built on these lines could have greatly profited from expensive lessons learned in counterinsurgency warfare in Malaya and the Philippines, as well as in French Vietnam.

But it was not from those conflicts, unfortunately, that the U.S. Army drew its inspiration for training ARVN, but rather from the Korean War, a conventional (that is, World War II–style) conflict in which the major fighting had ended in 1953. Most leaders of the new ARVN wished to develop a force oriented toward counterinsurgency, but MAAG was determined to construct a Vietnamese army that would be able to repel a massive, conventional Korea-type invasion from the North.[22] Laboring under their Korean concepts, the Americans built a force that was cumbersome and road-bound— like the French one before it. The leaders of this new conventional army had, of necessity, been rapidly advanced from much lower ranks and were not experienced at this type of command. Under them, ARVN developed some bad habits. It relied on massive firepower as a substitute for flanking movements on the ground.[23] After the fall of South Vietnam, a high-ranking ARVN officer wrote that "another shortcoming of ARVN units at battalion and lower levels was their failure to maneuver when being engaged. After the first contact, they tended to stop and wait for support rather than conduct probes and maneuver to attack or close in on the enemy. This shortcoming indicated a need for additional training for small-unit leaders."[24] Besides, forays into the countryside never lasted more than seven days, with the result that ARVN inflicted only minimal damage to Viet Cong bases and rest areas and learned relatively little about jungle fighting.[25]

This reluctance of the South Vietnamese Army to go after, find, and grapple with the enemy was really a reluctance to fight a kind of war for which it had neither been trained nor equipped. Besides, the Vietnamese had been at war almost all the time since 1941, and consequently many ARVN officers took a very long-range and hence non-urgent view of this particular phase of the conflict.[26]

This U.S.-model ARVN carried with it other major costs as well. The rapidly expanding officer corps took most of the country's best young men, leaving relatively unimpressive material for staffing the all-important police and the civilian administrations.[27] Funds and attention were diverted from police and grass-roots self-defense efforts that, especially in the early years of the republic, would have been the cheapest and most effective way to checkmate the guerrillas.

But probably the most serious long-term damage to South Vietnam from the ill-conceived construction of a conventional ARVN was erosion of support in the United States. Some maintain that the conventional strength of the ARVN prevented Hanoi from launching an over-the-border assault. This may well be true, and if so it was very unfortunate for the South Vietnamese, for U.S. support would have been much easier to muster and sustain in the face of a classic Korean War–style invasion. What is certain, however, is that the sheer size and budget of this conventional army and the consequent neglect of state-building made the army by far the most cohesive force in the country; thus political power came to mean control of the ARVN, and vice versa. Under both Diem and Thieu, as previously noted, men became generals more for their political loyalty to the government than for their military distinction, or even competence, on the battlefield, and they in turn appointed subordinate officers according to the same criteria all the way down the line.[28] With all the post-Diem coups and attempted coups of the 1960s, and with ARVN administering most of the country and supplying its most visible leaders—leaders who could not seem to win—it was easy to present to the American public a picture of South Vietnam as nothing more than a military dictatorship, and an inefficient one at that. (U.S. responsibility for the dominant political role ARVN played in South Vietnam—American encouragement of the assassination of President Diem—somehow escaped attention.) Partly because of its size and training, partly because of its politicization, ARVN never learned how to combat the Viet Cong with lasting effect, so that the fighting got beyond its ability to control. Thus, in the developing chaos following the murder of President Diem, the Americans rashly took up the burden of the ground war, for which they too were unprepared. Predictably, typically, Americans attributed this regrettable situation not to Washington policies but to South Vietnamese corruption and cowardice. Equally predictable was the slow erosion of support within the United States for its ever more massive, every more bloody involvement in Southeast Asia. In summary, the Americans first built ARVN for the wrong mission, then put it in control of the country, then became exasperated when ARVN did not win, and finally decided to abandon their allies to "the inevitable."

EQUIPMENT AND TRAINING

ARVN had a well-educated officer corps, but it was not a well-trained army. Programs and projects to overcome training deficiencies arose from time to time, often under U.S. prodding and guidance, but little came of them. When President Diem, for example, created ranger units, U.S. Special Forces advisers arrived to train them. Ranger training in the United States required nine weeks; the advisers suggested at least seven weeks, but in the end ARVN rangers received only a four-week course.[29] Throughout the 1950s and the 1960s, systematic training was often interrupted or postponed because of the demands of combat operations, protection duty, and similar requirements. Even after the beginning of "Vietnamization" in 1968, one-third of ARVN battalions did no training at all, less than half trained for two hours a week, about one-fifth of all ARVN units trained only 20 minutes a week, and much of this training was ineffective or of only marginal benefit.[30] It was not only duty demands that interfered with serious training; when forced to supply cadres for training centers and programs, military commanders, being naturally unwilling to lose any of their good officers, made a practice of sending less competent ones.[31] In sum, "The greatest obstacle in improving and training the armed forces was the lack of qualified leadership at all levels, both officers and noncommissioned officers."[32] But perhaps "even more devastating for the South Vietnamese Army was . . . the lack of camaraderie between individual soldiers; this, too, was a failure in training."[33]

ARVN's inadequate combat training (which undoubtedly caused many needless casualties over the long years of the war) was matched by deficient political training. The tendency to downplay or ignore completely the importance of political education of the armed forces is a grave weakness of all Western and Western-trained armed forces, and ARVN was no exception. In contrast with Communist armies, including the Viet Cong and the NVA, where no one was ever permitted to lose sight of the central fact that wars are waged to achieve certain political aims, Western armies normally separate military operations from political goals, and nowhere was this truer than in South Vietnam. The most visible result of the failure to educate ARVN soldiers about what the war was being waged for was ARVN's poor and sometimes counterproductive treatment of the peasantry. Especially when ARVN was operating in contested areas, its units not infrequently behaved more like an army of foreign occupation than a national army whose purpose was to protect and elevate the civilian population among whom it moved.[34] Thus, it was not uncommon for U.S. advisers to be eyewitnesses to what amounted to the looting of southern villages by ARVN units, in part a consequence of the absence of a regular system of supplying adequate food to the enlisted soldiers (more on this to follow).[35]

While the training and indoctrination of ARVN stayed at low levels, the size of the army increased inexorably. By 1972, out of a South Vietnamese population of perhaps 19 million, ARVN alone enrolled over 400,000 men; there were another 100,000 in other regular South Vietnamese military services, as well as over half a million in the territorial forces (Regional and Popular Forces—RF/PF, or "Ruff-Puffs").[36] Even with U.S. aid, maintaining all these men in service was an extremely heavy burden for the country, one that deeply distorted the entire economy. Machiavelli praised the Greeks and Romans for making war with armies that were small in size but excellent in training.[37] South Vietnam sought to protect its independence with exactly the opposite kind of army. Smaller armed forces—less expensive, more disciplined, and better trained—would have served South Vietnam much more effectively than greater and greater numbers. As in the rueful French reflection on their own experience in Vietnam, ARVN needed "fewer battalions but better battalions."[38] A more compact army would have increased the proportion of volunteers to conscripts, thus making it easier to imitate the Roman practices of strict discipline and constant training, and facilitating as well an improvement in the political awareness of the troops. The money and effort saved by keeping the numbers in ARVN within bounds could have been spent on improving security for the civilian population, especially through the buildup of the very inexpensive but not ineffective territorial forces. In a smaller, better army devoting greater attention to local security and self-defense, the degree of politicization in that army, or at least the consequences of it, would also have decreased.

Almost totally dependent on the United States for armaments, ARVN had problems in this area as well. The United States supplied ARVN with the World War II–vintage M-1 rifle; this weapon, excellent in itself, was much too heavy and clumsy for the slim and compact Vietnamese soldier. On the other hand, by 1965 the Viet Cong possessed the very good Russian-made AK-47 assault rifle, to which the M-1 was hopelessly inferior in firepower.[39] But 1965 was also the year of the great buildup of American forces in Vietnam, and Secretary of Defense McNamara was opposed to diverting any M-16 rifles, which were more than a match for the AK-47, or much of any other first-class equipment, to America's beleaguered ally. ARVN therefore did not begin obtaining the M-16 until the spring of 1967, and it was in short supply for years.[40] In General Westmoreland's view,

> ARVN thus long fought at a serious disadvantage against the enemy's automatic AK-47, armed as they [ARVN] were with World War II's semiautomatic M-1, whose kick when firing appeared to rock the small Vietnamese soldiers back on their heels. Armed with a light carbine, little more than a peashooter when compared to the AK-47, the South Vietnamese militia were at an even worse disadvantage.[41]

As General Ky, South Vietnam's vice president, trenchantly observed, "The big, strapping American GI carried a light, fully automatic Colt M-16 rifle into combat with hundreds of rounds of ammunition, a match for the enemy's AK-47 assault rifle. Until after the Tet Offensive of 1968, our small soldiers carried heavy, eight-shot American M-1 rifles [unwieldy for Vietnamese and] so obsolete that the U.S. National Guard did not want them."[42] During the Tet Offensive of 1968, in the avenues of Saigon Viet Cong automatic rifles were answered only by ARVN carbines and garands. This disparity in weaponry between ARVN and the VC had for years produced "both unfavorable battlefield performance and low morale."[43] Needless to say, nobody wanted to "waste" good M-16s on the hapless Regional and Popular Forces, the home guard, who did not receive them in numbers until 1970, just one example of a costly, persistent, incomprehensible lack of appreciation of RF/PF contributions and potential on the part of both the Americans and ARVN.[44]

ARVN'S U.S. ADVISERS

In the mid-1960s, in part because it was the wrong kind of army for the country it was supposed to protect, ARVN was visibly suffering from inadequate leadership, questionable morale, and an inability to guarantee security for an increasingly large percentage of the South Vietnamese people.[45] How did ARVN's U.S. advisers respond to this lamentable and dangerous situation? The notorious "can do" attitude of most U.S. Army advisers of those days meant that all problems were seen as correctable, and this contributed to many over-optimistic reports. Feeling (rightly) that there was very little they could do to affect the general political situation in the country, advisers concentrated on teaching the Vietnamese about what they knew best: the weapons and tactics of a conventional army. Reflecting a very serious general weakness of American society then and now, the U.S. Army at the beginning of its involvement in Southeast Asia had no Vietnamese-language training program, and the number of U.S. officers who could speak and understand Vietnamese always remained miserably inadequate. Consequently, U.S. advisers tended to like and trust a South Vietnamese officer if he could speak decent English. (If he drank bourbon, so much the better.[46]) The South Vietnamese had been taking orders from white men for an awfully long time; U.S. advisers were therefore urged by their superiors to establish "rapport" with ARVN officers, and confrontation would seem to indicate its absence. In these circumstances, U.S. advisers often failed to demand the removal of even a clearly ineffective ARVN commander, because they feared it would look bad on their own records. Thus "rapport" became a dangerous concept.[47] More unfortunately, most U.S. advisers served for only one year, or even less. Just as he was getting to know the ARVN commander whom he was advising, the American officer would have to leave and be replaced by a new one who probably knew little of the language or what was really going on and who could thus be manipulated or circumvented by the local ARVN leaders.[48] The U.S. policy of short terms of service in South Vietnam meant that, in general, the Americans learned relatively little about that unhappy country. As one acute and devastating observation had it, the Americans did not fight a ten-year war in South Vietnam; they fought a one-year war ten times.

CORRUPTION AMONG THE SOUTH VIETNAMESE

No one can deny the existence of a great deal of corruption in South Vietnam, a condition found in other Southeast Asian nations—not least including North Vietnam—and indeed in the Third World as a whole (not to mention such places as Louisiana, Rhode Island, and New Jersey, just for examples).

Within ARVN, corruption was to a great extent the result of the fixed salaries of ARVN personnel being devastated by the inflation caused by the insurgency and the presence of hundreds of thousands of Americans in the country. In the words of Jeffrey Clarke, "between 1964 and 1972 consumer prices in South Vietnam rose 900 percent and the price of rice 1400 percent while incomes rose only about 300 percent for officers and at most 500 percent for enlisted men. . . . As a result a full colonel in the South Vietnamese Army saw his [real] monthly salary fall from about US$400 to US$85; an Army captain, from US$287 to US$61; and a private, from US$77 to US30.[49] One consequence of the ravages of this inflation was that by 1969 an ARVN private made half as much as a common laborer.[50] Thus, as an ARVN officer wrote afterward, "corruption was necessary for survival in South Vietnam's war-ravaged economy."[51]

There is even more to this sad story. Sun Tzu had insisted: "Pay heed to nourishing the soldiers!" But as Robert K. Brigham notes, "the number of non-combat related illnesses was unusually high in the ARVN because of poor nutrition in the field . . . one of the most astonishing aspects of the ARVN food program was that the cost of meals was deducted from the pay of infantry soldiers."[52] The author continues: "On average, then, an ARVN private eating with his unit in 1964 was forced to spend nearly one-third of his entire annual salary on food. Since most ARVN soldiers were supporting their entire extended family, this was a system designed to fail and to leave ARVN searching for alternative food sources."[53]

An ARVN captain commented on this depressing situation: "Look at the U.S. soldier: he is well-fed, well-paid, well-supported, gets good housing, doesn't have to worry about the safety of his wife and family while he is away, gets R&R trips and sometimes a trip home, and he can leave for good in one year. The average ARVN soldier is not well-supported, makes very little money, and may live in squalor even when he is on leave, and knows he will be in the army for many years to come."[54] And General Nguyen Cao Ky, vice president of South Vietnam, wrote that "a U.S. combat ration—one meal—contained 3800 calories—almost twice what a typical Vietnamese soldier got for a whole day. . . . We had no post exchanges, no movies, no cold beer, and we fought for the duration, for twenty years, for however long the war continued, until death, disease, or disfigurement ended our service."[55]

Consider, finally, that in 1966 South Vietnam had only 1,000 qualified doctors, and of these 700 had already been forced into the armed forces. By the last year of the war, due to Congress slashing U.S. aid, ARVN medics found it necessary to wash and reuse disposable bandages and syringes.[56]

The failure to provide ARVN soldiers with proper medical care and even sufficient food was a patent, shameful scandal, the enormity of which merely underlines the determination of so many of that army's officers and enlisted men to persevere in their resistance to the conquest of their state by the Viet Cong and the North Vietnamese.

One needs always to keep in mind the fact that while corruption in South Vietnam was openly admitted, and talked and written about ad nauseam, no Western reporters ever talked about corruption in North Vietnam because of the totalitarian controls in that state. It was only after the war ended in 1975 that the vast scale of Communist corruption both in North Vietnam and afterward in "reunited" Vietnam became painfully apparent (as eventually also happened in Communist China and the former Soviet Union). It escaped quite a few American reporters and politicians, then and now, that political totalitarianism is the very essence of corruption.

But the fundamental question is this: Does the corruption, grand or petty, practiced by many South Vietnamese really prove that the whole population of South Vietnam deserved to be abandoned by their American allies and handed over to one of the cruelest and most incompetent—and most corrupt—dictatorships in Asia?

THE QUESTION OF DESERTION

Despite all the many challenges confronting ARVN, the campaign against the guerrillas was going reasonably well as 1962 drew to a close, and there was very little danger that the northern-inspired insurgency would shatter ARVN or overthrow the Diem government. Then in 1963 came the disturbances orchestrated by certain Buddhist and pseudo-Buddhist elements and the murder of Diem, events that struck ARVN like a typhoon. After the killing of Diem, coup followed coup, purge followed purge, ARVN morale, discipline and performance deteriorated, the Communists undertook operations in main-force units, and South Vietnam's republican experiment seemed perilously close to collapse. In light of this emergency, the Johnson Administration decided in the spring of 1965 to insert massive numbers of U.S. troops into South Vietnam. This decision meant that material assistance to ARVN would be deemphasized, and thus the South Vietnamese Army was reduced to the status of an auxiliary force in its own country. Saigon was saved, for the time being, but the root problems afflicting ARVN remained unsolved. The assumption of the burden of the war by the Americans meant that they would begin to suffer relatively large numbers of casualties, something no democracy can sustain over an extended period of time without visible progress toward victory, but the Americans did not know with what yardstick progress in a guerrilla war could be measured. Protracted large-scale U.S. participation in the war also presented the leaders in Hanoi (and their American sympathizers) with a valuable opportunity to attack the nationalist credentials of the South Vietnamese government (as President Diem had foreseen). Finally, although ARVN forces were consigned to smaller, less glamorous operations, they consistently suffered more casualties than the Americans: In proportion to population ARVN lost 40 men killed to every one American killed, a fact that rank-and-file U.S. soldiers were disinclined to acknowledge, and the American media completely ignored, because they didn't know about it.

In light of all the problems confronting the young republic and its equally young army, that ARVN suffered from a high level of desertion should be no surprise. The monthly gross desertion rate reached an all-time peak in the fall of 1968, at 17.2 per thousand; it eventually leveled off at 12 per thousand, but desertion was always higher than that figure in combat infantry units.[57]

Desertion had many causes. South Vietnam conscripted young men for very long periods without regard for the consequences.[58] The government kept lengthening the term of service for draftees, but did not do an effective job of explaining why. By 1968, young Vietnamese were drafted for the duration of the war, and leave policies were very stringent.[59] Poor pay, inadequate housing, substandard food, the wrenching pain of family separation, a haphazard promotion system, the inattention of many officers to the conditions and problems of their men—all these factors contributed their share.[60] Robert Brigham, one of the principal students of ARVN, states that "low pay, high inflation, and lengthy military service made life in the army an impossible burden for many of South Vietnam's poor."[61] Desertion rates were highest among first-year servicemen, during the Tet holidays, at harvest time, and in units with poor commanders—indicating strongly that personal rather than political reasons were uppermost in the minds of those who left ARVN unlawfully. Vietnamese society, moreover, did not view desertion as a serious moral failing, and the Saigon government made only halfhearted efforts to discover and punish deserters.[62] A general amnesty for desertions in 1964 both expressed the government's less-than-stringent attitude toward the problem and taught future deserters to expect similar forgiveness.[63]

There can be little doubt that desertion seriously interfered with the combat readiness of ARVN; it also supplied much ammunition to the critics of U.S. involvement in the war on the side of an ally whose moral and political shortcomings were symbolized for them by these elevated desertion rates. One must, however, take note of several other interesting aspects of this desertion question. First of all, the Viet Cong suffered desertion rates comparable to those of ARVN.[64] Of course, American journalists never reported on conditions among the Viet Cong, because they were not welcomed in those circles, and even if they were it would have done them little good because the journalists spoke no Vietnamese. Second, desertion in the South Vietnamese Regional Forces and Popular Forces (RF/PF) was significantly less than in ARVN, whose units often lived and fought very far from home: One very interesting study notes that "desertion rates of regional forces who serve in their home provinces is considerably lower than that of the regular army, and the desertion rate of popular forces who serve in their own villages is lower yet."[65] Militia members did not desert to go home; they were already home. Third, thousands of deserters from ARVN eventually returned to their original units, or joined units closer to home, or entered the RF/PF, thus increasing the combat effectiveness of the territorial home defense forces.[66] Gross desertion rates do not reflect these realities. Arguably only 20–30 percent of ARVN soldiers listed as deserters actually were such.[67]

Perhaps most significant of all, *desertion* from ARVN hardly ever turned into *defection to the enemy*. During the Chinese civil war of the 1940s, whole units, even whole divisions, of Chiang Kai-shek's nationalist armies would change sides; in Vietnam, such a thing never happened at the big-unit level, and hardly ever even at the platoon level. Compared with the number of deserters, defectors from the Saigon government side to the Communists were remarkably few, a fact attested to by numerous trained observers.[68]

On the other hand, 200,000 Viet Cong and North Vietnamese soldiers not merely deserted their own cause but defected to the Saigon side between 1963 and 1972.[69] By 1969, as Arthur Dommen, among others, observes, the war for the support of the South Vietnamese had basically been won by the Saigon government and its American and other allies and "defections from the Communist ranks had reached an all-time high."[70] The number of enemy defectors to the southern side was roughly equal to nine NVA divisions by 1969–1970.[71]

Finally, consider that desertion rates were high partly because desertion was easy: the South Vietnamese soldier was fighting in his own country. It may be instructive to consider desertion figures from a conflict in which desertion was as easy for American soldiers as it was for South Vietnamese soldiers: the American Civil War. In June 1863, on the eve of Gettysburg—the largest battle ever fought on the continent of North America—the Army of the Potomac, the principal shield of the Union, was down to an effective strength of only 75,000, because over 85,000 of the men on its rolls had deserted.[72] During the last two years of that conflict, desertion in the Federal forces approached 330 per thousand. As for the Confederates, the total authorized strength of their armies in December 1864 was 465,000; of that number 187,000 (400 per thousand) were listed as absent without leave.[73] On September 23, 1864, President Jefferson Davis publicly stated that two-thirds of Confederate soldiers were absent, "some sick, some wounded, but most of them without leave." Absenteeism, for all reasons, ran to 49 percent in the Army of Tennessee and 60 percent in Robert E. Lee's Army of Northern Virginia.[74]

SOUTHERN CASUALTIES

"In the last six years of the war, 1969–1975," states Robert Brigham, "there were over one million ARVN soldiers serving in eleven infantry divisions, making the ARVN one of the world's largest armies."[75] If the U.S., out of its 2015 population, maintained an army in Vietnam proportionately equal to that of ARVN, it would have had fifteen million troops there in any given year, thirty times the actual number at its very highest.

Thanks largely to the inaccurate reporting of the war by the American news business in Vietnam, "the American people at home were left with the impression that American soldiers were doing practically all of the fighting."[76] The facts were radically different. During the entire South Vietnam conflict between 1954 and 1975, 57,000 American personnel lost their lives there, a number almost exactly equaled by the number of Americans who died in highway accidents in the U.S *in 1970 alone*. The Americans incurred an average of 4,000 military deaths per year. The comparable figure for the Korean War was 18,000 U.S. military deaths per year, and for World War II 100,000 per year. From 1954 to 1975, ARVN combat deaths were higher than those of the Americans every single year. In all, approximately 250,000 ARVN died in combat, and 499,000 were wounded. Some authorities give higher figures, and it is essential to keep in mind that these casualty statistics for ARVN *do not include casualties among the territorial forces* (see below) nor of course among civilians.[77] Table 4.1 compares American military casualties with all South Vietnamese military casualties (including the Air Force and Navy), but *excluding the territorials*.[78]

But to observe that South Vietnamese Army casualties were higher than those of the Americans tells only a part of the real story. The population of

Table 4.1.   Allied Casualties

YEAR	KILLED IN ACTION		WOUNDED IN ACTION	
	American	South Vietnamese	American	South Vietnamese
1965	1,369	11,242	3,308	23,118
1966	5,008	11,953	16,526	20,975
1967	9,377	12,716	32,370	29,448
1968	14,489	27,915	46,797	70,696
1969	9,414	21,833	32,940	65,276
1970	4,221	23,346	15,211	71,582
1971	1,381	22,738	4,767	60,939
1972	300	39,587	587	109,960
1973	237	27,901	24	131,936
1974	207	31,219		155,735

South Vietnam was many times smaller than that of the United States. If American military casualties had been in the same proportion to the population of the United States as ARVN's were to the population of South Vietnam, the Americans would have suffered not 57,000 deaths but 2.6 million. How can one comprehend this figure? What is the meaning of "2.6 million American military deaths?" This is the meaning: through all the wars the Americans fought from the War of Independence to the fall of Saigon, including both sides in the Civil War as well as World War I, World War II, and Korea—a period of almost exactly two hundred years—American military fatalities amounted to less than 1 million. During the long fight against an armed Communist takeover of South Vietnam, ARVN alone (excluding the territorials, whose casualty rates were higher) suffered, in relation to the South Vietnamese population, more than forty times as many fatalities as the Americans.

THE TERRITORIALS

As for the unappreciated territorials, by the end of 1969 they numbered 475,000, including the Popular Forces, which consisted of 184,000 in 1975.[79] Popular Forces usually comprised 30-man platoons defending their own villages or hamlets, while Regional Forces, organized in companies of 100, served in their home provinces (but more on this below).[80] Official *Communist* sources state that by 1975 the South Vietnamese government had armed an additional 400,000 persons in the People's Self-Defense Forces (PSDF), composed of persons too old or too young for normal military or militia life (there were in fact many times that number). [81] Richard Hunt wrote that "as measured by combat deaths, service with the RF/PF was more dangerous than with ARVN or U.S. forces. With the exception of 1968, the Regional and Popular forces had a higher combat death rate than the South Vietnamese or American armies. In 1970, for example, the rate was 11 per thousand for U.S. ground forces and 16 for ARVN. The RF/PF rate reached 22." [82]

During the 1972 Easter Offensive (to be discussed), RF units conducted themselves very well against regular North Vietnam Army units (whom territorials, as home-guard militia, were never intended to fight) in the battle of Hue and elsewhere. By 1973, when the last American combat units were gone, territorial forces numbered over half a million. [83] The heavily populated Mekong Delta was mostly under the control of these "Ruff-Puffs." Receiving only 2–4 percent of the war budget, the territorials accounted for 30 percent of VC and NVA combat deaths, and were thus "the most cost-efficient military force on the allied side." [84]

One of the truly incomprehensible and damaging falsehoods bleated endlessly about the entire Vietnamese conflict period is that South Vietnam fell because the government had no popular support and its armed forces would not fight. It would have been very easy for the American media to obtain data on the relationship of ARVN and territorial casualties to those of U.S. forces; but this was, for some reason, never considered worth doing. Yet clearly, and irrefutably, as Andrew A. Wiest states, "That RF/PF [Territorial] forces continued to fight at all is a testament to the tenacity of the South Vietnamese population and serves as further indication that there existed a true reservoir of support for Southern nationalism—a reservoir that both the United States and South Vietnam failed to cultivate sufficiently." [85]

ON THE EVE OF TET

When Viet Cong insurgents became a serious problem in the late 1950s, local self-defense forces had not been prepared to meet the challenge, and so ARVN, originally set up to fight a Korea-style war, was thrown into a conflict for which it too was ill-prepared. Politicization of the higher command levels, thorough penetration of ARVN by Viet Cong agents, low technical and tactical proficiency of both soldiers and officers due to inadequate training, the overlapping responsibility and divided authority in part fostered by President Diem to protect himself from a possible coup—all these factors prevented ARVN from rooting out the southern insurgency before it approached the proportions of a national emergency.

As one of the results of the U.S.-backed 1963 coup against President Diem, ARVN had to administer the country as well as to defend it. The

generals in command of army and country were, with some notable exceptions, in power because they had distinguished themselves not in military
combat but in political intrigue, or at least political loyalty. They possessed
neither the technical ability to command large numbers of armed men nor the
political talent to ameliorate the woes of a war-torn and underdeveloped
society and a poorly nourished soldiery.

By 1967, Diem was dead and the generals were in control; many of the
old problems had predictably become worse, while newer ones were added.
A persistent shortage of commissioned and noncommissioned officers was
aggravated by the practice of assigning the best people to headquarters. Orders often went unobeyed, training deficiencies remained unsolved, and political education was insufficient. U.S. advisers found their Vietnamese
counterparts always willing to listen but not always willing to change.[86]
Indeed, to some extent ARVN resembled less a national army that a feudal
alliance of local armies. Political power rested on command of troops. The
movement of a division out of one command area into another therefore
became a major political consideration, and as a consequence flexibility in
the deployment of ARVN units was severely limited. The Communists were
aware of this weakness and often took advantage of it by conducting their
operations along the boundaries between ARVN military regions, or by running across the boundaries of one region into another.[87]

One cannot refrain, however, from observing that if the fighting efficien-
cy of a state's army is the benchmark of the moral worth of that state and its
people, then "Hitler would have had one of the most desirable political
systems in the mid–twentieth century."[88]

However that may be, with all its manifest difficulties and shortcomings,
as 1967 neared its end, ARVN "had held a politically troubled country together in the face of ever-increasing enemy strength. Few organizations in
the world could have done so well."[89] Indeed, in terms of its size, and its
relationship with the general population, ARVN had become "a genuine
people's army."[90] Of this army, the First ARVN Division was arguably the
best; Secretary of Defense Clarke Clifford said the First was "comparable in
quality to any U.S. Army division."[91] And one high-ranking ARVN commander has written that "the paratroopers [the Airborne Division, all volun-
teers] were the bravest soldiers of the armed forces."[92]

And well before the end of that same year—1967—Hanoi's leaders had
reached two conclusions: (1) they could not defeat the Americans militarily;
(2) they could still win the war politically, if they could convince the
Americans that the South Vietnamese were not viable long-term allies. The
most effective way to accomplish this would be to cause ARVN to break
apart. It had long been Communist strategy to avoid U.S. forces and concentrate on ARVN. Now, as the New Year holidays (Tet) of 1968 approached,
Hanoi prepared to administer a master-stroke against ARVN, a blow that it

hoped would precipitate the departure of the Americans and thus open the road to the conquest of the South. The next chapter will examine the effects of the great Tet Offensive of 1968 on ARVN, the South Vietnamese population, and the American news media.

NOTES

1. Ronald Spector, *Advice and Support: The Early Years of the U.S Army in Vietnam* (New York: Free Press, 1985), p. 131; Ellen Hammer, *The Struggle for Indochina, 1940–1955* (Stanford, CA: Stanford University Press, 1966), p. 287; Henri Navarre, *Agonie de l'Indochine* (Paris: Plon, 1956), p. 46; Douglas Pike, *PAVN: People's Army of Vietnam* (Novato, CA: Presidio, 1986), p. 8.

2. Spector, *Advice and Support*, p. 255.

3. James L. Collins, *The Development and Training of the South Vietnamese Army, 1950–1972* (Washington, DC: U.S. Army Center of Military History, 1975), p. 97.

4. Spector, *Advice and Support*, p. 282.

5. Allan E. Goodman, *An Institutional Profile of the South Vietnamese Officer Corps* (Santa Monica, CA: RAND, 1970), p. 9.

6. Ibid.

7. Ibid., p. v.

8. Collins, *Development and Training*, pp. 78–79.

9. Guenter Lewy, *America in Vietnam* (New York: Oxford University Press, 1978), p. 170.

10. Goodman, *Institutional Profile*, p. vi.

11. Ibid., p. 9.

12. Dennis J. Duncanson, *Government and Revolution in Vietnam* (New York: Oxford University Press, 1968), p. 290.

13. Spector, *Advice and Support*, p. 278.

14. See Gordon W. Prange, *At Dawn We Slept* (New York: Penguin Books, 1982), pp. 108–109.

15. Lewy, *America in Vietnam*, p. 170.

16. G. H. Turley, *The Easter Offensive: Vietnam 1972* (Novato, CA: Presidio, 1985), p. 146.

17. Thomas C. Thayer, *War without Fronts* (Boulder, CO: Westview, 1985), p. 68.

18. Ibid., pp. 60–63.

19. Arthur J. Dommen, *The Indochinese Experience of the French and the Americans: Nationalism and Communism in Cambodia, Laos and Vietnam* (Bloomington, IN: Indiana University Press, 2001), p. 637.

20. Denis Warner, *The Last Confucian: Vietnam, Southeast Asia and the West* (Harrmondsworth, England: Penguin, 1964), p. 108.

21. Bruce Palmer, Jr., *The 25-Year War: America's Military Role in Vietnam* (Lexington: University Press of Kentucky, 1984). See also Harry Summers, *On Strategy: A Critical Analysis of the Vietnam War* (Novato, CA: Presidio, 1982).

22. Andrew A. Wiest, *Vietnam's Forgotten Army: Heroism and Betrayal in the ARVN* (New York: New York University Press, 2008), p. 22.

23. Lewy, *America in Vietnam*, p. 182.

24. Nguyen Duy Hihn, *Lam Son 719* (Washington, DC: U.S. Army Center of Military History, 1979), p. 161.

25. Duncanson, *Government and Revolution*, p. 182.

26. Maj. Gen. Richard Lee, quoted in Collins, *Development and Training*, p. 75.

27. Sir Robert Thompson, *Defeating Communist Insurgency: Experiences from Malaya and Vietnam* (London: Chatto and Windus, 1966), pp. 58–62.

28. Douglas S. Blaufarb, "The Sources of U.S. Frustration in Vietnam," in *Lessons from an Unconventional War*, ed. Richard A. Hunt and Richard H. Shultz, Jr. (New York: Pergamon, 1982), p. 150.

29. Spector, *Advice and Support*, p. 354.

30. Thomas Thayer, "How to Analyze a War without Fronts," *Journal of Defense Research* (Fall 1975), p. viii; Thayer, *War without Fronts*, p. 71.

31. Collins, *Development and Training*, p. 122; Dong Van Khuyen, *The RVNAF* (Washington, DC: U.S. Army Center of Military History, 1980), p. 72; Thayer, *War without Fronts*, p. 72. Edward Luttwak writes: "Military history is often written without even mentioning how the soldiers on each side were trained; yet that is routinely the decisive factor in the strength of armies"; *The Grand Strategy of the Byzantine Empire* (Cambridge, MA: Harvard University Press, 2009), p. 269.

32. Collins, *Development and Training*, p. 75.

33. Robert K. Brigham, *ARVN: Life and Death in the South Vietnamese Army* (Lawrence, KS: University Press of Kansas, 2006), p. 45.

34. Lewy, *America in Vietnam*, pp. 177–178.

35. Stuart A. Herrington, *Silence was a Weapon: The Vietnam War in the Villages* (Novato, CA: Presidio, 1982), p. 211.

36. Collins, *Development and Training*, p. 151.

37. Machiavelli, *The Art of War*, Book VI.

38. Paul Ely, *Lessons of the War in Indochina,* vol. 2 (Santa Monica, CA: RAND, 1967), p. 219.

39. Lewy, *America in Vietnam*, p. 164; Collins, *Development and Training*, p. 47.

40. Collins, *Development and Training*, p.101.

41. Westmoreland, *A Soldier Reports*, p. 158.

42. Nguyen Cao Ky, *Buddha's Child: My Fight to Save South Vietnam* (New York: St. Martin's, 2002), p. 336.

43. Wiest, *Vietnam's Forgotten Army*, p. 55.

44. Lewy, *America in Vietnam*, pp. 166–167.

45. Spector, *Advice and Support*, p. 353.

46. Steven Hosmer, Konrad Kellen, and Brian Jenkins, *The Fall of South Vietnam: Statements by Vietnamese Military and Civilian Leaders* (New York: Crane, Russak, 1980), p. 84.

47. Collins, *Development and Training*, pp. 120–130.

48. Spector, *Advice and Support*, pp. 291–293; Cao Van Vien et al., *The U.S. Adviser* (Washington, DC: U.S. Army Center of Military History, 1980).

49. Jeffrey J. Clarke, *Advice and Support: The Final Years, 1965–1973* (Washington, DC: U.S. Army Center of Military History, 1988), p. 503.

50. Brigham, *ARVN*, p. 60.

51. Lam Quang Thi, *The Twenty-Five-Year Century: A South Vietnamese General Remembers the Indochina War to the Fall of Saigon* (Denton, TX: University of North Texas Press, 2001), p. 321.

52. Brigham, *ARVN*, pp. 56–57.

53. Brigham, *ARVN*, p. 58.

54. Brigham, *ARVN*, p. 50.

55. Nguyen Cao Ky, *Buddha's Child,* p. 336.

56. Brigham, *ARVN*, p. 69.

57. Collins, *Development and Training*, p. 92.

58. Brigham, *ARVN*, p. 1; see also Wiest, *Vietnam's Forgotten Army*, p. 23.

59. Soldiers in the Chinese People's Liberation Army during the Korean War (and probably at other times) had no definite enlistment period and no clear way to get out of the PLA besides death. See Alexander George, *The Chinese Communist Army in Action* (New York: Columbia University, 1966).

60. Lewy, *America in Vietnam*, p. 173.

61. Brigham, *ARVN*, p. 18; see also Wiest, *Vietnam's Forgotten Army*, p. 23.

62. Collins, *Development and Training,* p. 60.

63. Dong Van Khuyen, *The RVNAF*, p. 152.

64. Pike, *PAVN*, p. 244.

65. Brian M. Jenkins, *A People's Army for South Vietnam* (Santa Monica, CA: Rand, 1971), p. 9; and see Lewy, *America in Vietnam*, p. 173.

66. Thayer, *War without Fronts*, p. 75.

67. Brigham, *ARVN*, p. 49.

68. Pike, *PAVN*, p. 244; Lewy, *America in Vietnam*, p. 172; William E. Le Gro, *Vietnam from Ceasefire to Capitulation* (Washington, DC: U.S. Army Center of Military History, 1981), p. 34; George Tanham, *Communist Revolutionary Warfare: From the Vietminh to the Viet Cong* (New York: Praeger, 1967), maintains that even among ARVN members taken prisoner by the enemy, few changed sides. "Hardly ever did an ARVN soldier defect to the enemy"; William C. Westmoreland, *A Soldier Reports*, p. 252.

69. Thayer, *War without Fronts*, p. 202. A very good study on Viet Cong and NVA defectors is Jeannette A. Koch, *The Chieu Hoi Program: in South Vietnam, 1963–1971* (Santa Monica, CA: RAND, 1973).

70. Dommen, *Indochinese Experience*, p. 709.

71. Lewis Sorley, *Reassessing ARVN* (Lubbock, TX: Texas Tech University, 2006), pp. 22–23.

72. Bruce Catton, *The Army of the Potomac: Glory Road* (Garden City, NY: Doubleday, 1952), pp. 102 and 255.

73. Allan Nevins, *The War for the Union: The Organized War, 1863–1864* (New York: Scribner's, 1971), p. 131.

74. Donald Stoker, *The Grand Design: Strategy and the U.S. Civil War* (New York: Oxford University Press, 2010), p. 389.

75. Brigham, *ARVN*, p. x.

76. Westmoreland, *A Soldier Reports*, p. 251.

77. Thayer, *War without Fronts*, pp. 105–106; Todd, *Cruel April*, p. 234; Charles Hirschman, Samuel Preston, and Vu Manh Loi, "Vietnamese Casualties during the American War: A New Estimate," *Population and Development Review* 21 (December 1995), pp. 783–812; David A. Savitz, Nguyen Minh Thang, Ingrid E. Swenson, and Erika Stone, "Vietnamese Infant and Child Mortality in Relation to the Vietnam War," *American Journal of Public Health*, v. 83 (1993), pp. 1134–1138. Many American scholars accept these figures: see, for example, Ronald Spector, *After Tet: The Bloodiest Year in Vietnam* (New York: Free Press, 1993) and Guenter Lewy, *America in Vietnam*.

78. Adapted from figures from the Office of the Comptroller, Department of Defense. Ira A. Hunt, Jr., presents slightly different figures: see his *Losing Vietnam: How America Abandoned Southeast Asia* (Lexington, KY: University Press of Kentucky, 2013), p. 105.

79. DAO, *Final Assessment*, 9:10.

80. W. Scott Thompson and Donaldson Frizzell, eds., *The Lessons of Vietnam* (New York: Crane, Russack, 1977), p. 257.

81. The Military History Institute of Vietnam, *Victory in Vietnam*, Trans. Merle L. Pribbenow (Lawrence, KS: University Press of Kansas, 2002), p. 334; Jenkins, in *People's Army*, advocated combining the Regional Forces, the Popular Forces, and the People's Self-Defense Forces under one command and giving them better training and weapons; among other effects, this would have allowed ARVN to be smaller and less expensive.

82. Richard A. Hunt, *Pacification: The American Struggle for Vietnam's Hearts and Minds* (Boulder, CO: Westview, 1995), p. 253.

83. Hoang Ngoc Lung, *The General Offensives of 1968–1969* (Washington, DC: U.S. Army Center of Military History, 1981), p. 150; Westmoreland, *Soldier Reports*, p. 159; Hunt, *Pacification*, p. 214; Ngo Quang Truong, *Territorial Forces* (Washington, DC: U.S. Army Center of Military History, 1981), p. 77; Le Gro, *Vietnam from Ceasefire*, p. 330; Collins, *Development and Training*, p. 151.

84. Thomas C. Thayer, "Territorial Forces," in Thompson and Frizzell, *Lessons of Vietnam*, p. 258.

85. Wiest, *Vietnam's Forgotten Army*, p. 75.

86. Spector, *Advice and Support*, pp. 344–348.

87. Lewy, *America in Vietnam*, p. 184; for further discussion of weaknesses at the top of ARVN, see Lewis Sorley, *A Better War: The Unexamined Victories and Final Tragedy of America's Last Years in Vietnam* (New York: Harcourt, Brace, 1999).

88. *The Economist*, May 6, 1972, p. 12.

89. Westmoreland, *Soldier Reports*, p. 250.

90. Dommen, *Indochinese Experience*, p. 901.

91. Thomas Cantwell, "The Army of South Vietnam: A Military and Political History, 1955–1975." Doctoral Dissertation, University of New South Wales, 1989, p. 311.

92. Lam Quang Thi, *Twenty-Five Year Century*, p. 306.

Chapter Five

The Tet Offensive and the
Ho Chi Minh Trail

"Most of what people hear about the Tet Offensive is wrong."—James S. Robbins, *This Time We Win*

The Tet Offensive of 1968 is arguably the most important series of events in · the entire Vietnamese conflict between 1954 and 1975. A close consideration of the origins, the outcome, and the consequences of the Offensive casts a great deal of light on the true nature of that conflict and why it ended in the way that it did, light that is revealing but not comforting.

ORIGINS

Between 1965 and 1967, only 3 percent of American GNP was devoted to the war in Vietnam. Only one eligible American male in fifty was drafted; only half of these went to Vietnam; one in 50 who went to Vietnam died there. At the height of the involvement, only one-third of 1 percent of all Americans—one out of every three hundred at most—were in Vietnam. Between 1960 and the summer of 1967, 13,000 Americans had been killed in action, fewer than the number of Americans who had died in the United States during those same years as the result of accidental falls, and a *mere 4 percent of the number of Americans who had died in automotive accidents.*[1]

For the Communists the war had been of a dramatically different nature. North Vietnamese casualties were five times as great as allied casualties.[2] North Vietnamese deaths were almost ten times American deaths.[3] The Hanoi regime was in fact requiring its own people to endure a casualty rate nearly twice that suffered by the Japanese in World War II. In 1969 General

Giap told a European interviewer that between 1965 and 1968 alone, Communist military losses totaled six hundred thousand.[4] The equivalent for the U.S. in 2015 would be at least six million war deaths. The lack of real progress against the Americans and ARVN, despite these vast sacrifices, was seriously hurting morale.[5] With the allied forces increasing in strength and skill all the time, the leaders in Hanoi could only conclude that the war had become a stalemate at best. If something drastic were not undertaken to reverse this situation, the future from the Communist viewpoint could only worsen.[6]

Accordingly, as early as the spring of 1967, meticulous preparations began in Hanoi for an offensive in 1968.[7] The campaign would have two major goals. The first was to crumple up main ARVN units. The second was to capture the large cities of South Vietnam, with the aid of a mass civilian uprising against the Thieu government. Indeed, according to James Wirtz, "the primary objective of the Tet Offensive was to win the war by instigating a general uprising"; this concept of an end to the war in a massive civilian revolt "represents the major Vietnamese contribution to the theory of [Maoist] people's war."[8] Through these events the state of South Vietnam would come close to paralysis, and the Americans, disillusioned and disheartened, with nothing much left to defend, would go home. Thus, General Giap would have his latter-day Dien Bien Phu; as in 1954 one spectacular battle had destroyed the will of the French political class to continue the war (not so very hard to do), so fourteen years later another spectacular battle would surely rock the resolve of the Americans.

It was in this context that Hanoi made the decision to launch a major offensive during the sacred Tet holidays, which in previous years had been a period of truce. In January 1968, the fourteenth Plenum of the North Vietnamese Communist Party Central Committee set out the objectives of the coming Tet offensive: "Annihilate and cause the total disintegration of the bulk of the puppet army [ARVN], overthrow the puppet regime at all administrative levels, and place all government power in the hands of the people [i.e., the Communist Party]."[9]

WHY WAS TET A SURPRISE?

In his valuable study of the Tet Offensive, James J. Wirtz wrote that

> the North Vietnamese leadership was surprised not only by the U.S. intervention [during and after 1965] but by the scope and pace of the buildup of ground forces. . . . They had made a crucial mistake in figuring that the United States would not intervene decisively to save the Saigon regime. In fact, U.S. intervention was probably the first major surprise of the war (the other instances

being the Tet Offensive and the 1972 Christmas Bombing of Hanoi and Haiphong).[10]

The Tet Offensive, even though it involved the deployment of several scores
of thousands of guerrillas and regular troops, took the Americans and their
allies almost completely off guard. This is not as mysterious as it might
seem. Surprise is an integral part of warfare. Recall for example just these
twentieth-century surprises: the 1940 German Ardennes offensive that resulted in the fall of France, the 1941 German invasion of the USSR, the 1941
attack on Pearl Harbor, the1943 invasion of Sicily, the 1944 Normandy landings, the 1944 Battle of the Bulge, the 1950 North Korean onslaught, the
1950 Chinese intervention in Korea, the 1954 capture of Dien Bien Phu, and
the 1973 Egyptian offensive against Israel.

From late 1967 onward, a great deal of information—from prisoners,
defectors, South Vietnamese agents, intercepted or monitored communications—was in fact reaching the allies that some very big event was about to
take place. But this information, suggesting that the Viet Cong were going to
throw away their advantages of guerrilla warfare and expose themselves in
large numbers in the cities, seemed to contradict common sense: it was too
good to be true. U.S. intelligence analysts "usually treated captured enemy
documents that called for urban attacks and a revolt against the South Vietnamese government as part of an active deception campaign intended to draw
U.S. attention and resources away from the developing threat along the border, especially at Khe Sanh."[11] Khe Sanh was an American firebase in Quang
Tri province, close to the borders of both Laos and North Vietnam. Now, the
Americans knew—or thought they knew—all about Dien Bien Phu, and
interpreted the fighting around Khe Sanh, where 6,000 American Marines
and ARVN troops were besieged by 20,000 North Vietnamese regulars, as an
attempted replay of that earlier battle.[12] As Wirtz observes, "The siege of the
U.S. firebase at Khe Sanh, aimed to preoccupy the U.S. Command on the eve
of the offensive, was the final initiative in the effort to keep U.S. forces
separated from ARVN."[13]

Then, on January 23, North Korean forces seized the USS *Pueblo* in
international waters, further distracting both Saigon and Washington from
the coming offensive.

THE "GENERAL UPRISING"

But there is a much more important reason why Tet was a surprise to the
Americans (and to a lesser degree, the South Vietnamese). Wirtz points out
that "for the allies to predict the Tet Offensive, they would have to overcome
probably the toughest problem that can confront intelligence analysts; they
would have to recognize that the plan for a Tet offensive *rested on a commu-*

nist mistake.[14] Thucydides wrote that "in practice we always base our preparations against an enemy on the assumption that his plans are good. Indeed
it is right not to rest our hopes on a belief in his blunders."[15] Machiavelli
counseled that "the commander of an army must always mistrust any manifest error which he sees the enemy commit, as it invariably conceals some
stratagem."[16] And Robert E. Lee advised that "it is proper for us to expect
[the enemy] to do what he ought to do."[17]

It was in this venerable and sensible tradition—making the assumption
that the enemy knows what he is doing—that the Americans and their allies
discounted the accumulating evidence of a coming offensive. The various
American and South Vietnamese intelligence units knew that the Viet Cong
lacked the manpower to destroy ARVN and take over South Vietnam. A
major Communist offensive would have a real chance of success only in the
event of a simultaneous, authentic popular revolt against the Saigon regime
and its defenders—the Communists' much-talked about "general uprising."
The Americans correctly believed, first, that a general uprising was not going
to happen; second, that without such a rising the Communist armed forces
could not possibly prevail; and third, *that the Communists side knew all this.*

Yes, but what if the Communist side *did not* know all this?

Because, as will be seen, very large segments—certainly a substantial
majority—of the South Vietnamese population did not support the VC, the
general offensive would be a failure, indeed a devastating one. But, assuming
the Hanoi leadership did not know that a general uprising was not going to
take place, *why didn't they know*? "The source of this error," writes Wirtz,
"can be linked to a breakdown in communication between junior cadre members and senior officials. In the aftermath of the offensive, captured junior
officers admitted that they never expected the urban population in their area
of operation to revolt."[18] As Wirtz reports, most post-Tet prisoners of war

> did not believe that the local population in *their* area would revolt in support of
> the attack, but they carried out their orders in the hope that their own assault
> would help to instigate a general uprising in *other* areas. These POW state-
> ments indicate that, even though local commanders in South Vietnam knew
> that civilians in their areas of operations did not overwhelmingly support their
> cause, senior communist commanders still launched the Tet offensive in the
> hope of instigating a general uprising.[19]

There were other serious breakdowns in communication. For Tet to be a true
surprise, the Communists needed to maintain the strictest secrecy about plans
and movements. But considerations of secrecy gravely interfered with requirements of coordination, equally essential if the hoped-for general uprising were going to materialize. Coordination of effort, however, was quite
inadequate: when, on the very eve of the attack, Hanoi made the highly
questionable decision to postpone the outbreak for 24 hours, many units in

the northern provinces of South Vietnam did not receive notification of that postponement. Hence, fighting in those places began prematurely, giving the allied forces in the rest of South Vietnam a very brief but very vital warning.[20]

The simplest explanation for these costly decisions in Hanoi is human error. But there is an alternative explanation for why the Communist leadership (1) insisted on launching a major offensive despite the massive widespread evidence available to it that a general uprising would not materialize and that the offensive would therefore end in disaster, and (2) then decreed a brief postponement of the offensive, news of which would inevitably fail to reach everyone. In 1944, Stalin exhorted the underground Polish Home Army to launch its long-prepared uprising against the Nazi occupation. He then refused to let near-at-hand Soviet forces go to the assistance of that civilian uprising, until the Germans had all but eliminated the potentially very troublesome Polish resistance organization, so that the Red Army would encounter no real obstacles to its occupation of Poland.[21] What if Hanoi believed—correctly, as it turned out—that the Americans would sooner or later tire of this war, and would find some pretext or other to abandon their South Vietnamese allies?[22] Would a newly installed Viet Cong regime in Saigon insist on negotiations regarding reunification with Hanoi on equal terms? Would such a southern regime welcome real reunification—that is, a Hanoi takeover—at all? But if the Viet Cong had ceased to be a serious force before the Americans left, then no negotiations with anybody would be necessary: reunification of Vietnam would merely mean the occupation of the South by the North Vietnamese Army—which is eventually what happened.[23]

THE FIGHTING IN SAIGON

South Vietnam's beautiful capital city was less than fifty miles from the Cambodian border. Between the time of the 1954 partition and the approach of the Tet Offensive, the population of that city had multiplied from approximately half a million to well over two million, and perhaps a million people more inhabited its suburbs. Thus as 1968 opened, at least one South Vietnamese out of every six lived in the Greater Saigon area. Yet in spite of its exposed geographical position and its massive population increase, in the midst of war Saigon was peaceful: not since the early days of the Viet Minh conflict in 1946 had the city experienced any real combat within its confines.

Despite many signs pointing to something big getting ready to happen, the American command declined to cancel the traditional Tet ceasefire, "by far the worst action taken by the Americans on the eve of the offensive."[24] Nevertheless, among the most important factors in the battle for Saigon was the redeployment of thousands of U.S. troops into and around the city just a few days before the outbreak. On January 10, General Frederick Weyand, U.S. commander of the III Corps, correctly predicted a massive Communist attack, and was largely responsible for preventing further movement of U.S. troops away from Saigon and other cities. General Westmoreland allowed Weyand to move 15 battalions closer to Saigon, troops that certainly made a tremendous difference in the coming struggle for the capital.[25]

During the Offensive, Communist forces attacked not only Saigon but 39 of 44 province capitals and 72 of 242 district capitals as well (a district was a subdivision of a province). They hit the headquarters of all four ARVN military regions into which South Vietnam was divided, and they targeted the ancient capital city of Hue, which would become the scene of some of the fiercest conventional combat of the entire Offensive.[26] Since South Vietnam was no police state, allied forces were unable to prevent the entrance into Saigon of VC shock units and sappers (explosives teams) disguised as civilian holiday makers. At the start, thirty-five Communist battalions—around fourteen thousand men—had gathered in greater Saigon, with perhaps another four thousand sappers inside the city proper. Their main targets were predictable: special units were assigned to assassinate President Thieu and U.S. Ambassador Ellsworth Bunker, as well as the chief of the National Police, the director of South Vietnam's Central Intelligence Agency, and the chief of the Saigon police force. Other groups were to identify and massacre the families of ARVN officers. Locations to be destroyed, occupied, or neutralized included of course the presidential palace, the Saigon radio station, ARVN headquarters at the vital Tan Son Nhut air base and the airfield itself, as well as Bien Hoa air base sixteen miles north of Saigon, the main Saigon prison, South Vietnamese Navy headquarters, and the U.S. and the Philippine embassies. Very few if any other U.S. installations were on the VC list. Those VC units that hit the presidential palace were dressed in ARVN uniforms. A number of other Viet Cong units assigned to Saigon were outfitted as riot police or other security forces.

For the Viet Cong in Saigon, everything went wrong. One VC unit succeeded in getting inside and temporarily taking control of the radio station and tried to play prepared tapes with the message that a general uprising was occurring and that the liberation of Saigon was at hand. But ARVN had set up a system for just such a contingency: they cut off the radio station's electric power, and so the tapes were not aired and nobody heard the great news; and the VC inside the station were killed. Three VC battalions attacked Ton Son Nhut air base but were beaten off after being badly mauled.[27] The force that was supposed to break open the main Saigon prison never reached it. Having failed to achieve or complete their assigned missions, many groups of guerrillas scattered, often randomly seeking refuge inside various structures or makeshift havens, where they were easily located, penned in, and wiped out. A large number of VC chose to make a stand on the grounds of the old French Phu To racetrack, where after serious fighting they were destroyed. The fierce efforts that some of these VC units made to hold on to captured areas or symbolic structures suggest their belief in the imminence of the often-proclaimed popular uprising, which of course never occurred.

More typically, a VC squad that made its way onto the grounds of the U.S. Embassy was soon completely wiped out. In point of fact, the U.S. Embassy was the least important of the VC targets from the viewpoint of the defense of the country or even of the capital. Nevertheless, the American media in Saigon devoted enormous amounts of attention to the fighting around the building. Unsurprisingly, much of the reporting about the embassy fighting was grotesquely inaccurate, as will be shown. But arguably the most important failure of the Offensive was that not a single one of the assassination units proved able to fulfill its assignment. (But as will be seen, this was not true of VC units assigned to murder the families of members of South Vietnamese security forces.)

These failures of the Viet Cong inside Saigon to achieve or even begin their missions can be explained easily. Few of the guerrillas in Saigon had any familiarity at all with that city—or with any city. Consequently, like the insurgents of Warsaw, Budapest, Algiers, Montevideo, Belfast, or Grozny, the VC were trying to fight in territory that was strategically very disadvantageous to them; but quite unlike those other insurgents, the urban landscape was completely strange to them as well. Consequently, many units composed of young country boys easily became lost in Saigon's streets and avenues and thus failed to keep rendezvous, find their assigned targets, and locate or identify their potential supporters. Many of the guerrillas taken prisoner were fourteen or even twelve years old, one of the first major appearances of the child-soldier phenomenon that would become so infamous later in Africa; these youngsters easily gave up valuable intelligence to their interrogators.

At the same time, Communist reserve units outside Saigon had been poised to come into the city to aid the insurgents already fighting within it, but they never arrived because on the second day of the offensive, General Westmoreland ordered U.S. units to block the roads and highways leading into Saigon.[28] This was by no means the least important element in the failure of the Offensive. From this timely blocking movement arises an important lesson for urban counterinsurgency:

> Cities that are descending into chaos must quickly be isolated from the surrounding countryside. Whatever the main source of urban turmoil—insurrection, terrorist attacks, or simple anarchy—outside reinforcements, supplies or sympathizers must be prevented from reaching the centers of urban disturbances. If reinforcements can be kept from urban centers [the guerrilla] units will eventually run out of ammunition, supplies and personnel as security forces systematically isolate and neutralize pockets of resistance.[29]

(At Hue, by contrast, the Communists had been able to insert reinforcements and strengthen their positions for several days. Regular formations of the North Vietnamese Army entered the city on January 31. It was not until February 23 that these units were defeated completely. More detail will soon follow.)

Witnesses to and close students of the Tet Offensive place the number of VC and NVA involved in the fighting all over South Vietnam at roughly eighty-four thousand. Estimated deaths among these range upward from thirty thousand; one authority places the number of killed or captured at forty-five thousand.[30] Many thousands of others were wounded. American combat deaths numbered four thousand, those of the South Vietnamese between four thousand and eight thousand.

Undoubtedly this statistical asymmetry is impressive. It is, however, much less than the full truth. In Don Oberdorfer's stark observation, "the Viet Cong lost the best of a generation of resistance fighters."[31] The import of that statement cannot be too heavily stressed: as Phillip Davidson points out, it is not just that losses among the Viet Cong were extremely heavy: they "were concentrated in their political leadership cadres who had surfaced during the attack. In truth, for all practical purposes, the Tet Offensive destroyed the Viet Cong."[32]

MASSACRES IN HUE

Beyond the complete military failure of Tet, Communist terror tactics during the battle strengthened the hand of the Saigon government all over South Vietnam. Most of the Viet Cong attacks in the cities were beaten off in two or three days, but one of the longest and bloodiest actions of the entire Vietnam war raged in the ancient capital city of Hue. Before and during the allied counterattack on the city, the Communists rounded up thousands of civilians—known anticommunists, students, Catholic priests,[33] nurses, low-level government employees, and their relatives. Perhaps as many as 2,800 of these were shot, bludgeoned to death, or actually buried alive—men, women, children, the old, the young.[34] Another 2,000 were never discovered or heard from again. Some American apologists for the Viet Cong would try to excuse these atrocities as merely the nervous vengeance of a defeated army or as justified retaliation against so-called oppressors of the people. Yet in the words of a distinguished American journalist, these mass murders were clearly "a deliberate slaughter, ordered from on high, for plain and specific purposes."[35] The grisly deeds at Hue received little attention in the American press, especially compared to its later fascination with the smallest details of My Lai. But there is no disputing that the deliberate bloodbath at Hue played a significant role in the popular backlash against the Viet Cong and the resulting rally to the Saigon government. Samuel Popkin wrote

> Before the Tet Offensive, 18-year-old villagers would lie and say they were 13 to get out of the draft. After the Tet Offensive, 13- and 14-year-olds would lie and say they were 18 to get into the draft before the Communists got to them. The perception of the craziness of what the Communists were doing was increased, and the idea that they were inevitable winners was so deflated that people changed very much how they felt.[36]

Inexplicably, the massacres at Hue received little notice and are now largely forgotten in the United States. But in the years following the Tet Offensive, the celebrated author James Jones[37] wrote that "whatever else they accomplished, the Hue massacres effectively turned the bulk of the South Vietnamese against the Northern Communists. In South Vietnam, wherever one went . . . the 1968 Tet massacres were still being talked about in 1973."[38] Douglas Blaufarb noted that "after Tet, the population had substantially abandoned the VC cause."[39] To make up their heavy losses, the VC drastically increased their forcible recruitment of peasants; at the same time, heightened mobilization by the South Vietnamese decreased the numbers available for this forcible Communist recruitment.

WHY DID THE TET OFFENSIVE FAIL?

Lists of the causes of the failure of the Tet Offensive will naturally vary somewhat, but any serious list would certainly have to include the return to the Saigon area, without an hour to spare, of U.S. troops that had previously been withdrawn, as well as the quick and effective shutting off of access routes into the city. Another key factor is that urban guerrilla warfare is almost an oxymoron: cities are no place to attempt to apply guerrilla tactics developed in the countryside, no matter how effective they may have been there.[40] It is precisely for that reason that American and Vietnamese intelligence operatives could not take seriously the indications that the Viet Cong guerrillas were going to emerge, going to reveal themselves, inside the cities of South Vietnam.

But there are at least two other fundamental reasons for the complete failure of the Tet Offensive, each being very instructive as to the true nature of this war. The first is the performance during Tet of the South Vietnamese Army. The second is the nature of that South Vietnamese society that Hanoi wished to conquer.

ARVN and Tet

Without the tenacity displayed by ARVN, Tet would almost certainly have been successful. Sympathizers with and apologists for the failure of the Offensive offered the view that the anticipated people's uprising in Saigon failed to occur because of the presence of ARVN units in the capital. Now, there is undoubtedly truth in that contention, but if it is true, shouldn't the leadership in Hanoi have taken that fact into consideration before launching the Offensive? (Or maybe they had?) It had long been predicted, indeed it was an article of faith in North Vietnam, that at the first appearance of real danger, ARVN would disintegrate. Now, it is true enough, and quite instructive, that in the hour of grave crisis the armies of Louis XVI, Nicholas II, and the Shah of Iran had wavered and then dissolved, and thus threw open the gates to revolution; so (notably) did the carefully recruited and heavily indoctrinated Communist forces in Budapest in 1956 and in East Germany, Romania, and Czechoslovakia in 1989. But ARVN did not disintegrate; quite to the contrary. Although most ARVN units were at half strength because of the Tet holiday truce (which the Communists impiously violated), they neither deserted, nor defected to the Communists. Instead, "they fought valiantly and ultimately drove the VC out of dozens of cities and towns."[41]

General Phillip Davidson, head of U.S. military intelligence in South Vietnam, later wrote that "the professionalism and steadfastness of ARVN during the Tet Offensive surprised not only the enemy, but the Americans and [the South Vietnamese] themselves as well."[42] Other competent observers have recorded that ARVN "came of age during the 1968 fighting,"[43] and that while the performance of ARVN units varied widely under the attack, "overall their stout resistance was an essential factor in Hanoi's military failure."[44] General Westmoreland later wrote:

> In the main, the Tet Offensive was a Vietnamese fight. To the ARVN, other members of the South Vietnamese armed forces, the militia, the National Police—to those belonged the major share of credit for turning back the offensive. Some individuals failed—an occasional commander proved incompetent; but overall, when put to the crucial test, no ARVN unit had broken or defected. The South Vietnamese had fully vindicated my trust.[45]

Note that General Westmoreland penned these words after the fall of South Vietnam; he had no points to win by excessively flattering anybody. And Andrew Wiest, a most careful student of ARVN, later wrote:

> That the South Vietnamese population did not rise up, that the ARVN fought bravely—more bravely than the Americans dared hope—was critical to the tactical success of the battle and portended well for the future of South Vietnam. In reality, most of the fighting and dying in the Tet Offensive, especially in the critical battles in Hue City, fell to the ARVN, a tragic victory won by a

nation that did not survive to tell its own story. It was the finest hour of the ARVN.[46]

(Pathetically—or comically—true to form, shortly after the outbreak of the Offensive John Kenneth Galbraith confidently assured President Johnson that there would soon be massive defections from ARVN to the Communist side.[47])

After Tet was over, the United States finally began giving ARVN good M-16 rifles, a match for the Communist AK-47 and much superior to the vintage rifles ARVN had always received before that.

The Nature of South Vietnamese Society

Another fundamental cause of the failure of the Tet Offensive is that most South Vietnamese did not wish it to succeed. This is a consideration quite distinct and independent from the unexpectedly sturdy showing—the decisive behavior—by ARVN and the territorials during the Offensive.

As we have seen, "the primary objective of the Tet offensive was to win the war by instigating a general uprising."[48] But that objective was far beyond possibility, either in Saigon or in the country as a whole, because by 1968 so much of the population was immune or even hostile to Communist appeals, all those members and adherents of important social groups some of whom we have encountered previously: the powerful indigenous religious sects, northern refugees, the Catholic community, the close-knit Chinese minority, the urban business and professional classes, employees of the South Vietnamese and U.S. governments, the relatives of victims of Viet Cong violence, the politically disengaged, and—above all—well over one million officers, soldiers, militiamen, and policemen, along with their families. Many of these groups were especially numerous in and around Saigon. (In contrast, according to a source very friendly to the Communist side, as late as 1974—as the Americans were clearly running out on the South Vietnamese—there were in all of Saigon only five hundred Communist activists.)[49]

This proposition—that most South Vietnamese were quite the opposite of enthusiastic supporters of the Viet Cong—would undoubtedly surprise or even annoy many Americans of today, but there is abundant evidence to sustain it. First, please recall from chapter 1 the number of Vietnamese who died fighting the Viet Minh between 1946 and 1954 in the uniforms of either the CEF or Bao Dai's Vietnamese National Army: 40,000 in the CEF (over 40 percent of all CEF killed and missing), 59,000 in the VNA,[50] a total of at least 99,000, equivalent to more than 1 million Americans in 2015. And recall further that 36 percent of the defenders of Dien Bien Phu had been

Vietnamese, and that Vietnamese paratroopers were volunteering to jump into that clearly doomed fortress complex until the very end.

All those Vietnamese, and their family members, who had borne arms against the Viet Minh and who found themselves on the free side of the partition line, would constitute the political and military foundation of the South Vietnamese state, powerfully reinforced by the million persons who fled across the partition line in 1954, the equivalent in 2015 of more than ten million Americans fleeing the U.S. in a few months. Moreover, Ellen J. Hammer has recorded that "as ICC [International Control Commission] staff members traveled around North Vietnam [after partition], they encountered many people who implored their assistance in leaving for the South, but it was too late"; hostility to the Communists in the northern provinces was real and widespread by 1954. Partly for that reason, Hammer continued, "the population of the South had no wish to live under communism as it was practiced in the North."[51] In 1966, the distinguished East Asian specialist Robert Scalapino offered these rough estimates of the South Vietnamese population: for the Communists, 15–20 percent; opposed to the Communists, 35–40 percent; apolitical, 40–50 percent.[52] CBS correspondent Charles Collingwood stated on national television in 1967 that "in secure [allied-controlled] areas there is intense dislike of the Viet Cong" and that a "CBS survey . . . confirms that the Viet Cong does not enjoy mass support outside the areas it controls."[53] One scholar very sympathetic to the Viet Cong states that the insurgency had the support of about one-third of the peasantry (everyone admits that the Communists were much weaker in the cities) in the late 1960s, with about one-third neutral.[54] Robert Thompson, deeply experienced with counterinsurgency, believed that free elections in 1968 would have seen the Communists win about a third of the vote.[55] And at the outset of the Tet Offensive, Communist headquarters in South Vietnam (COSVN) warned its followers that the Saigon government was supported by "an army of more than 1,200,000 stubborn, reactionary, and well-equipped soldiers," out of a total southern population of less than 19 million.[56]

In effect, the Tet Offensive, absolutely relying on a popular uprising and an ARVN collapse, had attacked in too many places and thus was sufficiently strong nowhere, because what the Viet Cong encountered was not only the chimera of enthusiastic popular support but the reality of widespread popular resistance. There is much agreement on this point. "The communists," wrote Wirtz, "soon discovered that they were not welcomed as liberators. Civilians ignored the call to stage a general uprising and generally failed to cooperate with the communists. Some civilians even jumped at the first opportunity to inform authorities of the whereabouts of VC units or to volunteer information about VC plans. The Tet Offensive definitely failed to unfold as anticipated."[57]

In his magisterial study of these events Arthur Dommen observes that nowhere in South Vietnam had the people risen up to support the NLF [Viet Cong]. . . . The South Vietnamese people, indeed, informed by what they had seen with their own eyes, had read about in their newspapers, and heard about on their radios, had concluded that the NLF did not stand for peace but for war; not for prosperity but for destruction; not for independence but for dependence.[58]

The one who bore the heaviest cost of this popular hostility was undoubtedly the youthful Viet Cong fighter. Even before Tet, Konrad Kellen had observed that "though told by his cadres that the south is already overwhelmingly controlled by the VC, he is likely to find on arriving that he is not welcomed by the local people and must camp out in the jungle. Often he is taken aback to discover that he must fight his fellow Vietnamese. Or, if this is not a surprise, that he must fight them in numbers greater than he had been led to expect."[59]

The failure of the civilian population to rise up in aid of the Viet Cong stunned Hanoi, officially at least.[60] Concerning the Tet Offensive, *Victory in Vietnam*, the official history of the North Vietnamese Army, published by the Military History Institute of Vietnam (Hanoi), states:

> We were subjective in our assessment of the situation, especially in assessing the strength of the mass political forces in the urban areas. We had somewhat underestimated the capabilities and reactions of the enemy and had set our goals too high. . . . When the battle did not progress favorably for our side and when we suffered casualties, rightist thoughts, pessimism, and hesitancy appeared among our forces.[61]

Translation: The popular uprising didn't happen, ARVN fought well, and our enormous casualties devastated our soldiers' morale.

Of course, after the failure of Tet the position of the Communists in South Vietnam deteriorated further. James Willbanks observes that "many South Vietnamese villagers, who heretofore had been at best ambivalent about joining Saigon's fight against the Communists, were shocked by what they saw as the excesses of the Communists during the 1968 attacks and joined the PSDF, taking up arms to protect their towns, villages and hamlets. By the end of 1969, over three million members had volunteered for the PSDF."[62] In early 1972 that number in the PSDF [People's Self-Defense Forces] had risen to four million—a figure of course quite separate from all those in ARVN, the territorials, and the police forces, out of a population of less than nineteen million.[63] In a word, said Robert Thompson, "the VC side of it is over. The people have rejected the VC."[64] A respected student of electoral processes around the world wrote in 1972 that the "vast majority" of South Vietnamese did not wish to see a Communist takeover of their country.[65] In 1974, Thompson maintained that "the GVN [Government of South Vietnam] was supported in its war aims by over 90 per cent of the population and the communists by less than 10 percent."[66]

Indeed, the lack of a mass revolt against the South Vietnamese government characterized not only Tet but also the Easter Offensive of 1972—and even the final conventional North Vietnamese Army invasion in 1975, when it was only too obvious to anyone with eyes to see that the South Vietnamese cause was lost.[67]

Perhaps the most telling testimony of all regarding what the majority of South Vietnamese wanted is this: in 1975, on the very eve of the fall of Saigon, no less than Northern Premier Pham Van Dong himself conceded (conservatively) that, after a Communist takeover of South Vietnam, from 50 to 70 percent of the southern population would need to be "persuaded" of the benefits of "reunification."[68] (Granted, he probably would not have publicly offered such an estimate just before the Tet Offensive.)

THE MEDIA

"In retrospect," according to NVA General Tran Do, "we didn't achieve our main objective, which was to spur uprising throughout the south. Still, we inflicted heavy casualties on the Americans and their puppets. . . . As for making an impact on the United States, it had not been our intention—but it turned out to be a fortunate result."[69] How did such an outcome occur?

In essence, the answer to that legitimate and fundamental question is this: With a few honorable exceptions, the American media reporting of Tet was not only full of errors, but was the exact opposite of what actually happened on the ground.

It is true that ill-informed or self-serving persons sometimes criticize the news media. It does not ineluctably follow, however, that all criticism of the news media is self-serving or ill-informed. Consider this: in 1994, Senator George Mitchell of Maine, the Democratic floor leader, stated that the American news industry was "more destructive than constructive than ever." Representative Barney Frank (D-Mass.) stated that "you people [reporters] celebrate failure and ignore success. *Nothing about government is done as incompetently as the reporting of it.*"[70] Suppose we allow, for the moment, that such comments by those two experienced political figures are not totally without merit, what did they mean? Did they not clearly mean that American reporters, operating amidst American culture and indeed in the American capital, fluent (so to speak) in the American language, are often unable to present American political events and their meaning to the American public correctly? But if such statements—and the persons who make them—are taken seriously, might it not then be utterly unreasonable to inquire whether the reporting and interpreting of events in Vietnam by American journalists, most of whom knew little about the military tactics of guerrilla warfare and less about the political tactics of Leninism, who were totally unfamiliar with the culture of Vietnam and who indeed spoke none of the indigenous languages, and not even French—is it in fact utterly unreasonable to inquire if such reporting may have sometimes failed to attain the level of perfect accuracy?

Consider further that during the Tet Offensive and afterward, neither *Time* nor *Newsweek* published a single article on ARVN. Apparently not even one positive story on the fighting performance of any ARVN unit appeared in any American newspaper. The Saigon government's unprecedented mass arming of the civilian population after the Tet Offensive revealed for all to see the true relationship among that government, the Viet Cong, and the South Vietnamese people. That was a tremendous story indeed, but the news media never presented it to the American public. Most importantly, the television networks in particular portrayed the Tet Offensive as an incomprehensible catastrophe for American forces, a collapse of security all over South Vietnam that was inexplicably unexpected, apparently total, and undoubtedly irredeemable. How could any regular viewers of the nightly network news shows be immune to the constant suggestion that the United States was enmeshed in a hopeless war against formidable foes, and all for the defense of ineffectual allies? Regular viewers of the Cronkite or Huntley-Brinkley newscasts saw more infantry combat during Tet (regularly punctuated by commercials for deodorants and bathroom tissue) than most U.S. troops in Vietnam at the time. [71] This "nightly portrayal of violence and gore and of American soldiers seemingly on the brink of disaster contributed significantly to disillusionment with the war." [72] George Will scathingly observed that "if the North could have seen that battle [Antietam] in living color [on television] it would have elected McClellan president [in 1864] and we would be two nations today." [73] Many newsmen portrayed South Vietnam as a land of corruption, crime, cowardice, and cruelty. All these elements were indeed easy to find in a war-torn South Vietnam open to minute and hostile scrutiny from the foreign press. North Vietnam was of course not subjected to anything even approaching such relentless scrutiny, but few journalists seemed to appreciate the consequences of that gargantuan asymmetry; at any rate the closed nature of the North meant that the failings and blemishes of the South were vastly magnified. Not infrequently, American reporters saved themselves the discomfort and danger of gathering stories on their own by purchasing them from tremendously helpful and wonderfully well-informed English-speaking Vietnamese in Saigon who after the war turned out to be—*of course, what else?*—agents of Hanoi. [74] And the influential Harrison Salisbury of the *New York Times* sent from Hanoi searing reports of supposed American bombing atrocities—atrocities he had himself not witnessed but information on which had helpfully been supplied directly to him by the North Vietnamese government. [75]

Because few reporters in Vietnam during the Tet Offensive had experienced or even viewed the tremendous destruction of cities during World War II, or in Korea, many of them, especially in formerly pleasant and peaceful Saigon, were deeply shocked and frightened at the violence they saw or heard around them. Consequently, most reporters imagined that everybody in South Vietnam was as overwhelmed by the Offensive as they themselves were. This inexperience and isolation of many reporters stimulated "the media's penchant for self-projection and instant analysis" so that major network "specials" on Tet "assume average South Vietnamese reactions [to Tet] were those of American commentators." [76] Take as an example the reporting of the Viet Cong attack on the U.S. Embassy in Saigon. The embassy had no military significance whatsoever. Had it been burned down or blown up, it would have had absolutely no effect on the outcome of the fighting in the capital city. Nineteen Viet Cong attacked the embassy compound and all of them were soon killed or captured; yet reporters turned this minor shootout into the most significant event of the entire war. "This little group [of VC at the embassy], numbering [less than] three hundredths of one percent of the total nationwide attack force, was destined to receive about three quarters of all the attention of the outside world in the first stunning hours of the Tet offensive." [77] On January 31, UPI stated that "as U.S. military police attacked Communist positions in the Embassy from the street level, helicopters took troops to the roof of the eight-story building to root them out floor by floor." [78] (The Embassy had six floors.) Peter Arnett and others informed the world that the VC had taken over the first floor of the embassy. [79] Later UPI stated that "there were unconfirmed reports the communists had taken over the first five floors of the [embassy]." [80]

All of these reports were completely false.

Alas, that is not the worst. The Tet Offensive produced probably the most famous photograph to come out of the entire war: it was the one in which the Saigon police chief Loan took out his pistol and executed Bay Lop, a VC prisoner, in the streets of Saigon. Bay Lop was in civilian clothes when captured during the Battle for Saigon, and thus had no claim whatsoever to treatment as a prisoner of war. Shortly before his capture, witnesses saw him executing a policeman, his wife, and three children. [81] The photograph of the terrorist's execution was plastered all over the front pages and television screens across America, often without even the most cursory explanation of the circumstances in which it had been taken. The photographer was Eddie Adams, a 35-year-old former marine and award-winning journalist. For years thereafter Adams stated that he deeply regretted having taken that picture. Now, whatever one's personal feelings about the incident, the question arises of how—*precisely how*—does a picture of a policeman shooting a blood-soaked, child-killing terrorist in the street of a city filled with violence prove that the U.S. was right to abandon the South Vietnamese?

Media coverage of the war, at the time and later, provoked devastating reactions from students of the Vietnam conflict: for example, Douglas Pike declared that North Vietnamese propaganda had "turned skeptical newsmen credulous, careful scholars indifferent to data, honorable men blind to immorality."[82] And notably, a very great deal of the most searing criticism of the reporting about Vietnam came from within the ranks of professional journalists.[83] One veteran newspaperman wrote that "drama was perpetuated at the expense of information."[84] Another journalist wrote that "the *New York Times* and many others had succeeded in creating an image of South Vietnam that was so distant from the truth as not even to be good caricature."[85] The *Economist* noted that many reporters believed everything claimed by the National Liberation Front (the VC) or Hanoi. ABC anchorman Howard K. Smith wrote that "the Viet Cong casualties were one hundred times ours. But we never told the public that."[86] Robert Elegant, editor of *Newsweek* and recipient of three Overseas Press Club Awards, charges that "the press consistently magnified the allies' deficiencies, and displayed almost saintly tolerance of those misdeeds of Hanoi it could neither disregard nor deny."[87] Elegant published a most authoritative and disturbing dissection of the failings of the American news industry during the Vietnamese conflict entitled "Vietnam: How to Lose a War," in the August 1981 issue of *Encounter*. And William V. Kennedy penned a devastating, root-and-branch analysis of media shortcomings in wartime.[88]

Now, in light of all these criticisms and charges, consider the following:

At an October 31, 1987 roundtable discussion of military ethics at Harvard University, moderator Professor Charles Ogletree, Jr., asked ABC news anchor Peter Jennings and Mike Wallace of CBS's "60 Minutes" if they would warn U.S. troops about to be ambushed by the enemy in a hypothetical war between the U.S. and "North Kosan." Jennings originally responded, "If I was with a North Kosanese unit that came upon Americans, I think I would personally do what I could to warn the Americans." But Wallace clucked that he and other reporters would "regard it simply as another story that they are there to cover," and stated "I'm at a little bit of a loss to understand why, because you are an American, you would not have covered that story." "Don't you have a higher duty as an American citizen," Ogletree asked, "to do all you can to save the lives of soldiers rather than the journalistic ethic of reporting fact?" "No," Wallace responded, "you don't have a higher duty . . . you're a reporter."

Jennings later expressed agreement with Wallace.[89]

Polling data strongly suggest that media presentation of the war had only a limited effect on the electorate. The same is not true, however, with regard to its effect on Washington Beltway elites, entangled as always in their provincial self-absorption.

What if American journalists had covered World War II the way many of them did Vietnam? What if Nazi spokesmen had been given the opportunity to declare to the American electorate that Allied bombing of Germany was a war crime? What if the media had characterized the entire Allied strategy in Europe as a failure because of the jolting surprise of the Battle of the Bulge? Would the appalling casualties at Normandy or Okinawa have been presented as showing President Roosevelt to have been an incompetent failure? Would a photograph of a Russian policeman executing an SS prisoner in the streets of Smolensk have proven that U.S. participation in World War II was immoral?

Regrettably, many journalistic interpretations of events in Vietnam were little worse than numerous accounts produced during the war, and long afterwards, by American academicians.

THE NEW HAMPSHIRE PRIMARY

Tet was not the only big story the media got wrong in 1968. In the March New Hampshire Democratic presidential primary, Minnesota Senator Eugene McCarthy challenged President Johnson's renomination over U.S. involvement in the Vietnam conflict. When the state Democratic ballots were counted, President Johnson had 49.6 percent, and Senator McCarthy had 41.9 percent. The instant analysts of the television media promptly declared that McCarthy had won a "moral" victory because his vote was "higher than expected." (By whom?) The word "moral" was quickly dropped and references appeared on the airwaves and in print to McCarthy's "victory" in New Hampshire. Here indeed was a big story: an incumbent President had been defeated in the country's first primary election by a member of his own party who had campaigned on an antiwar platform.

Among other consequences, this media interpretation of the outcome of the New Hampshire primary persuaded Robert Kennedy that it was politically safe for him to enter the presidential race on an anti-Vietnam platform. It also helped persuade President Johnson that he should not seek reelection. Thus was history altered by the media interpretation of what had happened in New Hampshire.

Now, it was the case that on the New Hampshire Democratic Primary ballot, only Senator McCarthy's name appeared. That is, President Johnson had not only received more votes than Senator McCarthy, but his votes were all write-ins. Such an event is extremely exceptional in U.S. elections. But somehow, this profoundly story-changing circumstance escaped comment. And here is perhaps the most notable aspect of Senator McCarthy's super-hyped antiwar victory, certainly the one that shines the worst possible light on how the media reported that event. Following the New Hampshire Democratic primary, inquiries among those who had voted in that contest revealed that a great many of them, when describing themselves as being "against the war," actually meant to say that they were dissatisfied with the apparently ineffectual nature of the policies the Johnson Administration was pursing in Vietnam; they wanted more vigorous efforts, they wanted victory, not stalemate, and they were certainly *not* voting for a rapid U.S. abandonment of the South Vietnamese. These persons outnumbered the properly described "antiwar" voters by about three to two. And of those Democrats who had voted for Senator McCarthy in the March primary, in the November election a plurality cast their votes for Governor George Wallace of Alabama.[90]

Arguably, the single most important American victim of media misreporting and misinterpretation was President Lyndon Johnson.

REFLECTION

The Tet Offensive was Hanoi's admission that the guerrilla insurgency in South Vietnam had failed. The new strategy—the urban offensive—"was intended to win the war through sparking a mass uprising, overthrowing the South Vietnamese government, and making the position of the U.S. military untenable. That was how the enemy defined victory, and none of it was achieved."[91] Tet was not primarily about sending a message to Washington, it was not aimed at public opinion in the U.S. It was a last-ditch effort to knock South Vietnam out of the war, and it failed. The Viet Cong had no withdrawal plans from Saigon, and fought tenaciously to hold on to places taken. This was for real. In the words of arguably the best American study of the Offensive, "The magnitude of the Communists' defeat in Tet was thus a direct reflection of their conceptual failings, erroneous premises, poor assessment, inadequate planning, and lackluster execution."[92] Indeed.

By 1969, writes Dommen, "the war for the support of the South Vietnamese had basically been won by the Saigon Government and its allies" and "defections from the Communist ranks had reached an all-time high."[93]

As Wirtz observes:

> once disrupted, the VC infrastructure was not easily replaced. Search-and-destroy operations also tended to drive VC main forces and NVA units into remote areas, separating them from the infrastructure and guerrilla units they needed for support. Thus the combination of disrupted logistics, increasing casualties, and a feeling among VC and NVA soldiers that the end of the war was not yet in sight resulted in a decline in the morale and combat capability of communist units.[94]

In terms of equipment, territorial control, popular support, and general self-confidence, the state of South Vietnam was much stronger after Tet than before. The Communists had begun their long-planned offensive against an unprepared and dispersed enemy by violating a sacred holiday truce. They had predicted the disintegration of ARVN and massive upheavals in the cities. Instead, the Viet Cong suffered irreparable losses. Tet was so costly to the Viet Cong that they had to regress to mainly small-unit actions; it would be years before Hanoi felt able to launch another major offensive, and then, in 1972 its instrument would be not the Viet Cong but the North Vietnamese Army. In summary, "the Tet Offensive was the most disastrous defeat North Vietnam suffered in the long war."[95] Truly, if the Vietnam war had been a conventional war, if it had been decided on the basis of military success and military failure, "it would have been over by mid-1968 with the defeat of the Communist forces."[96] And it was in fact the end *of one kind of war.* As Timothy Lomperis concluded, "More than just dealing a sharp military defeat to Communist forces, [Tet] destroyed an entire political-military strategy, a revolution of Maoist people's war."[97] For the Communist side, Tet "was the end of People's War, and essentially of any strategy built on guerrilla warfare and a politically inspired insurgency."[98] Henceforth regular North Vietnamese Army troops would have to assume an ever-increasing share of the war's burdens.

Thus, for the Viet Cong, the consequences of the Tet Offensive were profound and permanent. As Oberdorfer explains,

> among the Vietnamese people, the battles had created doubts about Communist military power. The Liberation Army [the VC] had attacked in the middle of the Tet truce when the South Vietnamese Army was on leave, and even so it had been able to achieve only temporary inroads. If the Communists were unable to take the cities with a surprise attack in such circumstances, they would probably be unable to do better at any other time.[99]

Or, in Douglas Blaufarb's more succinct summary, after Tet "the population had abandoned the VC cause."[100] In acknowledgment of this change, following Tet, President Thieu distributed hundreds of thousands of weapons to a greatly expanded militia, the People's Self-Defense Force. And desertions from the VC and the NVA reached a peak during the year after Tet.[101]

The Tet Offensive began as a surprise for the Americans and for the South Vietnamese and ended as a disaster for the Communists. "People's War" had failed. The South Vietnamese armed forces would keep on fighting for more than seven years after Tet—a period of time longer than the American Civil War or World War I or World War II. The final fall of South Vietnam required a massive invasion by the North Vietnamese Army, generously equipped by the Chinese and the Soviets, against South Vietnamese forces abandoned by the Americans. Thus, the utter nonoccurrence of the

General Uprising, which the Hanoi leadership predicted with such assurance, is the key to understanding both the true nature of the war, and hence the tragedy of the U.S. desertion of its South Vietnamese allies.

THE HO CHI MINH TRAIL

If the Ho Chi Minh Trail had not existed, it is very difficult to see how Hanoi could have launched either the Tet Offensive of 1968 or (especially) the Easter Offensive of 1972, and even the final assault of 1975. Indeed, all the serious problems allied forces encountered in the struggle for a free South Vietnam had their roots, to one degree or another, in the failure to stop Hanoi's permanent invasion of the South. The famous Trail went through "neutral" Laos and Cambodia. President Eisenhower had warned President Kennedy that Laos was the key to South Vietnam, and General Taylor told Kennedy as early as 1961 that the insurgents—the Viet Cong—could not be beaten as long as infiltration via their Laotian sanctuary went unchecked. [102]

The misnamed "Trail" was begun in 1959, and by a decade later had become a network of roads—10,000 miles in total length with an estimated 2,000-mile pipeline—down which poured thousands of troops and trucks every month. The construction of the Trail was in itself an epic. Built at the cost of vast sacrifice of human lives, through some of the most inhospitable territory to human beings in the world, the Trail was a victory over forbidding terrain, debilitating climate, physical exhaustion, and omnipresent insects, snakes, fungus, and infection. This logistical triumph would cost many Americans their lives and the South Vietnamese their freedom, needlessly so.

If the troops from North Vietnam who had infiltrated into South Vietnam in relatively small batches between 1959 and 1965 had all come in at the same time, it would have looked like a Korea-style invasion. Instead, the Trail confronted American and ARVN troops with a sort of slow-motion Schlieffen Plan, by which they were constantly being outflanked. [103]

Sir Robert Thompson, the distinguished and widely experienced British authority on insurgency, wrote this: "One further point which was a key element in the Vietnam war and one which people do not realize was probably its turning point was the Laos agreement of 1962. Because it kept the United States out of Laos and gave the North Vietnamese a free run it made the war [to defend South Vietnam] almost unwinnable." [104]

General Westmoreland and others wanted to cut the Trail on the ground by sending three divisions across Laos to the border of Thailand, a distance comparable to that between Washington and Philadelphia. The South Korea Demarcation (Truce) line is almost 150 miles long; in the 1950s the French built the Morice Line running almost 600 miles along the Algerian-Tunisian border and thereby effectively stopped guerrilla infiltration into Algeria; in the 1980s, the Moroccans built the Hassan line, a ten- to twelve-foot-high rock-and-sand anti-guerrilla wall with sensors and radar running hundreds of miles through Western Sahara (formerly Spanish Sahara). General Bruce Palmer advocated extending the Demilitarized Zone across Laos to Thailand; three U.S. divisions would hold this line, supported by intensive airpower. The U.S. navy would blockade North Vietnamese ports and threaten the coast with invasion; there would be no need for "strategic bombing" of the North. Thus the United States armed forces would execute a double mission: (1) block the infiltration and invasion into South Vietnam, and (2) train and equip a first-class ARVN. Cut off from replacements and heavy equipment, the Viet Cong must eventually wither away. Most of all, as General West-moreland wrote, "in defending well-prepared positions U.S. troops would suffer fewer casualties."[105] Ambassadors Lodge and Bunker agreed with the necessity and affirmed the ability to block the Laotian route into South Vietnam.[106]

The Johnson Administration, however, forbade any attempt to use ground forces to block the Trail across Laos; it intended to stem the tide of men and supplies by airpower alone. Accordingly, the Americans carried out the most intensive bombing campaign in the history of warfare. It was to no avail. The demands made upon American airpower were unrealistic. Traffic down the Trail was slowed at times, but not stopped. President Johnson later wrote that of course he was aware that "North Vietnamese and Viet Cong forces were enjoying almost complete sanctuary in Laos and Cambodia." But then why not put a stop to this? Because in 1962 President Kennedy had agreed to the "neutralization" of Laos and, in President Johnson's exact words, in May 1967 "we were all concerned that entering Laos with ground forces would *end all hope of reviving the 1962 Laos agreement, fragile though it was, and would greatly increase the forces needed in Southeast Asia.*"[107]

Leaving open the Ho Chi Minh Trail seemed to allow no alternative to massive bombing of North Vietnam. Why and how bombing would have a greater effect on the North Vietnamese than it had had on the British or the Germans in World War II were never quite made clear. In any event, North Vietnamese officials told Robert Shaplen that their Chinese-assisted forces shot down twenty-five hundred U.S. aircraft engaged in bombing the Trail.[108]

The failure both to close the Trail and to adopt any alternative strategy that would have neutralized its effects meant that the Communist forces could fight on interior lines, a tremendous advantage. It also meant that the Communists were free to invade South Vietnam continuously: the NVA's huge (and unsuccessful) 1972 Easter Offensive would have been quite im-possible without the Laotian springboard. It meant that when hard pressed by allied forces, the enemy could simply retreat into Laos or Cambodia. Thus the policies of the Johnson Administration—policies adopted for domestic political reasons, not military-strategic ones—made a lasting, or even a temporary, allied military victory impossible. And that fact, in turn meant that attrition—killing large numbers of North Vietnamese who came down the Trail into South Vietnam—would take longer than key segments of the American governing class would accept. Indeed, like the bombing of the North, attrition itself was a substitute policy forced on the allies through the failure to interrupt the Ho Chi Minh Trail. But "it was impossible to defeat North Vietnam decisively in South Vietnam without stopping the invasion" via that Trail.[109]

After the fall of Saigon, leading figures in Hanoi expressed the conviction that the Trail was the key to their success.[110] They are not alone in that opinion. Sir Robert Thompson stated that "if they [the North Vietnamese] had not had this unmolested avenue through Laos, the insurgency in Vietnam could have been stopped at any time in the early 1960s."[111] In essence, "Without it [the Trail]," wrote Thompson, "the [Communist] war could not have been waged."[112] Prominent Johnson Administration figures concur. "Surely," wrote William P. Bundy, "we could have held a line across Laos and South Vietnam with significantly fewer men than we eventually employed within South Vietnam, far less American casualties, and in the end much greater effect and less bloodshed in the South itself."[113] "In retrospect," stated Ambassador Bunker, "I am more certain than I was in 1967 that our failure to cut the Ho Chi Minh Trail was a strategic mistake of the first order."[114] And Walt Rostow declared that the failure to act against the Ho Chi Minh Trail in 1962 "may have been the single greatest mistake in United States foreign policy in the 1960s."[115]

The reader may pursue this topic in the appendix.

NOTES

1. Don Oberdorfer, *Tet!* (New York: Da Capo Press, 1984), p. 81; Hoang Ngoc Lung, *The General Offensives of 1968–1969* (Washington, DC: U.S. Army Center of Military History, 1981), p. 22.
2. William D. Henderson, *Why the Viet Cong Fought: A Study of Motivation and Control in a Modern Army in Combat* (Westport, CT: Greenwood, 1979), p. xv.
3. Hoang Ngoc Lung, *General Offensives of 1968–1969*, p. 21.
4. *Washington Post,* April 6, 1969. This was out of a total Vietnamese population of around thirty-six millions.
5. Henderson, *Why the Viet Cong Fought*, p. 23.
6. James J. Wirtz, *The Tet Offensive: Intelligence Failure in War* (Ithaca, NY: Cornell University Press, 1994), p. 46.
7. Oberdorfer, *Tet!* p. 45.
8. Wirtz, *Tet Offensive*, pp. 23 and 60.
9. The Military History Institute of Vietnam, *Victory in Vietnam: The Official History of the People's Army of Vietnam, 1954–1975*, tr. Merle L. Pribbenow (Lawrence, KS: University Press of Kansas, 2002), p. 214.
10. Wirtz, *Tet Offensive*, p. 2.
11. Wirtz, *Tet Offensive*, p. 83.

12. Whether or not the siege of Khe Sanh was intended as a distraction or was an integral part of Giap's offensive plans has been hotly disputed; see Wirtz, *Tet Offensive*, pp. 63, 81, and 98; and Gabriel Kolko, *Anatomy of a War* (New York: Pantheon, 1985), p. 305. Davidson rejected the view of Khe Sanh as merely a diversion; *Vietnam at War*, pp. 444–445. Consult also John Prados and R. W. Stubbe, *Valley of Decision: The Siege of Khe Sanh* (Boston: Houghton-Mifflin, 1991).

13. Wirtz, *Tet Offensive*, p. 63.

14. Wirtz, *Tet Offensive*, p. 84. My italics.

15. Thucydides, *The Peloponnesian War*, Chapter 3.

16. Machiavelli, *The Discourses*, chapter XLVIII.

17. Douglas Southall Freeman, *Robert E. Lee* (New York: Scribner 1997), p. 504.

18. Wirtz, *Tet Offensive*, p. 82.

19. Wirtz, *Tet Offensive*, p. 245; my italics.

20. Wirtz, *Tet Offensive*, p. 66.

21. Norman Davies, *Rising '44: The Battle for Warsaw* (New York: Viking, 2003); Tadeusz Komorowski [Bor], *The Secret Army* (New York: Macmillan, 1951); Stefan Krbonski, *Fighting Warsaw: The Story of the Polish Underground State* (New York: Minerva Press, 1968).

22. In 1962, North Vietnamese Premier Pham Van Dong told Bernard Fall that "Americans do not like long, inconclusive wars"; Fall, *Vietnam Witness, 1953–1966* (New York: Praeger, 1966). In his book *Big Victory, Great Task* (New York: Praeger, 1968), General Giap predicted that the United States would not maintain large numbers of troops in Vietnam for very long.

23. This is the view of, among others, Sir Robert Thompson; see his *Make for the Hills: Memories of Far Eastern Wars* (London: Leo Cooper, 1989), p. 155.

24. Wirtz, *Tet Offensive*, p.196.

25. Wirtz, *Tet Offensive*, p. 200.

26. Large areas of Hue were taken over by NVA regulars, and fighting there ended with the successful siege of the ancient citadel by U.S. Marines. For the fighting in Hue, see Eric Hammel, *Fire in the Streets: The Battle for Hue, Tet 1968* (Chicago: Contemporary Books, 1991); Keith William Nolan, *Battle for Hue: Tet 1968* (Novato, CA: Presidio, 1983); George Smith, *The Siege at Hue* (Boulder, CO: Lynne Rienner, 1999); Nicholas Warr, *Phase Line Green* (Annapolis, MD: Naval Institute Press, 1997); and see the chapter "Death in Hue" in Oberdorfer, *Tet!*

27. William Westmoreland, *A Solder Reports* (Garden City, NY: Doubleday, 1976), p. 326.

28. For Hanoi's official description of VC actions around Saigon, see Military History Institute of Vietnam, *Victory in Vietnam*, pp. 219–223.

29. James J. Wirtz, "The Battles of Saigon and Hue: Tet 1968," *Soldiers in Cities: Military Operations on Urban Terrain*, ed. Michael C. Desch (Carlisle, PA: Strategic Studies Institute, 2001), p. 83.

30. Phillip B. Davidson, *Vietnam at War: The History, 1946–1975* (Novato, CA: Presidio, 1988), p. 475; Ambassador Bunker cabled President Johnson that he believed thirty-three thousand had been killed and fifty-six hundred "detained"; *The Bunker Papers: Reports to the President from Vietnam, 1967–1973*, ed. Douglas Pike, 3 vols. (Berkeley: University of California Press, 1990), vol. 2, p. 334.

31. Oberdorfer, *Tet!* p. 329.

32. Davidson, *Vietnam at War*, p. 475.

33. See especially Oberdorfer, *Tet!*, pp. 213–214.

34. Oberdorfer, *Tet!*, p. 201; see also Allan Dawson, *55 Days: The Fall of South Vietnam* (Englewood Cliffs, NJ: Prentice-Hall, 1977), p. 92.

35. Oberdorfer, *Tet!*, p. 232.

36. Samuel Popkin, "The Village War," in *Vietnam as History*, ed. Peter Braestrup (Washington, D.C.: University Press of America, 1984), p. 102.

37. *From Here to Eternity* (1951), among other famous works.

38. "In the Shadow of Peace," *New York Times Sunday Magazine*, June 10, 1973, p. 17.

39. Douglas Blaufarb, *The Counterinsurgency Era*, p. 271. For more on how the Tet Offensive, and especially the atrocities in Hue, turned great numbers of South Vietnamese away from the VC, see Douglas Pike, *The Viet Cong Strategy of Terror* (Cambridge, MA: M.I.T. Press,

1970), and Samuel L. Popkin, *The Rational Peasant: The Political Economy of Rural Society in Vietnam* (Berkeley, CA: University of California Press, 1979).

40. See Anthony James Joes, *Urban Guerrilla Warfare* (Lexington, KY: University Press of Kentucky, 2007).

41. Wirtz, *Tet Offensive*, p. 224.

42. Davidson, *Vietnam at War*, p. 546.

43. Palmer, *Summons of the Trumpet*, p. 210.

44. Peter Braestrup, *Big Story* (Boulder, CO: Westview, 1977), vol. 1, pp. 448–449. William Colby, CIA station chief in Saigon and chief of the CIA's Far Eastern Division at the time of Tet, agrees; see his *Lost Victory*, chapter 14.

45. Westmoreland, *Soldier Reports*, p. 332.

46. Wiest, *Forgotten Army*, p. 97. "That the South Vietnamese, for all their faults, persevered is a strong reflection of their ability and strength, a strength that their advisers knew firsthand"; Wiest, *Forgotten Army*, p. 193.

47. Peter Braestrup, *Big Story*, vol. 1, p. 444.

48. Wirtz, *Tet Offensive*, p. 60.

49. Gabriel Kolko, *Anatomy of a War* (New York: Pantheon, 1985), p. 482.

50. Arthur J. Dommen, *The Indochinese Experience of the French and the Americans: Nationalism and Communism in Cambodia, Laos and Vietnam* (Bloomington, IN: Indiana University Press, 2001), p. 252.

51. Hammer, *A Death in November*, pp. 61 and 81.

52. Robert A. Scalapino in the *New York Times Magazine*, December 11, 1966, quoted in Fishel, *Vietnam*, p. 780.

53. Quoted in Fishel, *Vietnam*, pp. 653 and 659.

54. Kolko, *Anatomy*, p. 250.

55. Thompson, *No Exit*, p. 65. Race agrees that the Viet Cong were a minority; *War Comes to Long An*, p. 188 and passim.

56. Oberdorfer, *Tet!*, p. 255; the figure was a little high.

57. Wirtz, *Tet Offensive*, p. 224.

58. Dommen, *Indochinese Experience*, p. 670.

59. Konrad Kellen, *A Profile of the PAVN Soldier in South Vietnam* (Santa Monica, CA: RAND, 1968), p. 12.

60. Palmer, *Summons of the Trumpet*, p. 246; Wirtz, *Tet Offensive*, p. 224; Hoang Ngoc Lung, *The General Offensives of 1968–1969* (Washington, D.C.: U.S. Army Center of Military History, 1981), pp. 22–23. "Perhaps one of the most significant failures of the enemy's Tet offensive was the absence of popular support for the enemy forces which penetrated the cities, support which he had evidently anticipated and counted on"; Bunker, *Bunker Papers*, vol. 2, p. 549.

61. *Victory in Vietnam*, p. 224. "[ARVN's] fighting spirit and fighting experience varied, of course . . . but in general were comparable to ours"; Bui Tin, *From Enemy to Friend*, p. 95.

62. James H. Willbanks, *Abandoning Vietnam: How America Left and South Vietnam Lost Its War* (Lawrence, KS: University Press of Kansas, 2004), p. 57.

63. Lewis Sorley, *A Better War: The Unexamined Victories and Final Tragedy of America's Last Years in Vietnam* (New York: Harcourt Brace, 1999), p. 306.

64. Quoted in Sorley, *A Better War*, p. 317.

65. Penniman, *Elections*, p, 199.

66. Thompson, *Peace Is Not at Hand*, p. 127.

67. Timothy Lomperis emphasized this point in *The War Everyone Lost—and Won: American Intervention in Vietnam's Twin Struggles* (Baton Rouge: Louisiana State University Press, 1984), especially p. 169. In connection with the observation of Professor Lomperis, see also Victoria Pohle, *The Viet Cong in Saigon: Tactics and Objectives during the Tet Offensive* (Santa Monica, CA: RAND, 1969).

68. Malcolm Salmon, "After Revolution, Evolution," *Far Eastern Economic Review*, December 12, 1975, pp. 32–34; Duncanson, *Government and Revolution*, estimates that the Communists had the support of one in four Vietnamese. Shortly before the Easter Offensive, John Paul Vann observed that "the basic fact of life is that the overwhelming majority of the

population—somewhere around 95 per cent—prefer the government of Vietnam to a Communist government or the government that's being offered by the other side." Sorley, *Better War*, p. 348.

69. Wirtz, *Tet Offensive*, p. 61.

70. See the *New York Times*, October 1, 1994. My emphasis.

71. Oberdorfer, *Tet!*, p. 242.

72. Lewy, *America in Vietnam*, p. 434.

73. Davidson, *Vietnam at War*, p. 489.

74. Olivier Todd, *Cruel April: The Fall of Saigon* (New York: Norton, 1987), pp. 95, 253, 398; Robert D. McFadden, "The Reporter Was a Spy," *New York Times*, April 28, 1997, p. A-8; Larry Berman, *Perfect Spy: The Incredible Double Life of Pham Xuan An, Time Magazine Reporter and Vietnamese Communist Agent* (New York: Smithsonian Books, 2007).

75. Braestrup, *Big Story*, vol. 1, p. 495; Pike, *PAVN*, p. 242; Todd, *Cruel April*. See the account of the Salisbury reports in Lewy, *America and Vietnam*, pp. 400–401.

76. Braestrup, *Big Story*, vol. 1, pp. 162, 184, 531.

77. Oberdorfer, *Tet!*, p. 5.

78. Oberdorfer, *Tet!*, p. 30.

79. Oberdorfer, *Tet!*, p. 27.

80. Oberdorfer, *Tet!*, p. 31; see also pp. 27–28.

81. James S. Robbins, *This Time We Win: Revisiting the Tet Offensive* (New York: Encounter, 2010), pp. 154–155.

82. *Economist*, May 13, 1972, p. 34. Douglas Pike, quoted in Warner, *Certain Victory*, p. 18.

83. One must record that "those few TV newsmen who actually covered ARVN troops in combat were a good deal less disparaging in their broadcasts than their colleagues who did not"; Braestrup, *Big Story*, vol. 1, p. 475.

84. Braestrup, *Big Story*, vol. 1, p. 531.

85. Braestrup, *Big Story*, vol. 1, p. 716.

86. Davidson, *Vietnam at War*, p. 486.

87. Braestrup, *Big Story*, vol. 1, pp. 531 (quotation), 492, 716. See also Warner, *Certain Victory*, p. 205; Marc Leepson, "Vietnam War Reconsidered," *Editorial Research Reports*, March 1983, p. 195.

88. William V. Kennedy, *The Military and the Media* (New York: Praeger, 1993).

89. Robbins, *This Time We Win*, pp. 241–242.

90. *"Congressional Quarterly*'s Guide to U.S. Elections" (Washington, DC: *Congressional Quarterly*, 1975), p. 343; Philip E. Converse, Warren E. Miller, Jerrold G. Rusk, and Arthur C. Wolfe, "Continuity and Change in American Politics: Parties and Issues in the 1968 Election," *American Political Science Review*, vol. 53, (1969), pp. 1083–1105; Braestrup, *Big Story*, pp. 665–673.

91. Robbins, *This Time We Win*, p. 78.

92. Robbins, *This Time We Win*, p. 175.

93. Dommen, *Indochinese Experience*, p. 709.

94. Wirtz, *Tet Offensive*, p. 43.

95. Palmer, *Summons of the Trumpet*, p. 201. On the Viet Cong military debacle, see William J. Duiker, *The Communist Road to Power in Vietnam*, 2nd edition (Boulder, CO: Westview, 1996), p. 269; Lewy, *America in Vietnam*, p. 76; see also Thayer, *War without Fronts*, p. 92; Shaplen, *Bitter Victory*, pp. 188–189; Blaufarb, *Counterinsurgency Era*, pp. 261–262.

96. Pike, *PAVN*, p. 227.

97. Lomperis, *From People's War to People's Rule,* p. 321.

98. "People's War, as a banner that had led the Party through a generation of trials, was finished"; Lomperis, *From People's War to People's Rule*, pp. 341 and 340. "Never again was the Tet 1968 strategy repeated"; Kolko, *Anatomy of a War*, p. 334.

99. Oberdorfer, *Tet!* p. 155.

100. Blaufarb, *Counterinsurgency Era*, p. 271. See also Bunker, *Bunker Papers*, vol. 2, pp. 344, 346.

101. Kolko, *Anatomy*, pp. 371, 334; Thayer, *War without Fronts*, p. 92.

102. Taylor, *Swords and Plowshares*, p. 247. "Eisenhower added that Laos was the key to all southeast Asia" on January 19, 1961; Arthur Schlesinger, *A Thousand Days* (Boston: Houghton Mifflin, 1965), p. 163. Eisenhower said that the United States would have to act alone if necessary to close the Laotian invasion route; Johnson, *The Vantage Point: Perspectives on the Presidency, 1963–1969* (New York: Holt, Rinhart, Winston, 1971), p. 51. The joint chiefs told President Kennedy they opposed putting ground troops into Laos—there were just too many problems with such a situation. See Colby, *Lost Victory: A Firsthand Account of America's Sixteen-Year Involvement in Vietnam* (Chicago, IL: Contemporary Books, 1989), p. 194. But Norman Hannah says the military opposed intervention in Laos *to save Laos*, not intervention in Laos to save South Vietnam; *Key to Failure: Laos and the Vietnam War* (Lanham, MD: Madison, 1987), p. 271. "Eisenhower turned out to have been right. . . . Even though Laos was a remote and landlocked country, the North Vietnamese, as feared and hated foreigners, could not have waged a guerrilla war on its soil. America could have fought there the sort of conventional war for which its army had been trained"; Henry Kissinger, *Diplomacy* (New York: Simon and Schuster, 1994), p. 647.

103. This was the main concept for the invasion of France, developed by Alfred von Schlieffen, chief of the German General Staff from 1891 to 1905. Under the Schlieffen Plan, the French Army would have been outflanked and then destroyed by a vast wheeling movement of the German Army's massive right (northern) wing across neutral Belgium.

104. Robert Thompson, "Regular Armies and Insurgency," in Thomas Haycock, ed., *Regular Armies and Insurgency* (London: Croom, Kelm, 1979), p. 17.

105. William Westmoreland, *A Soldier Reports* (Garden City, NY: Doubleday, 1976), p. 148. True, the Polisario guerrillas were not the NVA, but then Morocco was not the United States. The quotation is in Bruce Palmer, *The Twenty-Five-Year War* (Lexington, KY: University Press of Kentucky, 1984), p. 185. Summers endorses General Palmer's conclusion that three divisions in Laos, with five along the DMZ, would have been sufficient to isolate the battlefield; Harry Summers, *On Strategy: A Critical Analysis of the Vietnam War* (Novato, CA: Presidio, 1982), pp. 122–123.

106. Palmer, *The Twenty-Five-Year War*, p. 105; Hannah, *Key to Failure*, p. 236. See Ellsworth Bunker, *The Bunker Papers: Reports to the President from Vietnam, 1967–1973*, ed. Douglas Pike, 3 vols. (Berkeley, CA: University of California Press, 1990). Mark Moyar, *Triumph Forsaken: The Vietnam War, 1954–1965* (New York: Cambridge University Press 2006), p. 323 and passim.

107. Johnson, *Vantage Point*, pp. 369, 370, my emphasis.

108. Robert Shaplen, *Bitter Victory* (New York: Harper and Row, 1986), p. 158.

109. Hannah, *Key to Failure*, p. xxv.

110. See especially Military History in Vietnam, *Victory in Vietnam*, passim.

111. Robert Thompson, "Regular Armies and Insurgency," p. 18.

112. *Make for the Hills: Memories of Far Eastern Wars* (London: Leo Cooper, 1989), p. 131.

113. Bundy is quoted in Hannah, *Key to Failure*, p. 183.

114. Bunker is quoted in Hannah, *Key to Failure*, p. 217; Bunker urged President Johnson to invade Laos; Hannah, *Key to Failure*, p. 236–237.

115. Rostow is quoted in R. B. Smith, *An International History of the Vietnam War*, vol. 2, *The Kennedy Strategy* (New York: St. Martin's, 1985), p. 102. See also Shaplen, *Bitter Victory*, pp. 148, 157; Douglas Pike, "Road to Victory," in *War in Peace*, vol. 5, edited by Robert Thompson (London: Orbis, 1984). See the discussion of an American barrier across Laos in Wirtz, *Tet Offensive*, pp. 120 ff. See also Bui Tin, *From Enemy to Friend: A North Vietnamese Perspective on the War* (Annapolis, MD: Naval Institute Press, 2002), p. 75. "The Trail undeniably lay at the heart of the war"; John Prados, *Blood Road: The Ho Chi Minh Trail and the Vietnam War* (New York: John Wiley, 1999), p. xiii.

Chapter Six

The 1972 Easter Offensive

Long before 1972, the war in South Vietnam had for all important purposes ceased to be a counter-guerrilla struggle. It had become instead a classic confrontation of heavily equipped, regular armed forces. Thus, whatever sympathy for the Viet Cong may still have existed in certain rural areas was now largely irrelevant. The outcome of the struggle over South Vietnam would henceforth depend on the prowess of the North Vietnamese Army, a "professional army of a Communist state operating outside its border in conventional style."[1] The coming Easter Offensive of 1972 would call forth battles bigger than any seen in the world since Korea, twenty years before, bigger than the battles of the Six Day War.[2]

The 1972 Offensive was "the greatest tribute yet paid to the progress achieved in the South over the previous three years,"[3] because the years after the Tet Offensive had been good ones for South Vietnam. Its army was better trained and better equipped, and its militia forces had increased in numbers, self-confidence and skill. If Hanoi did not interrupt this process of gradual consolidation, it would one day be too late.[4] Saigon was expecting a major move by the North in 1972, during Tet; the date was too early but the anticipation was quite sound. Hanoi had indeed decided to launch another knockout effort, along 1968 lines, with the purpose above all of making the United States break its ties with Saigon. Like 1968, 1972 was a presidential election year; perhaps Hanoi could force Richard Nixon out of the White House as it had (unexpectedly) forced out Lyndon Johnson.[5] As *The Economist* saw it, "After all, North Vietnam's leaders know that the election of Mr. McGovern [Senator from South Dakota, the 1972 Democratic presidential candidate] would give them a free hand throughout Indochina."[6] Typically, Hanoi was putting the finishing touches on its offensive plans while engaged in peace talks with the allies in Paris.

The 1972 Eater Offensive would indeed be a fearsome and impressive undertaking. The North Vietnamese Army was "the most efficient fighting machine in Asia."[7] The Hanoi leadership designed an invasion strategy that would best employ its new Russian tanks, surface-to-air missiles, and other sophisticated weaponry.[8] This would definitely be the largest operation the NVA had ever undertaken. Well aware that his Communist state was safe from any sort of invasion, General Giap denuded North Vietnam of troops in order to throw everything possible into his long-sought second Dien Bien Phu. Nothing was left behind in the North except civilian militiamen and two inexperienced divisions.[9] At the same time, the number of U.S. military personnel of all types still in South Vietnam was down to only 75,000 (from close to 600,000 in 1968), and decreasing; only a minority of them were in combat units.

Hanoi's design for the great Easter campaign had four distinct segments. First, there would be a furious major attack directly across the Demilitarized Zone, with its objective the city of Quang Tri, less than 20 miles from the North Vietnam border. Second, a big force would sweep out of Laos toward symbolic Hue. Third, from Cambodia would come a massive assault against the city of An Loc, which was slated to become the capital of the "liberated" areas of South Vietnam. A fourth and final thrust aimed at Kontum, in the central highlands, with the objective of eventually cutting South Vietnam in two.

The offensive began convulsively on March 30, with a powerful attack across the Ben Hai River into Quang Tri province. Defending that province was the Third ARVN Division, newly formed, untried as a cohesive force, and unprepared to receive a major onslaught. ARVN commanders in this northern danger zone lacked confidence in their ability to contain the NVA without U.S. advisers.[10] After enduring a tremendous pounding from greatly superior NVA forces, the Third Division embarked on a retreat out of Quang Tri city, which the NVA occupied on May 1, the only provincial capital to be taken by the North in the entire offensive. A retreat under fire is the most difficult maneuver for even the most cohesive and experienced and best-led troops. Panic soon afflicted several elements of the novice Third Division; tanks, trucks, and personal weapons were left behind, and many officers deserted their men. Retreating soldiers and fleeing civilians (who well re-membered 1968) choked Highway I from Quang Tri to Hue. NVA artillery ceaselessly hammered the defenseless, fleeing columns of refugees, killing or wounding at least 20,000.[11]

The attack against Hue also began on March 30. NVA units reached the outskirts of that city on May 1, the day Quang Tri fell. Most civil officials, painfully mindful of the massacres in Hue during the 1968 offensive, and alarmed by reports of mass killings in areas already taken in this Easter offensive, abandoned the city.[12] Yet, while Hue was only 40 miles south of

Quang Tri, its fate was to be far different. Not inexperienced troops but the crack Marine Division and the veteran First ARVN Division defended the ancient city. In addition, the area Ruff-Puffs (Territorials), mobilized under army command, would give a good account of themselves against superior NVA numbers and equipment. On the second of May, just as the siege of the city was really getting started, President Thieu placed in command of Hue and the whole northern front his best fighting general, 43-year old airborne-trained Ngo Quang Truong, a veteran of Bao Dai's old Vietnamese National Army, called by General Bruce Palmer "a tough, seasoned, fighting leader, probably the best field commander in South Vietnam."[13] General Truong stopped the incipient panic, established a new defense line, and held on. Early NVA successes in the Easter Offensive "depended directly on the military hardware donated by the Russians."[14] Nevertheless, the defenders of Hue were able to withstand this onslaught, with the indispensable aid of close support from U.S. Air Force, Navy, and Marine aircraft.

An Loc came under attack in the first week of April. Soon NVA and Viet Cong forces had the city completely surrounded. Saigon had to supply the defenders totally by air, despite anti-aircraft fire from Communist forces so murderous that not even helicopters could land. The city took a horrendous beating from NVA artillery, especially its famous Soviet-designed 130-mm field guns. On May 10, the attack went into a second phase, with seven Communist regiments pitted against 4,000 South Vietnamese defenders. Once again the awesome B-52s, the weapon Communist troops feared above all others in the allied arsenal, mauled the massed NVA units, and the 21st ARVN Division began moving to the relief of the city from the south. The besieging forces began withdrawing on May 15. The failure to take An Loc was "a major military and political setback for the Communists,"[15] a fact recognized by President Thieu when he promoted by one grade every single soldier who had participated in the defense of the city.

At Kontum, the fourth area of Communist offensive action, real fighting did not begin until May 14. Communist forces were spearheaded by some of the very good T-54 tanks that Hanoi had obtained from the Soviets. Nevertheless, fighting in a number of sectors devolved into savage hand-to-hand combat. The attackers renewed the assault on the May 21 and again on the May 25. President Thieu visited the battle area on May 30 to confer a promotion on the commanding officer and encourage the defenders. Thanks in part to timely assistance from American B-52s, the attack on Kontum ran out of steam by the end of the month.

Indeed it was clear before the middle of May that the offensive had degenerated into a stalemate. Hanoi had committed everything it had to the great Easter Offensive of 1972, but had attained not a single one of its objectives. Kontum was holding, Saigon was safe (during the entire 1972 offensive, "not one single incident in the whole of sprawling Saigon, not even a hand grenade in a bar" occurred).[16] Even the exposed and vulnerable Military Region I (the provinces right below the DMZ) was mostly in South Vietnamese hands. An Loc, marked out by the Communists to become the national capital of a southern counter-state, had stood fast. For all its impressive exertions, the NVA had little to show except the city of Quang Tri, but the South Vietnamese opened a counter-offensive on June 28 and retook the city a few weeks later. The Easter Offensive cost the NVA 100,000 casualties and General Giap his long-held command. Not only had the offensive been a vast and costly disappointment militarily, but the myth that a majority of South Vietnamese wanted the North to win had once again been exposed to all who would see.[17] It would require three years for the North Vietnamese Army to recover from its 1972 losses. Meanwhile the South was filled with reports of NVA tank crews who had been literally chained inside their vehicles.[18] In contrast, ARVN morale was at probably the highest level in the history of the state.[19] Not only had Southern forces successfully resisted the NVA attack, but in retaliation for the offensive President Nixon had at long last ordered the mining of Haiphong harbor, North Vietnam's essential reception area for Soviet aid.[20]

In retrospect, the reasons for the failure of the 1972 offensive are not hard to identify. General Giap had made a fatal error in trying to do too much; instead of concentrating his resources, perhaps at Quang Tri and An Loc, he began by dispersing his invasion on four fronts, as he had done, with equal lack of success and heavy casualties, during the attacks on the De Lattre Line in 1951 (like Hitler's multi-pronged invasion of the USSR). Seeking major victories all over South Vietnam, he ended by achieving none. For even the most seasoned commanders, the coordination of major movements of infantry, armor, and artillery is a signal challenge; for Hanoi's relatively inexperienced generals, it was next to an impossibility.[21] Additionally, the South Vietnamese had the inestimable assistance of the mighty B-52s, as well as the services of 25,000 tough South Korean soldiers.

Yet this assistance would have been for nothing, Giap's strategic errors and his commanders' awkwardness at modern conventional warfare would not have prevented a Communist victory, if the South Vietnamese armed forces, and especially ARVN, had not—once again, and indisputably—withstood the test.[22]

With proper equipment and leadership, South Vietnamese forces were undoubtedly a match for their adversaries.[23] Testimonials to the fighting qualities of the South Vietnamese are numerous and impressive. During the heaviest Easter Offensive action, General Creighton Abrams, commander of the few remaining U.S. forces in South Vietnam, exclaimed, "By God, the South Vietnamese can hack it!"[24] Lieutenant General William McCaffrey observed that "the ARVN soldier emerges as a remarkable individual who perseveres in spite of great hardship. He has earned a victory."[25] For Douglas

Pike, it was "the stubborn, even heroic, South Vietnamese defense" in which "ARVN troops and even local [RF/PF] forces stood and fought as never before" that halted the Easter Offensive in its tracks.[26] The tremendous importance of the defeat of the 1972 Offensive cannot be overstated. Consider these two weighty evaluations: first, in Sir Robert Thompson's opinion:

> The South Vietnamese people have fought on a scale and at a cost which far outweighs any contribution made by the United States and their resilience and stamina have been incomparable. There have been many ignorant critics of their fighting quality. No one of these critics would have believed in 1968 that over 500,000 American troops could be withdrawn and that South Vietnam would still stand and defeat a massive invasion which few other countries in the world could have withstood even with the support of American air power.[27]

Second, in his well-regarded study *Abandoning Vietnam*, James Willbanks writes:

> The South Vietnamese ultimately held out against everything the NVA could throw at them. In addition to inflicting a military defeat on the enemy, the ARVN defenders won a decisive psychological victory. They had stood up against the very best of the North Vietnamese Army, defeated them, and prevented them from establishing their "liberation government" in the South. President Thieu and his regime emerged from the crisis stronger than ever, at least on the surface. He and his army had been victorious. The victory seemed a turning point for South Vietnam. . . . When ably led, the South Vietnamese soldier fought hard and in many places well. The Vietnamese Marines in I Corps [northern South Vietnam] maintained discipline and order throughout the offensive, even when superior enemy strength caused them to abandon defensive positions. The besieged defenders in An Loc repeatedly threw back NVA human wave assaults, standing toe to toe with the Communist attackers, holding out longer than the French did at Dien Bien Phu.[28]

As Dale Andrade noted, "The people of South Vietnam had paid a terrible price for beating back the North Vietnamese, and they recognized the sacrifices of the military, particularly the Airborne and Marine Divisions. General Truong later summed up the feelings of his nation when he observed, 'These exploits remain forever engraved on their minds.'"[29]

The euphoria over the performance of Southern forces during the offensive unfortunately diverted attention from their faulty strategic deployment. President Thieu's obsession with the alleged necessity to "hold all places" instead of concentrating forces in and around crucial areas left South Vietnam with very inadequate strategic and tactical reserves, that is, without serious forces available to quickly reinforce an endangered area. If this situation remained uncorrected, it would have to result eventually in the most disastrous consequences.[30]

Nevertheless, the undeniable lesson of 1972 was that although it still had some serious weaknesses, ARVN had developed into an impressive fighting force—"The South Vietnamese could hack it." Sir Robert Thompson observed that "having seen quite a number of armies over the years, I am prepared to state that ARVN is now second only to Israel in this type of modern warfare in the western world."[31] The South Vietnamese Army had stood firm during the carefully planned and furiously mounted offensives of both Tet 1968 and Easter 1972. The Northern regime had done its best, and failed—twice. As long as it could be provided with replacement supplies and air support from the Americans, ARVN could clearly be counted on to defend the independence of the Southern republic indefinitely.

But—incredibly—American support was about to evaporate.

NOTES

1. Hammond Rolph, "Vietnamese Communism and the Protracted War," *Asian Survey* 12 (September 1972), pp. 785 and 789.

2. Sir Robert Thompson, *Peace Is Not at Hand* (New York: McKay, 1974), p. 97.

3. Sir Robert Thompson, *Make for the Hills: Memories of Far Eastern Wars* (London: Leo Cooper, 1989), p. 174.

4. Douglas Blaufarb, "The Sources of Frustration in Vietnam," in Richard A. Hunt and Richard H. Shultz, Jr., *Lessons from an Unconventional War* (New York: Pergamon, 1982), p. 147.

5. Guenter Lewy, *America in Vietnam*, (New York: Oxford University Press, 1978), p. 196.

6. . *Economist*, June 17, 1972, p. 16.

7. Ibid., April 15, 1972, p. 15.

8. G. H. Turley, *The Easter Offensive* (Novato, CA: Presidio, 1985), p. 27. The North's Soviet-made tanks were far superior to ARVN's U.S.-made light tanks; Jeffrey J. Clarke, *Advice and Support: The Final Years, 1965–1973* (Washington, DC: U.S. Army Center of Military History, 1988), p. 482.

9. *Economist*, April 27, 1972, p. 16.

10. Turley, *Easter Offensive*, p. 104.

11. Lewy, *America in Vietnam*, p. 197.

12. *Economist*, May 6, 1972, p. 39.

13. Bruce Palmer, Jr., *The 25-Year War: America's Military Role in Vietnam* (Lexington, KY: University Press of Kentucky, 1984), p.120. Truong had participated in Diem's extirpation of the Binh Xuyen back in 1955. He died in Virginia in 2007.

14. *Economist*, May 13, 1972, p. 31.

15. *Economist*, June 24, p. 28. See Lam Quang Thi. *Hell in An Loc: The 1972 Easter Invasion and the Battle That Saved South Vietnam* (Denton, TX: University of North Texas Press, 2009).

16. Thompson, *Make for the Hills*, p. 166.

17. *Economist*, May 6, 1972, p. 39.

18. "Over 3,000 North Vietnamese tank crews had had four to five months training at the Russian armoured school in Odessa"; Thomson, *Peace Is Not at Hand*, p. 111.

19. Stuart A.Herrington, *Silence Was a Weapon: The Vietnam War in the Villages* (Novato, CA: Presidio, 1982), p. 210.

20. Lewy, *America in Vietnam*, p. 198; Herrington, *Silence Was a Weapon*, p. 210.

21. Lewy, *America in Vietnam*, pp. 199–200; Lewis Sorley, *A Better War: The Unexamined Victories and Final Tragedy of America's Last Years in Vietnam* (New York: Harcourt, Brace, 1999), chapter 20.

22. "It is essential to emphasize first that air support would have been useless if ARVN had not held its ground and compelled the NVA to launch set piece attacks"; Thompson, *Peace Is Not at Hand*, p. 109.

23. William Le Gro, *Vietnam from Ceasefire to Capitulation*, p. 174; James Lawton Collins, Jr., *The Development and Training of the South Vietnamese Army, 1950–1972* (Washington, DC: U.S. Army Center of Military History, 1975), p. 122; Dave Richard Palmer, *Summons of the Trumpet: U.S.-Vietnam in Perspective* (San Rafael, CA: Presidio, 1975), p. 255.

24. Palmer, *25-Year War,* p. 122; Pike, in *PAVN: People's Army of Vietnam* (Novato, CA: Presidio, 1986), says ARVN fought "heroically." Sorley, in *A Better War*, gives the Territorials very high grades.

25. Sorley, *A Better War,* p. 339.

26. Pike, *PAVN*, p. 229.

27. Thompson, *Peace Is Not at Hand*, p. 168.

28. Willbanks, *Abandoning Vietnam*, pp. 155, 157–158.

29. Dale Andrade, *America's Last Vietnam Battle: Halting Hanoi's 1972 Easter Offensive* (Lawrence, KS: University Press of Kansas, 2001).

30. Harry Summers, *On Strategy: A Critical Analysis of the Vietnam War* (Novato, CA: Presidio, 1982), p. 138.

31. Thompson, *Peace Is Not at Hand*, p. 169.

Chapter Seven

The Americans Abandon the South Vietnamese

In 1968, the Politburo in Hanoi was desperate to bring the fourteen-year conflict with the South Vietnamese to a successful conclusion. It therefore tried to knock South Vietnam out of the war by having the Viet Cong seize the cities, provoke a popular uprising, and shatter ARVN. That effort failed utterly. Four years later, Hanoi tried to knock South Vietnam out of the war again, this time by a multipronged conventional invasion. That effort also failed utterly. The Communists had done their best in both offensives, the one by experienced guerrillas and the other by trained regulars, with little to show for their pains but great numbers of casualties and a strengthened, more self-confident South Vietnam. It was clear that, as long as the United States continued to support South Vietnam with air power, no Communist victory was possible in the short or middle term. Consequently, in 1973 North Vietnam went through the motions of signing a peace agreement with South Vietnam and the United States.

Even after the passage of decades, the asymmetries of the 1973 Paris agreements on ending the fighting in Vietnam remain hard to believe. Those agreements provided for (1) the withdrawal of all U.S. forces from the South and the cessation of all U.S. air attacks on the North; (2) the implicit recognition of Hanoi's right to maintain close to a quarter of a million Northern troops in the South; at the same time, in explicit violation of these agreements, 50,000 North Vietnamese regulars remained inside Laos and other thousands in Cambodia, all of whom could and did move quickly into South Vietnam; (3) the "enforcement" of this peace agreement by an International Control Commission, which included members from Communist Poland and Communist Hungary and could operate only through unanimity.[1]

How could ARVN hope to fill the place of the hundreds of thousands of U.S. troops that had been withdrawn from South Vietnam between 1968 and 1973? How long could South Vietnam survive the presence of hundreds of thousands of enemy soldiers within its borders? President Thieu signed the agreements only after brutal pressure had been brought to bear upon him, including a threat by President Nixon that if Thieu did not accept the situation, the U.S. would make an agreement with Hanoi alone. President Nixon wrote to President Thieu that "you have my absolute assurance that if Hanoi fails to abide by the terms of this agreement, it is my intention to take swift and severe retaliatory actions."[2] It was on the basis of this, and similar pledges and promises of continued U.S. help, that the government of South Vietnam, with very much reluctance, signed the 1973 agreements.

A few years later, former Secretary of State Kissinger wrote:

> We had no illusions about Hanoi's long-term goals. Nor did we go through the agony of four years of war and searing negotiations simply to achieve "a decent interval" for our withdrawal. We were determined to do our utmost to enable Saigon to grow in security and prosperity so that it could prevail in any political struggle. We sought not an interval before collapse but lasting peace with honor. But for the collapse of executive authority as a result of Watergate, I believe we would have succeeded.[3]

But, as one student of these events has observed, "the only part of the Paris agreements that was observed was the removal of U.S. forces."[4] The "peace" agreements in fact meant peace for North Vietnam and more war for South Vietnam. Or, as Arnold Isaacs wrote, "Unlike the Geneva agreement of 1954, which had given Vietnam an interval of relative peace, the Paris agreement of 1973 did not stop the fighting for a single hour."[5]

In March 1973, after numerous and blatant violations of the agreements by Hanoi, President Nixon stated: "We have informed North Vietnam of our concern. . . . I would only suggest that in light of my actions over the last four years . . . North Vietnam should not lightly disregard such expressions of concern."[6] It was soon apparent, however, that even if President Nixon might wish to take military action against North Vietnam, the U.S. Congress would not allow him. Increasingly agitated over continuing U.S. air strikes in Cambodia, Congress enacted legislation on June 30, 1973, cutting off funds effective August 15, 1973, for all "combat activities by United States military forces in or over or from off the shores of North Vietnam, South Vietnam, Laos or Cambodia." The President's options for retaliation against North Vietnamese violations of the peace agreement were even further restricted when Congress passed, over the President's veto, the "War Powers Resolution" on November 7, 1973. This measure required the President to consult with Congress before introducing any U.S. armed forces into hostile situations abroad.

The consequent cessation of U.S. air strikes provided Hanoi with the golden opportunity to improve its illegal (through neutral countries—not that anybody cared) highways into the South and greatly increase the traffic on them. Within one year of the Paris agreements, the North had infiltrated an additional 100,000 to 120,000 regulars into the South; during 1973 alone, the North Vietnamese Army increased its tanks and artillery in the South four-fold.[7] All of this was completely forbidden by the ceasefire agreements, and should have been stopped by the International Control Commission, charged with overseeing compliance. Yet while that Commission kept careful watch on U.S. supplies to the South, North Vietnam made it completely clear that under no circumstances would it allow the Commission to impede, or even observe, the enormous flow of men and materiel it was sending into the South. Indeed, the Communists would not even permit Commission members to enter the territories they controlled. In light of this absurd situation, the Canadian members of the Commission announced in May 1973 that they would no longer participate and were in fact leaving Vietnam.

In contrast, observes Robert Thompson, "The restrictions on South Vietnam were as near absolute as they could be made. The South was fully open to public scrutiny of its every action through television cameras and, just after the ceasefire, one of the largest posses of reporters ever seen, many of them hostile and ready to report any misdemeanor."[8]

In summary, first the Paris agreements placed severe limits on U.S. military aid to the Government of Vietnam, and then Congress forbade any military activity at all. There were no limits on international Communist assistance to North Vietnam or North Vietnamese assistance to their own forces in the South. All this outside aid could now reach Communist forces in South Vietnam unhindered by allied air, land, or sea operations. Consequently, "In South Vietnam, the [Hanoi forces] are rapidly developing their strongest military position in the history of the war."[9]

Of course, the grand assumption which had finally led President Thieu to agree to the Paris ceasefire was that Richard Nixon would be president through the end of 1976 and his successor, whoever he might be, would honor the public and private pledges to South Vietnam made by his presidential predecessor. As it turned out, Nixon was forced to resign the presidency in August 1974. His successor, Gerald Ford, was at first unaware of the written pledges Nixon had made to Thieu and then unable to persuade Congress to honor those pledges.[10]

A venerable authority on Vietnamese affairs once wrote: "If there had never been a Watergate, there would be a South Vietnam today."[11] Quite possibly that is true. But former Secretary of State Dean Rusk insisted that "the Paris peace agreements of 1973 were in effect a surrender. Any agreements that left North Vietnamese troops in South Vietnam meant the eventual takeover of South Vietnam."[12]

ARVN ON THE STRATEGIC DEFENSIVE

At the end of January 1973, ARVN had an assigned strength of about 450,000 men. Of these, about 153,000 were in 13 infantry divisions and another 20,000 in the Ranger groups; in addition there were about 325,000 personnel in the Regional Forces and about 200,000 in the Popular Forces.[13] This muster of one million personnel, out of a total population of under twenty million, is quite impressive (equal to a U.S. military establishment of fifteen million in 2015). But it is deceptive in its implications. The radical weakness of ARVN lay in the fundamental difference between its mission and that of the enemy. In accordance with the defensive strategy—"hold every inch"—prevailing after the peace agreements, ARVN was spread extremely thin, holding fixed positions all over South Vietnam, as it had been doing for the previous twenty years, and as the French had done before them. In contrast, as Arthur Dommen points out, "the [Northern] commanders could move their forces around the ARVN's fixed positions and concentrate an overwhelming force anywhere so as to seize an objective of their choosing."[14] ARVN was in a perilous situation that could not last: "the enemy was free to pick his targets, concentrate his forces and attack at will [the same strategy used by Mao Tse-tung against the Chinese Nationalists during the Chinese civil war after 1945]. [The enemy] was doubly free to do so as ARVN did not have the capability to interfere with North Vietnam's massive staging activities along South Vietnam's western borders."[15]

All this was happening because the South Vietnamese had no strategic reserve. The Airborne and the Marine divisions were supposed to be that national strategic reserve: elite, professional formations, mobile and powerful, capable of moving quickly to any danger point or emergency situation anywhere in the country. Some have said that the North Vietnamese had no equals to the South's Airborne and Marine Divisions; Robert Thompson declared that "by 1972, the First, Marine, and Airborne divisions [of South Vietnam] were three of the best in the world."[16] Interestingly, the majority of the members of the Marine Division had their origins north of the 1954 partition line.[17] The Airborne were all volunteers. Some Airborne elements would wage guerrilla war against the Northern conquerors in the jungle-covered mountains of Central Vietnam for years after the fall of Saigon in 1975.

But these elite divisions did not function as a national strategic reserve, available to be sent wherever needed. Instead they were assigned, like the rest of the South Vietnamese forces, to the permanent defense of exposed areas.[18] Arguably, Thieu's hold-everywhere policy was politically necessary, but in terms of overall strategy it was disastrous. Cao Van Vien observed that it became very easy for the enemy "to concentrate a force five or six times greater than ours at any remote place and with abundant fire support overwhelm an outpost at will. To attempt to hold all remote outposts, therefore, amounted to sacrificing a substantial number of troops who could be employed effectively elsewhere."[19]

It was precisely this ability of the North Vietnamese to pick their target and assemble overwhelming numbers against it that caused Robert Thompson to observe that "in all the arguments about the fighting quality of the South Vietnamese soldier, it has to be remembered that, in nearly every action fought, the numerical superiority of the NVA was locally greater. They would not have attacked if that had not been the case."[20]

CONGRESS CUTS OFF AID

Not content with forbidding U.S. military action in Vietnam, Congress began to make drastic cuts in aid to the South Vietnamese. For fiscal year 1973, Congress had appropriated $2.8 billion in assistance of all kinds to South Vietnam. For FY 1974, that amount was slashed to $700 million, and was scheduled to be reduced to a mere $300 million for FY 1975. Congress's choking off of assistance to South Vietnam to below operating levels represented "a decision that seriously undermined South Vietnamese combat power and [the] will to continue the struggle."[21] These massive and unexpected cuts dangerously reduced or completely eliminated many capabilities of ARVN and other military branches "in the face of an increasingly grave enemy threat."[22] The last Southern offensive operation took place in May 1974. After that, lack of fuel, spare parts, and ammunition continually reduced ARVN's mobility. As early as February 1974 aid reduction was seriously affecting ARVN artillery; eventually artillery batteries in the Central Highlands that had been previously firing 100 rounds daily were reduced to firing only four. By that summer each ARVN soldier received only 85 bullets *per month*, less than three bullets per day.[23] North Vietnamese sources have accepted these figures as valid.[24]

In the Mekong Delta, the most populous part of the country and the area where the Communists had always been weakest, cutbacks to the navy forced it to deactivate half its units, thus uncovering that whole strategic area. The shortage of new radio batteries resulted in a reduction of army radio communications by 50 percent. Aircraft flew fewer missions, and many planes ceased to fly at all, because they lacked replacement parts. About half of ARVN's truck force was out of commission for lack of fuel and parts. Even the bandages of the wounded and the dead had to be washed and used again.[25] And, as previously noted, while President Thieu's "defend all areas" policy meant that ARVN lacked an available strategic reserve, the army's mobility declined even further owing to ever-increasing shortages of transport, fuel, and spare parts.[26]

Quite beyond these measurable effects, a close student of ARVN writes that "the psychological damage of the aid cuts was almost certainly greater than the real. To military and bureaucratic elites that gravely lacked self-confidence, the cuts were a symbolic act of American abandonment, a blow from which the South Vietnamese leadership never recovered."[27]

In contrast to massive cuts in aid from the United States to South Vietnam, during the post-ceasefire period North Vietnam continued to receive "more than adequate military and economic aid, primarily from Moscow and Peking."[28] While U.S. support was withering, Hanoi was thus able to send hugely increased amounts of supplies, petroleum products, weapons and over 100,000 new troops into the South. It is at the very least open to question that the North Vietnamese Army would have been victorious without abundant Chinese and Soviet help.[29]

Ambassador Ellsworth Bunker later wrote:

> I gave Thieu three letters personally from President Nixon committing us, in case of a violation of the Paris agreements by the other side, to come to their assistance. Well, the other side violated the agreements almost from the first day they signed them . . . but we never came to their assistance, because Congress refused to appropriate the money. The result was, and as each day went by, the South Vietnamese had fewer guns, fewer planes, fewer tanks, diminishing ammunition with which to fight, while the North was being fully supplied by the Soviets and the Chinese. The result was inevitable.[30]

Years afterward, former Secretary of Defense Melvin Laird wrote: "Without U.S. funding, South Vietnam was quickly overrun. We saved a mere $257 million a year and in the process doomed South Vietnam, which had been ably fighting the war without our troops since 1973."[31] (Whatever had happened to President Kennedy's inaugural pledge to "pay any price"?)

Two careful students of the fall of South Vietnam conclude: "The weight of the evidence shows that had the United States kept the promises made in writing to [President Thieu] to convince him to sign the Paris Accords [of 1973], the Republic of South Vietnam could have survived."[32] Instead, James Willbanks wrote, "The United States neither stayed the course (as we did and continue to do in South Korea) nor provided the promised support to the South Vietnamese," with consequences all too predictable and dire.[33]

NOTES

1. See the texts of the agreements in Department of State *Bulletin*, February 12, 1973, pp. 169–188. One can read an interesting version of how the agreements came about in Henry Kissinger, *White House Years* (Boston: Little, Brown, 1979), esp. pp. 1301–1477. But see also Nguyen Tien Hung and Jerrold L. N. Schecter, *The Palace File: Vietnam Secret Documents* (New York: Harper and Row, 1986).

2. Guenter Lewy, *America in Vietnam* (New York: Oxford University Press, 1978), pp. 202–203; Nguyen Tien Hung and Schecter, *Palace File,* esp. pp. 149ff.

3. Kissinger, *White House Years,* p. 1470.

4. Stephen T. Hosmer, Konrad Kellen, and Brian M. Jenkins, *The Fall of South Vietnam: Statements by South Vietnamese Military and Civilian Leaders* (New York: Crane, Russak, 1980), p. 30.

5. Arnold R. Isaacs, *Without Honor: Defeat in Vietnam and Cambodia* (New York: Vintage, 1984), p. 12.

6. Robert Thompson, *Peace Is Not at Hand* (New York: McKay, 1974), p. 154.

7. William Le Gro, *Vietnam from Ceasefire to Capitulation* (Washington, DC: U.S. Army Center of Military History, 1981), p. 78.

8. Thompson, *Peace Is Not at hand,* p. 140.

9. Defense Attaché Office, *RVNAF: Final Assessment* (Washington, DC: U.S. Government Printing Office, 1975), p. 11.

10. Arthur Dommen, *The Indochinese Experience of the French and the Americans: Nationalism and Communism in Cambodia, Laos and Vietnam* (Bloomington, IN: Indiana University Press, 2001), pp. 895ff.

11. Douglas Pike in Peter Braestrup, ed., *Vietnam as History* (Washington, DC: University Press of America, 1984), p. 88.

12. Dean Rusk, *As I Saw It: A Secretary of State's Memoirs* (London: I. B. Tauris, 1991), p. 431.

13. Dommen, *Indochinese Experience,* p. 889.

14. Dommen, *Indochinese Experience,* p. 896. See also Hunt, *Losing Vietnam,* p. 168.

15. Hosmer, *Fall,* p. 132. "While North Vietnam could prepare interminably for an offensive with little fear of a preemptive strike, and then pick the time and place of its attack, Saigon was forced to remain forever vigilant, maintaining a thinly spread defensive network all over South Vietnam"; Dale Andrade, *America's Last Vietnam Battle: Halting Hanoi's 1972 Easter Offensive* (Lawrence, KS: University Press of Kansas, 2001), p. 487.

16. Thompson, "Vietnam" in Robert Thompson, ed., *War in Peace* (London: Orbis Publishing, 1981), p. 193; Thompson goes on to state in 1989 that the three divisions that recaptured Quang Tri "were at this time about the best fighting divisions in the western world"; *Make for the Hills: Memories of Far Eastern Wars* (London: Leo Cooper, 1989), p. 177. See also Olivier Todd, *Cruel April: The Fall of Saigon* (New York: Norton, 1987), p. 438.

17. Lam Quang Thi, *The Twenty-Five Year Century: A South Vietnamese General Remembers the Indochina War to the Fall of Saigon* (Denton, TX: University of North Texas Press, 2001), p. 273.

18. Dommen, *Indochinese Experience,* p. 889.

19. Cao Van Vien, *The Final Collapse* (Washington, DC: U.S. Army Center of Military History, 1983), p. 39; see also The Military History Institute of Vietnam, *Victory in Vietnam: The Official History of the People's Army of Vietnam, 1954–1975,* trans. Merle Pribbenow (Lawrence, KS: University Press of Kansas, 2002), p. 386.

20. Thompson, *Peace Is Not at Hand,* p. 74.

21. Le Gro, *Vietnam,* p. 88.

22. Defense Attaché Office, *RVNAF: Final Assessment,* p. 1.2.

23. Lewy, *America in Vietnam,* p. 208. "The results of these cutbacks coupled with inflation were immediately felt on the battlefield. Each infantryman, for example, could only spend one hand grenade and eighty-five bullets per month. Each 105-mm howitzer, the main artillery weapon in our arsenal, could now fire only ten rounds per day"; Lam Quang Thi, *Twenty-Five Year Century,* p. 318. General Westmoreland accepts these figures: see *A Soldier Reports,* p. 397.

24. See, for example, Van Tien Dung, *Our Great Spring Victory* (New York: Monthly Review Press, 1977), pp. 17–18.

25. Lewy, *America in Vietnam,* p. 208; Dong Van Khuyen, *The RVNAF* (Washington, DC: U.S. Army Center of Military History, 1980), pp. 287–288; Le Gro, *Vietnam,* pp. 84–87.

26. Hosmer, *Fall,* p. 12.

27. James H. Willbanks, *Abandoning Vietnam: How America Left and South Vietnam Lost Its War* (Lawrence, KS: University Press of Kansas, 2004), p. 285.

28. *Final Assessment*, p. 12.

29. Dommen, *Indochinese Experience*, p. 867.

30. Lewis Sorley, *A Better War: The Unexamined Victories and Final Tragedy of America's Last Years in Vietnam* (New York: Harcourt Brace, 1999), p. 373.

31. Melvin Laird, "Iraq: Learning the Lessons of Vietnam," *Foreign Affairs*, Nov.–Dec., 2005, p. 26.

32. Nguyen Tien Hung and Schecter, *The Palace File,* p. 354.

33. Willbanks, *Abandoning Vietnam*, p. 257.

Chapter Eight

Retrenchment and Collapse

At the end of 1974, the defenses of South Vietnam were strongest in Military Region (MR) I, containing Hue and Da Nang. This area was under the protection of the First ARVN Division, the Marine Division, and the Airborne Division, all elite units, plus two others. But at the same time, defending forces in the Central Highlands consisted only of two overstretched divisions.

In December 1974, the NVA struck the biggest blow so far in violation of the Paris agreements: an overwhelming assault on Phuoc Long province, next to Cambodia on the border of MR II and MR III, about 75 miles northeast of Saigon. ARVN counterattacks were unsuccessful. Southern troops who had families in the provincial capital or among the refugees disappeared from the ranks of their units to rescue them—a harbinger of things to come. [1]

The conquest of Phuoc Long was one of the most decisive events of the entire war. It was the first time that an entire province had fallen to the Communists. But the South Vietnamese received a much more severe shock when the President of the United States failed to make any response to this dramatic escalation of Northern aggression: indeed, President Ford, in his first State of the Union message, did not even mention Vietnam. A few days later, he announced that he could foresee no circumstances in which the United States would return to the struggle. This declaration that the United States would do nothing to preserve South Vietnam, in which it had invested so much blood and treasure, shook the South Vietnamese like nothing since the murder of President Diem; now their American mentors had not only cut them off materially but had disowned them publicly. [2] Above all, Ford's statement convinced Hanoi that the hour had indeed arrived to attempt the final conquest of the South. [3] North Vietnamese Army Colonel Bui Tin observed that "when Ford kept the B-52s in their hangars, our leadership decided on a big offensive against South Vietnam."[4]

In the spring of 1975, confronted by open abandonment at the hands of their American allies, South Vietnam's leaders decided that a completely new defensive strategy had to be adopted. It was this decision that would result, within a remarkably brief time, in the total defeat and occupation of South Vietnam.

THE FALL OF BAN ME THUOT

With their forces having to a significant extent recovered from the costly failure of the 1972 Easter Offensive, and greatly excited by the increasingly obvious American determination to abandon the South Vietnamese, the Hanoi leadership planned to make big gains during 1975. The essence of the Northern strategy was to mount another effort to cut South Vietnam in two across the Central Highlands, then make some thrusts in the direction of Saigon. Close to 180,000 North Vietnamese combat troops entered South Vietnam from the beginning of September 1974 to the end of April 1975.[5] Saigon was unable to counter this massive influx effectively, having neither a mobile reserve nor a second strategic line of defense. Even if there had been such a reserve, the lack of fuel and spare parts resulting from the severe reductions in U.S. assistance would have prevented its efficient deployment.

The key to the Northern offensive was the city of Ban Me Thuot, capital of Darlac province, about 40 miles east of the Cambodian border in the lower end of the highlands (MR II). Defending the city was the 23d ARVN Division, a punishment unit for disciplinary cases and other troublesome soldiers. The Communists planned to take Ban Me Thuot by employing all their old and successful tactics: ruse, surprise, and overwhelming numbers. Attacks were launched against Pleiku and Kontum, important posts to the north of Ban Me Thuot. ARVN intelligence informed General Phu, commanding at Ban Me Thuot, that the attacks to the north of him were intended by the enemy to be distractions. Refusing to believe this, Phu stripped Ban Me Thuot of troops in order to defend Pleiku and Kontum.[6] Because they could choose the times and places of their attacks, while Saigon had to defend everything, the Hanoi forces were almost always able to assemble overwhelming numbers at any point, and that is what happened at Ban Me Thuot. The Northerners had a superiority of 2.2 to 1 in heavy artillery, and at least 5 to 1 in overall personnel.[7] In earlier years, besieged Ban Me Thuot would have been supplied by air, but the rise in world oil prices and the cutback in U.S. aid made that impossible, while the Communist ring around the city rendered reinforcement by truck exceptionally difficult. Accordingly, on

March 11, 1975, Ban Me Thuot fell. This disaster was to change the whole war and indeed seal the destiny of South Vietnam.

During these dark days, the government of South Vietnam, although recognized by 80 foreign states, was finding itself increasingly without friends and alone in the world. The last U.S. ground combat troops had left South Vietnam by October 1972. and all American advisers were gone by June 30, 1973.[8] In fact, the South Vietnamese fought on alone for more than two and a half years, a longer period than that between Pearl Harbor and Normandy, or between Fort Sumter and Gettysburg.

For 20 years the Hanoi leadership had told the world that the fighting in South Vietnam was between an indigenous, broadly based popular uprising and the tyrannical regime—first Diem's and then Thieu's—that had provoked it. Substantial elements of the U.S. media had accepted and peddled this line, and thus it penetrated an ever-increasing segment of the American people and their elected representatives. In February 1975, the month before the fall of Ban Me Thuot, a high-ranking delegation of South Vietnamese leaders went to Washington to plead for aid, only to be refused an audience by Senate Majority Leader Mike Mansfield and by Minority Leader Hugh Scott. When the U.S. Congress appropriated only $700 million of an original $1 billion authorization for defense assistance to South Vietnam, it "had an erosive effect on the morale of the Republic of Vietnam armed forces."[9] Massive aid cutbacks, and the clearly expressed hostility to South Vietnam that lay behind them, induced "a growing psychology of accommodation and retreat that sometimes approached despair"[10] and thus "made defeat inevitable."[11]

Aware that the tactics used against Ban Me Thuot could and would be employed elsewhere, high-ranking ARVN officers approached President Thieu with demands for a major shift in strategy.[12] On March 14, three days after the fall of Ban Me Thuot and two days after the House Democratic Caucus rejected President Ford's plea for emergency supplemental aid to the South Vietnamese, President Thieu announced to ARVN leaders his new strategy. Ban Me Thuot, declared Thieu, must be retaken at all costs; it must be the northern anchor for a consolidated defense of Military Regions III and IV (the Saigon area and the Mekong Delta). In order to accomplish this task, Military Regions I and II (the five northernmost provinces and the Central Highlands), with the exception of the strongholds of Hue and Da Nang, would have to be stripped of troops and abandoned to the enemy.

The decision to give up the "defend everything" policy and instead to retreat from the north and center and concentrate in the south was not at all a bad one in itself: 7 of ARVN's 13 divisions were deployed in MR I and MR II, defending only one-fifth of the population. A consolidated South Vietnam based on MRs III and IV would constitute a state of well over 13 million people. "A redeployment of our forces," wrote General Cao Van Vien, "should have been carried out by mid-1974." [13]

Clearly, the new concentration strategy depended on the successful extrication and redeployment of ARVN forces from the northern provinces in the teeth of NVA attacks—the key assumption being that ARVN divisions in the northern area could carry out a sustained, massive fighting retreat, one of the absolutely most difficult operations known to warfare.

Cao Van Vien [14] was at this time the chairman of the Joint General Staff. He later wrote: "If some revolutions are essentially a collapse of the old order, and others are the product of individual human actions, the Vietnamese revolution is quintessentially an example of the latter." [15] The truth of this statement finds its confirmation in the series of really disastrous decisions and movements in March 1975 that in a matter of a few weeks completely unraveled the fabric of the South Vietnamese Army that had been fighting for twenty-one years.

The Airborne Division, along with the Marines, had long been the most elite units in the South Vietnamese armed forces. Rushed to the defense of Quang Tri province during the Easter Offensive, the Airborne Division had done good work, but had suffered thousands of killed and wounded. By the spring of 1975, therefore, it was really a new division, filled with relatively unseasoned replacements and lacking the old spirit of self-confidence. [16] Morale was depressed further because while the home base of the Airborne was in the south, where the families of its members lived, after the 1973 Paris agreements it had been committed to a static defense of Military Region I, the far north. The Airborne was nevertheless the symbol of determined resistance to any Northern invasion of MR I. On March 14, as the overture to Thieu's new strategy, General Truong was ordered to send the Airborne Division from Da Nang to Saigon, preparatory to an offensive to retake Ban Me Thuot. This was indeed "a most disastrous" [17] decision, because to replace the redeployed Airborne troops, the crack Marine Division was moved out of Quang Tri down to Da Nang. This shift left the symbolic old capital of Hue with inadequate protection. Equally important, the transfer of the Airborne Division convinced many that a second partition of Vietnam was coming, and provoked a tremendous movement of refugees southward, a human flood that would make the defense of Hue and Da Nang impossible. [18] In the judgment of the U.S. Defense Attaché Office, "The disintegration of RVNAF [Republic of Vietnam Armed Forces] in MR I can be attributed principally to President Thieu's ill-timed mid-March decision to withdraw [the Airborne Division] from Quang Nam Province [Da Nang]." [19]

DEBACLE IN THE CENTRAL HIGHLANDS

The first major phase of the withdrawal from the Central Highlands began on March 16. ARVN units from Kontum and Pleiku were to move south and east. The troops in Pleiku were set on their way without anyone having informed the civilian authorities in that town. When people realized what was happening, panic enveloped the population. Physicians abandoned their hospitals, policemen shed their uniforms, arson and looting broke out.[20] Everyone wanted to join the ARVN troops in leaving the highlands. Inexplicably, no one in authority in Saigon had imagined that a massive exodus of civilians would seek to join the retreating columns of soldiers, becoming entangled with them and bringing any movement to an effective halt. Any retreat from Kontum and Pleiku, through extremely rough country over secondary roads and inadequate or even broken bridges, would in the best of circumstances have been tremendously difficult; with the enemy not only pursuing but somehow all around, with crowds of panic-stricken civilians clogging the roads and blocking army vehicles, it was impossible. The retreat soon disintegrated into anarchy. Tanks and oxcarts became hopelessly entangled, young soldiers jostled venerable farmers, frantic parents searched for lost children, the roar of engines competed with the cries of terrified animals, officers lost control of their units—all while great numbers of helpless civilians and soldiers were being slaughtered by indiscriminate fire from NVA artillery as well as wayward bombs dropped by South Vietnamese aircraft. The confusion, panic, and tragedy of the withdrawal from the Central Highlands surpass Hemingway's compelling portrayal of the retreat of the Italian army before the Austrians and Germans during the Battle of Caporetto. Of the 400,000 civilians who fled Kontum, Pleiku, and other places, perhaps only 100,000 made it out; this was "the worst bloodbath of the war."[21] Of the 60,000 troops who set out from Pleiku and Kontum, only 20,000 reached safety, making this "the greatest disaster in the history of ARVN."[22] As Cao Van Vien later wrote, with stunning understatement, "The apparent total indifference with which the United States and other non-Communist countries regarded this tragic loss reinforced the doubt the Vietnamese people held concerning the viability of the Paris Agreements."[23]

The retreat from the highlands was unfolding with essentially no plans, with poor intelligence—nobody was even sure which bridges were standing and which were down—and a total lack of preparation for handling hundreds of thousands of civilian refugees. Many good aircraft were left behind for the enemy at Pleiku (as later at Da Nang).[24] Even the most basic military tactics for a retreat, such as "leapfrogging"—in which some units stand and face the enemy while others retreat behind them, those previously retreating then taking a stand while the former defending units fall back behind them, and so on—were forgotten. The retreat from Pleiku and Kontum "must rank as one of the worst planned and worst executed withdrawal operations in the annals of military history."[25] In the end, nearly all the military units that began the withdrawal disintegrated. Faced with this and similar catastrophes in MRs I and II, many high-ranking ARVN officers took their own lives.[26]

The unannounced ARVN pullout from Kontum and Pleiku meant that RF/PF units in these areas were to be left behind and exposed to the advancing North Vietnamese Army. News of this abandonment spread rapidly over South Vietnam and had the predictable effect on the morale of territorial units everywhere.[27]

During the attack on Ban Me Thuot, the retreat from the Central Highlands, and the consequent Northern invasion of MR I, the Thieu government made no effective effort to communicate its plans or expectations to the people of South Vietnam. Nobody knew what was going on, and so the rumor mill inevitably began rolling.[28] The most widespread of these rumors was that Thieu had made a deal with Hanoi: in return for the northern provinces Hanoi would guarantee the neutrality of the remainder of South Vietnam.[29] Such rumors were sped along, where they were not actually created, by Communist agents who had infiltrated both ARVN and the civil administration (as during the Cold War the West German establishment was thoroughly penetrated by East German spies). These agents included at least one general, Nguyen Huu Hanh; not until after the final surrender of Saigon did anyone realize how numerous and destructive those Communists who had found niches within the Saigon government had been.[30]

The rumors of a deal between Thieu and Hanoi paralyzed top military commanders, who were reluctant to waste the blood of their troops in resisting the inevitable.[31] For twenty years the Communists had propagandized in vain that ARVN was on the verge of collapse and defection. Now in the spring of 1975 it was like some incredible nightmare coming true.

The lack of planning, communication, and leadership would all almost certainly have caused Thieu's redeployment to come unraveled in the end. But an "excessive preoccupation with secrecy," in order not to alert the enemy as to what was about to happen, precluded arrangements for an orderly withdrawal, including even attention to the repair of roads and bridges leading to the south.[32]

But the disintegration of ARVN was spurred most of all by the anxiety of the soldiers in MRs I and II to take care of their families. In an effort to overcome the most fundamental cause of desertion in the army, the Thieu government had made it a policy to permit and even encourage families of soldiers to live near military bases. As one student of ARVN wrote, "For ARVN troops, the close proximity of family members was the only reason to carry on the fight. 'The presence of our families was so important to us . . . we stayed energized for the war only by thinking that we were in the service of our families. I had refused to join my unit until I had permission to bring my family along. I know others felt the same way.'"[33]

General Lam Quang Thi has left this description:

> One of the biggest drawbacks of the South Vietnamese Army was its lack of strategic mobility caused by the unresolved problem of servicemen's families. The soldiers fought to defend their villages, their cities and their families and a great number of them would desert and stay behind rather than join their retreating units, even at the risk of being captured and killed by the enemy. To move the First Division south to defend Da Nang would require the prior evacuation of servicemen's families. This had not been done because there was no long-range planning and because of indecision and continuous flipflops at the highest echelons of the government and the Army. Further, the entire evacuation of the families would have disclosed our plan to the enemy and would have also adversely affected the morale of the civilian population. As a result, ARVN was caught up in a dilemma which remained unresolved until the very end.[34]

Thus when the withdrawals were ordered, those civilians living near army units were exposed to capture and reprisal at the hands of the advancing NVA. Memories of what had happened at Hue during Tet 1968 were too fresh in everyone's mind for any soldier to be able to contemplate the capture of his family by the Communists with anything but despair. Besides, if one believed the rumors that Thieu had agreed to a new partition, it was imperative that one's family be moved far enough south to wind up on the non-Communist side of any new dividing line. Accordingly, many soldiers left their units and the line of retreat to try to find their families and take them to safety.[35]

While soldiers sought to remove their families from the Communist path, the same rumors of a new partition produced an inundation of refugees. The numbers of these civilians and their panic overwhelmed any chance of directing them south in an organized way. Almost the entire population of Quang Tri province, for example, jammed the road to Hue.[36] When it became clear that Hue could not be held, over a quarter of a million civilians struggled to escape farther south to what they supposed was the safety of Da Nang.[37] Their headlong flight away from advancing enemy units clogged the inadequate highways, while their desperation communicated itself to those troops who were still in some sort of orderly arrangement.

During the whole period of the second Vietnamese war, huge flights of refugees took place toward the allied lines and away from the Communists. The meaning of this constant direction of refugee flight has been a subject of bitter controversy. Apologists for the Hanoi side have often insisted that refugees fled toward the allies in order to escape bombing or artillery fire directed toward Communist areas, and in many instances this was undoubtedly true, especially in periods when it seemed that the allies were winning. But the exodus of refugees southward in March 1975 suggests quite a different explanation. In March 1975, the B-52s were long gone, and the South Vietnamese air force, with little fuel and no spare parts, was less than a shadow of its former self. The massive and increasingly disorganized military withdrawals signaled to all who would see that the Saigon government was in mortal peril, and that, at the least, the whole northern half of South Vietnam was going to pass into the hands of the NVA. Nevertheless, from Quang Tri south to Hue, from Hue south to Da Nang, from Da Nang toward Saigon (360 miles[38]), always the rolling tide of refugees flowed inexorably southward, in front of, alongside, or just behind a clearly beaten ARVN. There seems no other plausible explanation for this phenomenon but that millions of South Vietnamese simply did not wish, whether from anti-Communist or anti-northern sentiment, or from whatever mixture of motives and fears, to be placed in the power of the Hanoi regime. Hard evidence on this question is limited, but three careful students of the refugee phenomenon conclude that "fear of the NLF [VC] and North Vietnamese forces and their Communist ideology and practices was the most important motive for refugee movement and was expressed by Catholic and non-Catholic alike."[39] The fact that refugees during the last weeks of South Vietnam's existence were disproportionately Catholic, northern, and urban, makes more plausible the belief that political motives were at least as important as considerations of safety in these flights. And since 1975, at least 1.5 million persons have fled what used to be South Vietnam, the equivalent of 21 million Americans leaving the United States today. There is no way of knowing how many more might have wished to leave but for one reason or another were unable to do so.

Whatever our judgment on this question, it is clear that the disintegration of the South Vietnamese armed forces in MRs I and II was the result not of the actions of the enemy, but of a collapse of morale. This collapse was due, first, to the repudiation of the South Vietnamese by their former American allies, and, second, to the inexplicable failure of the Thieu government to adequately deal with or even anticipate the enormous effusion of refugees let loose by ARVN's efforts to retrench southward.

THE CAPTURE OF HUE AND DA NANG

President Thieu had originally thought to hold on to Hue and Da Nang while pulling out of the rest of the northern provinces, but the flood of refugees and the efforts of soldiers to find and remove their families made a defense of Hue impossible. On March 24, Thieu ordered the evacuation of Hue and the regroupment of its forces at Da Nang, a distance of about 50 miles. (From

Baltimore, MD, to Washington, DC, is 40 miles.) It was impossible to remove anything approaching a majority of the troops, not to speak of the refugees, from Hue by ship. The First ARVN Division, pride of the army, attempted to reach Da Nang by road, but was smashed to pieces south of Hue between March 24 and 26. Hue was the historical capital of Old Annam. Its occupation by the Communists, not through conquest but through collapse, accompanied by the shattering of the First Division, administered a psychological blow to ARVN from which it would not be able to recover in time.[40] It was amidst the disaster at Hue that the North Vietnamese Politburo met in Hanoi and made the decision to try to conquer the entirety of South Vietnam in 1975 with a concerted, all-out drive to Saigon before the arrival of the rains.

All eyes now shifted to the drama of Da Nang, the next major stronghold south of Hue. Da Nang was supposed to be the most heavily defended city in South Vietnam, even though the principal force around it, the 3rd ARVN Division, had been badly mauled during the Easter Offensive. By late March 1975 "the entire population of the Central Highlands, more than one million civilians, had joined the ARVN forces streaming toward Da Nang."[41] Attempts were made to stage a major airlift; many were fortunate enough to escape, but too often soldiers in fear of their lives ordered women and children off the crowded planes to make room for themselves.[42] Soon all chance of escape by air disappeared when the airfield, with almost 200 planes on it, was overrun by crowds of refugees. Panic gripped the city. Many of the soldiers newly arrived in Da Nang had become separated from their units, many units were without officers, commanding generals had left the scene, and no one came or rose up to impose order and infuse purpose into the demoralized defenders. The despairing members of the elite Marine units made no efforts to defend the city; indeed, some of them engaged in looting and some even shot their own officers.[43] Communist artillery shelling of the city increased, if possible, the chaos and terror. Thousands fled into the sea, some in small fishing craft, many swimming in hopes of reaching some vessel; untold numbers drowned or eventually went insane from drinking sea water. In all, perhaps 60,000 people died trying to escape from Da Nang.[44] The bursting, bleeding, wailing city, scene of the arrival of the first U.S. Marine combat contingents exactly ten years before, fell on March 30. More than 100,000 soldiers, enough if properly commanded to have defended Da Nang indefinitely, were taken prisoner.

The Communists did not conquer MR I and MR II; those areas were abandoned. That was according to Thieu's plan. What was not according to plan was that the South Vietnamese forces in those regions would be destroyed as fighting units. Yet out of seven divisions stationed in those areas on March 1, only about 40,000 men were able to regroup in MRs III and IV by April 11, including only 4,000 troops from the once-mighty Marine Division. Many officers had been killed or captured or had disappeared, seriously undermining whatever effectiveness remained to these troops. These numbers represented an unparalleled disaster for South Vietnam. A question mark had always hung over the existence of the South Vietnamese Republic; always before the question had been expressed as "How many years?" Now the question came down to "How many weeks?" One must emphasize: This drastic change in South Vietnam's survival prospects resulted not from a protracted battle but from a brief debacle. On April 2, Secretary of Defense James Schlesinger said that what was going on in South Vietnam was not a great offensive but a collapse, "with very little major fighting."[45] The next day, as if in cruel confirmation of this pronouncement, Dalat, site of the South Vietnamese West Point, was abandoned without a struggle.

Where would ARVN make a stand? *Would* ARVN make a stand? Or was the war already over?

Deserted by their American allies, running out of gasoline and ammunition while the Soviets and Chinese poured vast amounts of both into Hanoi, distracted by waves of rumors and floods of refugees, shattered by the disaster of the withdrawal in the north, the morale of ARVN and other military formations was close to rock bottom. But even in this grimmest hour, it began to seem that the Hanoi offensive had reached its culminating point and that the red tide was ebbing. In the provinces of Tay Ninh, Long Khanh, Binh Long, and Binh Duong—a belt of territory stretching from the Cambodian frontier to the northeast of Saigon—fierce ARVN resistance, displaying "countless instances of great tenacity in defense and awesome valor in combat, even in the face of overwhelming firepower and numbers," forced NVA pullbacks.[46] The Rangers, once an elite formation, had deteriorated badly in the previous few years. But at Duc My camp, Rangers fought furiously against hopeless odds. The 22nd ARVN Division waged an excellent defense of coastal Binh Dinh province. On the South China Sea coast, Ninh Thuan province was the site of President Thieu's home village and of the key Phan Rang airbase; Airborne and ARVN infantry elements put up a heroic defense there. The first big NVA assault on the base began on April 9, and a week later the largest NVA attacking force in the history of the war overwhelmed the defenders. During these battles of the spring offensive, defeated ARVN forces were not allowed to surrender; instead they were forced to "adhere to the people"—that is, they had to proclaim that they were defecting to the Communists. When surrendering ARVN units engaged in this semantic exercise, Hanoi publicized to the world that they had "changed sides."[47]

It was at Xuan Loc, the last stop on the main highway to Saigon, only 30 miles away, that ARVN units put up probably the best fight of their 20-year struggle for independence, winning the grudging admiration even of the Communists.[48] The town was defended by the 18th ARVN Division, nobody's idea of a prize unit. Yet the 18th held on through a tremendous artillery pounding. "The soldiers fought hard," notes Willbank, "because they were not worried about their family members, most of whom had been evacuated to Saigon before the main battle began."[49] According to the official North Vietnamese military history, "The battle [of Xuan Loc] turned into a hard, vicious struggle. Our units suffered heavy casualties."[50] Arguably, Xuan Loc was "the war's bloodiest battle."[51]

Determined to take Xuan Loc and viewing it as a meat grinder in which to destroy irreplaceable enemy troops, the NVA poured in everything it could gather together. Eventually four NVA divisions encircled the town, while the 18th ARVN Division had been reduced in effect to the size of one regiment.[52] Nevertheless, after a twelve-day siege, surviving elements, including Regional and Popular Forces, were able to cut their way out of Xuan Loc on April 21 and reassemble for the final defense of Saigon.[53] If only the evacuation of the north had been half as orderly and determined as the withdrawal from besieged Xuan Loc.

On April 21, 1975, the same day that Xuan Loc fell, President Thieu announced his resignation.

By the end of the first week of April, ARVN had been largely broken up and other RVNAF formations were badly demoralized. Nevertheless, most of the South Vietnamese population, in the Saigon area and the Mekong Delta, were still in the hands of the republic. In Saigon the situation was perilous. A classic battlefront encircled the capital, no more than 30 miles and in some places less than 20 miles from center city. Only 30,000 troops, including Territorials, were available to defend the capital, while the NVA and VC had up to 16 divisions available for the siege, equipped with the latest weapons, including surface-to-air missiles.[54] The voice of the Viet Cong, Liberation Radio, began calling once again on the people of Saigon to rise up against their oppressors. Once again, as in 1968 and 1972, the inhabitants of the city remained uncannily impervious to their opportunities to show enthusiasm for a Communist victory. By April 20 a quiet had settled over the battlefields. The Communist forces tightened their noose and the defenders contemplated their situation and awaited a miracle—or rather, awaited help from their American allies. Most South Vietnamese generals were aware that, just as the American B-52s had made all the difference in the 1972 offensive, they could stop this 1975 offensive dead in its tracks.[55] Late in March, ARVN leaders pleaded with Washington for some B-52 raids on the huge concentration of northern troops inside South Vietnam, raids that could have broken North Vietnamese military power for years.[56] But the U.S. Congress had slammed the door on any military help to its one-time ally and was firmly tightening the faucet on continued financial assistance as well. Nevertheless, so deep was the belief within ARVN, from top to bottom, that the Americans would not abandon them in this their hour of gravest trial, that the B-52s would suddenly come back and break up the NVA in confusion, that

ARVN's plans and efforts in its own defense undoubtedly suffered as a result. [57] President Thieu himself believed up until almost the last day that the Americans would not, after so many years and so many billions of dollars and so much young blood, condemn his countrymen to a Communist conquest that the Americans could prevent merely with the dispatch of a small part of their magnificent air power. [58]

THE EVACUATION OF SAIGON

During the month of April, the United States evacuated 130,000 Vietnamese from Saigon, not only government and military figures and their families, but many persons of more humble estate as well. Most of these were employees of the U.S. government and their dependents, or persons who had openly sided with the Saigon government or identified themselves as opposed to a Communist conquest of their country. They and their families faced certain persecution, and worse, if they fell into the hands of the Communist forces. Twelve thousand were lifted out of the besieged capital in the last two days of the evacuation alone, April 28 and 29. This was no mean accomplishment, and other scores of thousands got out of the city and the country on their own. But the episode has left behind it much bitter controversy. Some have charged Graham Martin, the last U.S. ambassador, with lack of planning and foresight, and much else. [59] As the days of Saigon were visibly dwindling to a few, the evacuation became more and more a scene of disorganization, betrayal, and tragedy. At Ton Son Nhut air base, guards had to be bribed to let civilians get near evacuation aircraft. [60] Some Americans gave up their seats on busses going to the evacuation sites at the U.S. Embassy to terrified Vietnamese, confident that they themselves would not be left behind. [61] But the scene at the embassy itself was truly awful. Thousands of Vietnamese, many of them women with young children in their arms, believing themselves to have been promised escape, or simply filled with fear at what would be visited upon them by the Communists, clamored, begged, and wept in front of the embassy gates to be let inside the grounds and carried to safety. As they slowly retreated, floor by floor, up to the roof of the embassy and its helicopter landing pad, Marine guards had to use tear gas and rifle butts to restrain these crowds of desperate Vietnamese civilians.

The Americans left behind more than broken pledges to suffering allies. They left behind Vietnamese employees of the U.S. Information Agency, mainly women, as well as South Korean General Rhee Dai Yong and other Korean officers, all of whom had been promised certain airlift out of suffering Saigon.

They left behind computers and tapes with the names and addresses of Vietnamese who had helped the Americans in one way or another, including

Vietnamese agents of the United States who had infiltrated the Viet Cong. [62] They left behind the files of over 200,000 ex-Communists who had changed sides over the years and supported the Saigon government. [63]

The Americans were not alone in this bacchanal of betrayal. Taiwan abandoned hundreds of its citizens who were intelligence agents. [64] Airlifts to Australia of adopted Vietnamese orphans were halted by the government of that country after Hanoi protested. [65] British ambassador John Bushnell refused to take any of his Vietnamese staff with him (reports say he referred to them as "coolies"). [66] The Canadian embassy informed all its Vietnamese employees that they and their dependents would be taken out of Saigon the following day, but the next morning when the Vietnamese and their families arrived, the embassy was empty. [67]

THE SURRENDER

In accordance with the South Vietnamese constitution, President Thieu's resignation was followed by the swearing in of aged Vice President Tran Van Huong. But enormous pressure was building for him to hand power over to General Duong Van Minh ("Big Minh"). Some believed that the Communists would be willing to negotiate with Minh, and thus perhaps something could be saved. Others believed that Minh was the man to organize a final stand at Saigon, turning the city into an Asian Stalingrad that would win the admiration of the Americans and shame them into at last saving the allies they had deserted. [68] The last hope of the South Vietnamese now was to hold on until Congress decided to send some aid. General Thi wrote that French officers arrived in Saigon to advise Thieu on last-ditch plans to hold the city. [69] But on April 23, President Ford told a Tulane University audience that the war was over for the Americans, even while the South Vietnamese were still fighting to defend Saigon.

On April 28, one week after Thieu's resignation, Huong gave up his office, and the National Assembly chose Minh as the new president of South Vietnam. By then serious efforts were being made under General Nguyen Van Toan to organize the defenses of Saigon and the surrounding area. [70] In the whole Mekong Delta region, containing almost half of the total population of South Vietnam, ARVN and the authority of the Saigon government were intact: not one of the region's 16 provincial capitals, not even one single district capital (districts were subdivisions of provinces) was in Communist hands. [71] In the other direction, at Lai Khe, 30 miles north of Saigon, the Fifth ARVN Division was fighting hard and getting ready to attempt a breakthrough to the capital city. [72] And the rains were coming! Any day, any hour now, the rainy season would break over Saigon and the whole south, the rainy season that made infantry movements so difficult and tank advances impossible—the rains that would save Saigon.

But at 10:20 a.m. on April 30, Saigon time, President Minh—assassin of Diem—broadcast a call to all the armed forces to cease resistance. At the conclusion of his message, the heavens opened and the rains began. Soon the first North Vietnamese tanks crashed through the gates of Independence Palace. Although elements of the South Vietnamese military, notably the Airborne, would carry on guerrilla warfare for several years, the Republic of South Vietnam had ceased to exist.

Minh's surrender order triggered the suicide of many high-ranking military and police officials.[73] And those pilots of the South Vietnamese air force who were able to reach neither the Seventh Fleet nor Thailand crashed their American-built fighter planes into the South China Sea.[74]

Of these events Henry Kissinger wrote: "On May 1, 1975, the day after Saigon fell, the House of Representatives refused to approve a request by [President] Ford for $327 million for the care and transportation of Indochinese refugees. Congressional leaders for weeks had argued against efforts to save Vietnamese, and now the House turned down refugee relief for those who had already been saved."[75]

NOTES

1. Cao Van Vien, *The Final Collapse* (Washington, DC: U.S. Army Center of Military History), p. 51.

2. Ibid., pp. 67–68.

3. William Le Gro, *Vietnam from Ceasefire to Capitulation* (Washington, DC: U.S. Army Center of Military History, 1981), pp. 138–39; Alan Dawson, *55 Days: The Fall of South Vietnam* (Englewood Cliffs, NJ: Prentice-Hall, 1977), p. 27; Guenter Lewy, *America in Vietnam* (New York: Oxford University Press, 1978), p. 211; William J. Duiker, *The Communist Road to Power in Vietnam,* 2nd ed. (Boulder, CO: Westview, 1996), p. 309. The Communists were deeply impressed with the nonevents after Phuoc Long; see Tran Van Tra, *Concluding the Thirty-Years War* (Rosslyn, VA: Foreign Broadcast Information Service, 1983), p. 134.

4. Stephen Young, "How North Vietnam Won the War," *Wall Street Journal,* 3 August 1995.

5. Lewy, *America in Vietnam*, p. 213.

6. Le Gro, *Vietnam*, p. 149; Vo Nguyen Giap, *How We Won the War* (Philadelphia, PA: Recon, 1976), p. 49; Alan Dawson, *55 Days: The Fall of South Vietnam* (Englewood Cliffs, NJ: Prentice-Hall, 1977), p. 47.

7. Lam Quang Thi, *The Twenty-Five Year Century: A South Vietnamese General Remembers the Indochina War to the Fall of Saigon* (Denton, TX: University of North Texas Press, 2001), p. 335.

8. Bruce Palmer, Jr., *The Twenty-Five-Year War: America's Military Role in Vietnam* (Lexington, KY: University Press of Kentucky, 1984), p. 121; Hunt, *Pacification*, p. 246.

9. Defense Attaché Office, *RVNAF Final Assessment*, June 15, 1975 (Washington, DC: U.S. Government Printing Office, 1975), p. 16-B-1.

10. Lewy, *America in Vietnam*, p. 208.

11. Cao Van Vien, *Final Collapse*, p. 7.

12. Duiker, *Communist Road to Power*, pp. 310–311.

13. Cao Van Vien, *Final Collapse*, p. 80.

14. "General Vien, with long combat experience in the South Vietnamese Army, was a fine soldier and an extraordinary military leader. He remained loyal to President Thieu, supported American policy to the best of his ability, cooperated willingly with the American high command, and took care of his soldiers—all together no mean list of accomplishments. He survived the war and was granted asylum in the United States, where he [wrote] a history of the war for the U.S. Army Center for Military History. On 20 January 1982 Vien became a naturalized American citizen in an Alexandria, Virginia, courtroom. In my opinion our country gained a brave, decent man"; Palmer, *Twenty-Five-Year War*, p. 195.

15. Ibid., p. 325.

16. Le Gro, *Vietnam*, p. 61.

17. W. Scott Thompson, "The Indochinese Debacle and the United States," *Orbis* 19 (Fall 1975), p. 996.

18. Cao Van Vien, *Final Collapse*, p. 110.

19. *RVNAF Final Assessment*, p. 22. "When the Quang Tri population began to migrate south, everyone somehow came to the same conclusion: Thieu and the Americans have sold out to the Communists. People believe that Thieu has made a deal with the Communists, giving them the northern part of [South Vietnam] in exchange for some guarantee that they will leave Saigon and the Delta alone. There are numerous conspiracy theories going around now, all of which tell the average South Vietnamese soldier that to fight and die in such a rigged contest is stupid"; Stuart A. Herrington, *Peace with Honor? An American Reports on Vietnam 1973–1975* (Novato, CA: Presidio Press, 1983), p. 128.

20. Denis Warner, *Certain Victory: How Hanoi Won the War* (Kansas City: Sheed, Andrews and McMeel 1978), pp. 60–61.

21. Gerald C. Hickey, *Free in the Forest: Ethnohistory of the Vietnamese Central Highlands, 1954–1976* (New Haven, CT: Yale University Press, 1982), p. 281.

22. Stephen Hosmer, Konrad Kellen, and Brian M. Jenkins, *The Fall of South Vietnam: Statements by Vietnamese Military and Civilians Leaders* (New York: Crane, Russak, 1980), pp. 193–194.

23. Cao Van Vien, *Final Collapse*, p. 67.

24. Herrington, *Peace with Honor?*, p. 123.

25. Hosmer et al., *Fall of South Vietnam*, p. 194.

26. Cao Van Vien, *Final Collapse*, p. 118.

27. Cao Van Vien and Dong Van Khuyen, *Reflections on the Vietnam War* (Washington, DC: U.S. Army Center of Military History, 1980), p. 128.

28. Cao Van Vien, *Final Collapse*, pp. 109–110.

29. Herrington, *Peace with Honor?*, p. 128.

30. Dawson, *55 Days*, p. 13; Cao Van Vien, *Final Collapse*, p. 146.

31. Warner, *Certain Victory*, p. 70.

32. Cao Van Vien, *Final Collapse*, p. 94.

33. Robert K. Brigham, *ARVN: Life and Death in the South Vietnamese Army* (Lawrence, KS: University Press of Kansas, 2006), p. 118.

34. Lam Quang Thi, *The Twenty-Five Year Century*, p. 358.

35. Defense Attaché Office, *RVNAF Final Assessment*, p. 16-B-5.

36. Le Gro, *Vietnam*, p. 155. "Well over 100,000 refugees fled southward to Hue"; *RVNAF Final Assessment*, p. 1.8.

37. Dawson, *55 Days*, p. 108.

38. Washington, DC, to Charlotte, NC, is 400 miles.

39. Le Thi Que, A. Terry Rambo, and Gary D. Murfin, "Why They Fled: Refugee Movements during the Spring 1975 Communist Offensive in South Vietnam," *Asian Survey* 16 (September 1976), p. 863.

40. Dawson, *55 Days*, p. 147.

41. Brigham, *ARVN*, p. 124; Lewy, *America in Vietnam*, p. 213. "Thousands of civilian refugees were fleeing south toward Da Nang along QL-1, making an orderly military evacuation impossible"; *Final Assessment*, p. 1–9. "The sheer number of refugees was overwhelming and their state of mind precluded any attempt at orderly extrication"; Cao Van Vien, *Final Collapse*, p. 115.

154 Chapter 8

42. Warner, *Certain Victory*, p. 74.

43. Ibid. "Bui Tin, speaking from the enemy's perspective, said that a key step for the allies to win the war would have been 'to train South Vietnam's generals. The junior South Vietnamese officers were good, competent and courageous, but the commanding general officers were inept'"; Lewis Sorley, A *Better War: The Unexamined Victories and Final Tragedy of America's Last Years in Vietnam* (New York: Harcourt Brace, 1999), p. 382.

44. Ibid., p. 75.

45. Le Gro, *Vietnam*, p. 171.

46. Ibid., pp. 170, 172.

47. Dawson, *55 Days*, p. 134.

48. Van Tien Dung, *Our Great Spring Victory*, pp. 165ff. See also Merle L. Pribbenow, *Victory in Vietnam: The Official History of the People's Army of Vietnam 1954–1975* (Lawrence, KS: University Press of Kansas, 2002), pp. 407–408.

49. James H. Willbanks, *Abandoning Vietnam: How America Left and South Vietnam Lost Its War* (Lawrence, KS: University Press of Kansas, 2004), p. 264.

50. *Victory in Vietnam*, p. 407.

51. Sorley, *A Better War*, p. 378.

52. Le Gro, *Vietnam*, pp. 173–175; Dawson, *55 Days*, pp. 234ff.

53. Cao Van Vien, *Final Collapse*, pp. 132–133.

54. Dawson, *55 Days*, has 10 NVA divisions besieging Saigon, p. 298; Le Gro, *Vietnam*, p. 177, places 16 NVA divisions in Military Region III (which included Saigon); Cao Van Vien, *Final Collapse*, says 15 combat divisions attacked Saigon, supplemented by others, p. 129.

55. Hosmer et al., *Fall of South Vietnam*, p. 133.

56. "I am certain that, had we continued to receive American fire support, we could have stopped and crushed the NVA's offensive during the critical months of February, March and April 1975"; Lam Quang Thi, *Twenty-Five-Year Century*, p. 290.

57. Ibid., pp. 237–238; Cao Van Vien, *Final Collapse*, p. 5. "Thieu refused to believe that the United States would not intervene, even after Congress passed legislation forbidding the White House to do anything. His self-imposed delusion, fueled by Nixon's repeated promises, prevented the South Vietnamese from developing a cogent, workable strategy within a framework of resource-constrained circumstances, that followed the cessation of U.S. military aid"; Willbanks, *Abandoning Vietnam*, p. 284.

58. Truong Nhu Tang, *A Viet Cong Memoir* (New York: Vintage, 1985), pp. 137–138; Dong Van Khuyen, *The RVNAF* (Washington, DC: U.S. Army Center of Military History, 1980), p. 387.

59. See, for example, Dawson, *55 Days*.

60. Ibid., p. 307.

61. Ibid.

62. Dawson, *55 Days*, p. 352; Warner, *Certain Victory*, p. 246.

63. Warner, *Certain Victory*, p. 203.

64. Dawson, *55 Days*, p. 359.

65. Ibid., p. 306.

66. Ibid., p. 305.

67. Warner, *Certain Victory*, p. 237.

68. Dawson, *55 Days*, p. 305; Cao Van Vien, *Final Collapse*, pp. 132–133.

69. Lam Quang Thi, *Twenty-Five-Year Century*, p. 381–382; see also Brigham, *ARVN*.

70. Hosmer et al., *Fall of South Vietnam*, p. 247.

71. Cao Van Vien, *Final Collapse*, p. 140.

72. In the event, this effort was defeated by the well-armed and numerous NVA; the 5th Division's commander, Brig. Gen. Le Nguyen Vy, committed suicide after his failure.

73. Dawson, *55 Days*, pp. 1–17.

74. Herrington, *Peace with Honor?*, p. 146.

75. Henry Kissinger, *Years of Renewal* (New York: Simon and Schuster, 1999), p. 546.

Chapter Nine

Reflections on the Fall of
South Vietnam

HOW NORTH VIETNAM WAS ESTABLISHED

The totalitarian dictatorship in North Vietnam had its origins in a coup in Hanoi in the last days of World War II. The coup, by the small but well-organized Viet Minh that included only one Vietnamese out of every 6,000,[1] took place during a power vacuum made possible by the indifference of the Japanese occupation forces to local events following Japan's unexpected surrender. Not only did Japanese troops not interfere with the Viet Minh coup, they in fact gave much invaluable help to them. It is to say the least very difficult to imagine how there would have been a Viet Minh "revolution" had there not previously been a Japanese occupation. Soon thereafter, Chinese Nationalist forces assisted Ho's regime to stabilize itself, while the Viet Minh began the systematic assassination of political rivals. Subsequently the Viet Minh regime was strengthened by French failure either to seriously negotiate with it or to do what was necessary to defeat it.

The French expulsion of the Viet Minh from Hanoi resulted in a guerrilla conflict, a very difficult type of struggle for any regular army to overcome. Generous aid to the Viet Minh from Communist China was of course an indisputable key to the outcome of the struggle. Among other important factors was the unparalleled instability of French political and military leadership. Viet Minh victories, moreover, were won first of all through their numerical superiority: the French would neither send sufficient numbers of troops from France, nor construct a really effective Vietnamese National Army. And beneath all these factors was the continuing French underestimation of their foes: the disaster at Cao Bang and Lang Son, and most especially the defeat at Dien Bien Phu, for examples, resulted from deliberate French initiatives. If the French had done in Vietnam in the late '40s what they did in Algeria in the late '50s—sending great numbers of regular soldiers, raising a very large indigenous armed force, and isolating the insurgents from outside assistance—if the French had done these things in Vietnam, the struggle there would undoubtedly have had a very different outcome.

DIEM

The contemporary image of Ngo Dinh Diem is dramatically different from the one held by those who worked with, or fought against, him. At one time or another the Japanese, Bao Dai, Ho Chi Minh, two American administrations—almost everybody but the French—wanted Diem for an ally or at least an instrument. Appointed in June 1954 as prime minister of a truncated state collapsing on every side, within a very short time and against all odds Diem established a functioning government.

Critics then and now pronounced his government not "democratic" enough, as if the Hanoi-guided insurgency was some sort of civil rights protest, and as if the expedient of appointing trusted relatives and friends to office in dangerous times had been invented by Diem. And consider the irony that a handful of American presidential appointees conspired with the army of a foreign country to overthrow the internationally recognized government of that country because, at least officially, those appointees considered it insufficiently democratic.

But arguably nothing contributed to the fall of President Diem more powerfully than the astoundingly incompetent misreporting of events in the summer of 1963, specifically that "the" Buddhists, who were "90% of the population," were all alienated from the government. In fact, of course, there were incomparably more Buddhist immolations after than under Diem. And the American media soon became bored with them.

Diem's death came not from the hands of his enemies in Hanoi but of his allies in Washington. This shameful act, "this unprecedented betrayal of an ally," required that powerful opponents of U.S. support for a coup in Saigon had to be overridden—in fact unconstitutionally circumvented.[2] The overthrow of Diem clearly refutes the charge that he ran a tight police state, and his murder suggests that he was much more popular than the *New York Times* wished to admit. (Or else why not put him on trial or just deport him?) In Anne Blair's damning judgment: "Diem was overthrown because he would not be a puppet."[3] Not long after Diem's death, the arch-plotters Henry Cabot Lodge and Averell Harriman came to understand, to a degree, the magnitude of their errors. It was a great pity they did not know in 1963 what they knew in 1964.

The name of Ngo Dinh Diem has been defaced, perhaps beyond restoration, by the endless canting of half truths and ignorant vituperation and utter nonsense. But even if one accepts all the criticisms of Diem at their most extreme, the failure to determine, even to consider, what—that is, who—would follow Diem, and the casual assumption that any government would perform better than his, surely ranks as one of most disturbing episodes of U.S. foreign policy in the entire Cold War. The murder of Diem eliminated the only Southern political figure the Communists really feared and opened the door wide to the chaos that engulfed South Vietnamese politics, requiring order to be restored and maintained by an essentially military government. (And South Vietnam would not be the last instance in which Washington, having adjudged the incumbent friendly government not up to democratic standards, abandoned it only to find its place taken by avowed enemies of the United States.)

After the betrayal of Diem, many in the United States continued to find the South Vietnamese government unworthy of their support because it, like Diem's, was insufficiently democratic—this in South Vietnam, to whose venerable culture Western-style democracy was utterly alien, in a region of the world where functioning democracies were notably scarce, where the French had in a century of rule made no effort to establish democratic forms, and whose territory was torn by both insurgency and invasion. Does anyone wish to declare that North Vietnam won the war because it was a model democracy? The truth is, of course, that President Thieu held office as result of elections immeasurably more competitive and honest than any in North Vietnam or in very many members of the United Nations, including the Mexico of the 1960s and 1970s (at least). "However repressive the Saigon regime may have appeared, there was more freedom in the South than in the North."[4] Indeed, the level of freedom of expression in South Vietnam did it much harm, because ARVN soldiers knew about demonstrations and riots in the U.S. (which the American news industry presented as representative of American public opinion, as if the media had never heard of Gallup polls) and heard Communist propaganda all the time, while the members of the North Vietnamese Army knew nothing except what Hanoi told them.

It is indeed remarkable that vehement and relentless criticisms of the South Vietnamese for their admitted shortcomings in the field of civil rights came from the political class of the United States, a country millions of whose citizens were at that very time (1963) denied their constitutionally guaranteed right to vote and which had, just two decades before Diem's murder, rounded up scores of thousands of American citizens, solely because of their race, and dumped them into "relocation" camps.

And it is as certain as anything can be in politics that if President Diem had been able to thwart his assassination in 1963, or if Cabot Lodge and Averell Harriman had known in 1963 what they learned later, the relationship of the United States to the Vietnam conflict would have evolved in a profoundly different direction. At the very least, whatever his faults, Diem's reputation should not depend on the opinions of those who advocated or profited from his murder.

ARVN

For some Americans, to denigrate ARVN is a necessity, because if ARVN was indeed a decent fighting organization—right up to the very end—then the abandonment of South Vietnam was a great error, and a shameful wrong.

The Army of the Republic of Vietnam—ARVN—had been trained by the Americans for the wrong kind of war and given second-rate equipment. The high educational requirements for officership were ill-advised. Army pay and medical care became more and more inadequate. Many in ARVN were literally undernourished, their families unsupported by the government. Using weapons inferior to those of the VC and the NVA, ARVN suffered huge casualties, proportionately many times higher than those of the Americans. The assassination of President Diem produced years of confusion and disorder within its ranks. And in the U.S., ARVN continuously received ill-informed criticism on the subject of desertion. In light of all its problems, Hanoi predicted that the 1968 Tet Offensive would result in the collapse of ARVN.

Hanoi's other prediction was that the disintegration of ARVN would be accompanied by a massive popular uprising in favor of the Communists. The South Vietnamese and the Americans were completely surprised by the offensive because they knew that no popular uprising was going to occur. (Many VC cadre also knew this.) But the biggest surprise of all was on the Communist side: ARVN on the whole stood fast, and the civilian population evidenced very little support for the Communist effort: no ARVN collapse, no civilian uprising, no Viet Cong victory.

Having failed spectacularly in its effort to take over South Vietnam through Viet Cong efforts, four years later Hanoi launched the 1972 Easter Offensive, a massive conventional invasion by the well-trained, Soviet-equipped North Vietnamese Army. Safe from any American land or amphibious attack on its territory, North Vietnam made a supreme effort, throwing the great bulk of its best forces into the assault. Major U.S. ground units were almost completely gone from South Vietnam by spring 1972; thus the impact of the Communist invasion fell almost exclusively on ARVN and the territorial forces. The South Vietnamese did not collapse but, on the contrary, the 1972 Offensive, like that of 1968, resulted in complete failure for the Communist side. As a consequence, morale within the South Vietnamese armed forces and the civil population reached an unprecedented high.

All this would change, drastically and irretrievably, as a result of the so-called peace agreement of 1973 and South Vietnam's abandonment by the Americans—an abandonment that came *after* the massive Communist failures of 1968 and 1972. And despite being deserted by the Americans, in the last years of the conflict ARVN would fight on stubbornly, suffering its highest losses of the entire twenty-year conflict.

GEOGRAPHY

The decisive weakness of South Vietnam was, arguably, its geography. In the first place, South Vietnam was too extensive for proper defense. The territory between the 17th parallel and Saigon was sparsely populated, but the political necessity of defending prestigious Hue imposed great burdens on ARVN, overstraining its resources and exposing it to constant flanking movements from Laos and Cambodia. There was no reason in military logic why South Vietnam had to attempt with such difficulty to hold so much territory in the Central Highlands: after all, it was the French who had drawn the partition line. Saigon's 1975 decision for retrenchment, therefore, was a good idea in itself, only much too late.

But geographical disadvantage meant much more: If Vietnam had been an island like Taiwan, or an archipelago like the Philippines, or a peninsula like Malaya or South Korea, the fighting there would have proceeded and ended differently. But, as an open society sharing a border with a totalitarian enemy and outflanked by its enemy's sanctuaries, South Vietnam was in the gravest position. That is to say, the fatal weakness for South Vietnam was the Ho Chi Minh Trail.

The entire allied strategy—if that is the term—put together by President Johnson and his advisers, was wrong. Refusal to shut down the Ho Chi Minh Trail meant that South Vietnam had to face continuous invasion, at times and places of the enemy's choosing, so that the invaders were always numerically superior to South Vietnamese forces at the points of contact. Consequently, it was impossible for ARVN to maintain a true strategic reserve. The failure to cut off the invasion routes into the South led to the massive but essentially ineffective U.S. bombing campaign and to the so-called "attrition strategy," inadequate substitutes both of which helped to undermine American confidence in the conduct of the war. Those who maintain that the Ho Chi Minh trail was Hanoi's war-winning weapon include Ellsworth Bunker, Dwight Eisenhower, Henry Kissinger, Bruce Palmer, Douglas Pike, Harry Summers, Maxwell Taylor, Robert Thompson, William Westmoreland, even poor Henry Cabot Lodge, and—yes!—the Hanoi Politburo.[5] Yet, despite the Communists having been granted almost complete control of the timing and location of their attacks, their massive offensives of 1968 and 1972 suffered resounding defeat.

Nearly as egregious a blunder as leaving the Trail open was Washington's refusal to threaten the territory of North Vietnam. The allies could have occupied a secure foothold in Quang Binh province in southern North Vietnam as a buffer for the South and a base from which to threaten further occupation of Northern territory. With little difficulty, moreover, the U.S. Navy could have presented North Vietnam with a permanent threat of an amphibious invasion.[6] In Vietnam, the U.S. faced no opposition on the sea, and General MacArthur's landing at Inchon in 1950 showed how crushingly effective a behind-enemy-lines amphibious operation could be. It would not have been necessary to actually launch a major amphibious attack on North Vietnam; all that would have been required was to present a credible threat to do so. But on the contrary, the Johnson Administration publicly trumpeted time after time that it would make no direct ground or amphibious attack against North Vietnamese territory, that the regime in Hanoi was safe no matter what it did or did not do. Hence the North was free to attack the South wherever and whenever it chose, and with all available forces. In this manner, U.S. passivity yielded the initiative permanently to the enemy side.

Even with constant reassurances from President Johnson that the U.S. would not launch any invasion of the North, "The North Vietnamese," as Merle Pribbenow writes, "were so afraid that the U.S. might launch an amphibious assault against North Vietnam itself that for some time [during the Easter Offensive] they held back their entire strategic reserve—two divisions, six main force regiments, and a provisional division formed using cadet officers from all their military schools—to defend against a possible attack against the 'panhandle' of southern North Vietnam rather that committing this force to the offensive. Those two reserve divisions could have made a real difference in the northern theater if they had been committed immediately when Quang Tri fell."[7] Clearly the presence of a real threat of U.S. amphibious invasion could have changed the course and outcome of the war. But by 1975 this U.S. threat—actually existing only in the minds of the Hanoi Politburo—had disappeared, and North Vietnam was thus free to employ every available soldier in its massive and final offensive into South Vietnam.[8]

By refusing to adopt a forward defense of South Vietnam, by bombing North Vietnam for years while failing both to close the Trail and to threaten to move into southern North Vietnam, the Johnson Administration revealed its strategic bankruptcy and in effect signed South Vietnam's death warrant.

President Johnson is arguably the most inept war leader in American history. Choosing the next day's bombing targets in the White House basement (if you bomb North Vietnam, why not at least threaten to invade it?), declining to close the Ho Chi Minh Trail, foreswearing the option of threatening a landing in North Vietnam (all this for domestic electoral purposes, not military), failing to offer the American people a comprehensible justification for the manner in which the war was being waged, unwilling to employ the moral and patronage powers of the Presidency to impose discipline upon the members of his own party (perhaps Johnson's greatest sin in the eyes of many Democrats was that he sat in John F. Kennedy's seat), and yet still refusing to end American participation in the conflict, Johnson saved neither his Administration nor his party[9] nor the South Vietnamese. But the final judgment (if such a thing is possible) on President Johnson must take into account that he inherited the U.S. involvement in Southeast Asia, and above all, he inherited the chaos produced by the assassination of Diem, which crime Johnson had opposed.

THE AID CUTOFF

Many blamed the fall of South Vietnam entirely on the South Vietnamese. Of course! They could not make it on their own without the help of the U.S. military; therefore, they were unworthy of assistance. Few people ever made that sort of observation about the West Germans, who gladly received U.S. troops onto their territory for over four decades, or about the South Koreans, among whom substantial American combat forces have been based for nearly seven decades.

The very defeat of South Vietnam implied to some Americans that that state was not politically viable. But, in contrast to the profound misperception widespread even today, South Vietnam did not fall to the pajama-clad guerrillas of American mythology; the final conquest of South Vietnam was accomplished by the regular North Vietnamese Army, one of the best-equipped forces in Asia at the time, an army engaging in one of the largest conventional military operations seen in that part of the world since the defeat of Imperial Japan. The "peace" of 1973 had eventually removed all U.S. forces from South Vietnam, but allowed many scores of thousands of North Vietnamese regulars to remain there, and then 200,000 more entered in late 1974 and early 1975.

And *of course* the South Vietnamese were defeated. President Thieu had signed the staggeringly one-sided "peace" agreement because President Nixon had promised, by word and by document, to punish any North Vietnamese violations. But after 1973 the U.S. Congress slashed aid to South Vietnam, while Communist powers continued their substantial help to the North. The consequences were embarrassingly predictable. If two armies of approximately equal size, drawn from the same ethnic background, are engaged in mortal combat, and one army has all the ammunition and gasoline it needs, and the other does not, which army could be expected to win? Lewis Sorley wrote: "Only when the United States defaulted on its commitments to South Vietnam, while North Vietnam's communist allies continued and indeed greatly increased support to their client state, were our unfortunate sometime allies overwhelmed and defeated."[10] Ira A. Hunt writes: "The United States reneged on almost all the pre-peace treaty promises made to South Vietnam."[11] Or, in the words of Colonel William Le Gro, present in South Vietnam until the last days: "The reduction to almost zero of United States support was the cause [of the collapse]. We did a terrible thing to the South Vietnamese."[12] It was the ARVN retrenchment effort in 1975, provoked by the American abandonment, that caused the collapse of South Vietnam: no abandonment, no retrenchment, no collapse.

But quite aside from these facts: if— again, as many Americans believe, or at least repeat—if the government of South Vietnam was so thoroughly corrupt, so bereft of supporters, if its army and its territorial militias were so unwilling to fight, if South Vietnam was, in a word, so utterly rotten, why then was such a massive Northern invasion necessary? Why didn't the Politburo in Hanoi just sit tight and wait for the rotted fruit to fall off the diseased tree?

SOUTHERN OPPOSITION TO THE COMMUNISTS

One of the most common, and inexplicable, errors prevalent in the United States regarding the Vietnam conflicts is this one: because the North eventually conquered the South, the Viet Minh and the Viet Cong must always have been highly popular there.

We have already seen that opposition to Communist domination of Vietnam had deep roots. In the war against the Viet Minh, for one example, the airborne units were the elite of the regular French forces (the CEF), and about half of these paratroopers were Vietnamese. This is a fundamental consideration. Recall that Martin Windrow pointed out, "Today it is little appreciated that the war as a whole [1946–1954], and the battle of Dien Bien Phu itself, were far from being clear-cut confrontations between Europeans and Indochinese, but involved significant numbers of Vietnamese fighting under French command."[13] And John McAlister wrote that by the spring of 1954 about 300,000 Vietnamese, in Bao Dai's Vietnamese National Army or in the CEF, were fighting against the Viet Minh; "this French capacity to mobilize substantial Vietnamese manpower for military purposes at the beginning as well as at the conclusion of the war suggests an important commentary on the revolution in Vietnam."[14] (Other authors set Bao Dai's army at 300,000.)

Resistance to Communist conquest persisted and indeed increased after the southern Vietnamese established their own state in 1954. Sorley notes that "the price paid by the South Vietnamese in their long struggle to remain free proved grievous indeed. The armed forces lost 275,000 killed in action. Another 465,000 civilians lost their lives, many of them assassinated by Viet Cong terrorists or felled by the enemy's indiscriminate shelling and rocketing of cities, and 935,000 more were wounded."[15] In fact, some of the best fighting by Southern forces took place in the desperate last weeks of the war, as for example at Xuan Loc. "To the very end they [the South Vietnamese] gave no indication that they chose of their own free will to live under Communism."[16]

The defeat of the Tet and Easter Offensives conclusively showed the shallowness of southern support for and the depth of southern resistance to a Communist takeover. The final collapse of South Vietnam may prove the ineptness of the ARVN high command, but not that ARVN and the territorial forces did not fight. And if the Americans had maintained their commitment to South Vietnam for just a few more years, many well-trained younger officers would have assumed leadership positions in ARVN.

The hostility of the majority of South Vietnamese to the Communist side is the main reason why, after their final victory in 1975, Hanoi never held internationally observed free elections in the former South Vietnam: "The paramount point," observes Thompson, "which comes through the whole of the Vietnam war, including the period after the ceasefire, is that the North Vietnamese and the Vietcong never had any hope of winning the South politically through elections."[17] Indeed, as we have seen, in 1975 the premier of North Vietnam, Pham Van Dong, famously observed that between 50 and 70 percent of the population of South Vietnam would need to be persuaded of the benefits of "reunification."[18]

In the aftermath of the fall of South Vietnam, untold numbers continued to suffer from the triumphant Hanoi regime's punitive policies as well as from its armed conflicts with Laos, Cambodia, Thailand, and China. The numbers we do have tell a grim story. Between 1975 and 1997, an estimated 859,000 persons fled Vietnam via the South China Sea (the pathetic "boat people") and survived; an unknown number perished at sea.[19] Among these boat people were possibly 40,000 former inhabitants of Saigon's Chinese suburb of Cholon who drowned in the sea or were enslaved by pirates.[20] The North Vietnamese executed at least 65,000 South Vietnamese, a number equal to over 950,000 Americans in 2015. Another 400,000—soldiers, officers, diplomats, professionals, students, priests, and their relatives—were kept in prison camps where 200,000 died, proportionately equivalent to the death of every man, woman, and child in the cities of Washington, DC, Baltimore, and Philadelphia combined.[21] In 1997 former NVA colonel Bui Tin stated, "there are now over two million Vietnamese who are refugees from their own country."[22] Sir Robert Thompson bitterly reminds us that "there were no 'boat people' fleeing north from General Thieu."[23]

The great exodus of South Vietnamese from their own country, the decades of corruption, stagnation, deprivation, persecution and execution that followed the fall of Saigon—does not all this strongly suggest that those millions of Vietnamese who had resisted Communist conquest for twenty years had been right?

The final conquest of South Vietnam was the achievement not of indigenous insurgents but of the North Vietnamese Army—after the Americans had created the wrong army for the South Vietnamese, colluded in the murder of its civilian leadership, left the Ho Chi Minh Trail wide open, assured North Vietnam that it need fear no American invasion, and then abandoned the South Vietnamese to their fate. Yet in spite of all these undeniable facts, somehow for many Americans the final defeat of the South Vietnamese seems to justify the U.S. desertion of its allies. Maybe the principal fault of the South Vietnamese was that they had far too much faith in their American allies.

In the mid-1980s, a former U.S. Army officer felt compelled, like many hundreds of Americans before and after him, to return to that strange, tragic, beautiful land of Vietnam. He spent most of his time in the place he knew best, Saigon. As he walked the familiar streets, or sat in cafes, Vietnamese would surreptitiously approach him and slip pieces of paper into his newspaper or book or pocket, and move quickly away. In the evenings when he returned to his hotel room, he would gather up all these slips of paper and read them. They were always the same: "Dear President Reagan—Please help me! Please help me to come to America."

THE VICTORS

Accompanying the vilification of Diem (indeed essential to it) was the quasi-sanctification of Ho Chi Minh. For one (admittedly egregious) example, George McGovern, Democratic presidential nominee in 1972, equated Ho Chi Minh with George Washington.

From the vantage point of our own day, it is not easy to grasp why Ho exercised such a great allure on so many Americans at the time. It is not clear why they saw Ho as more legitimate than Diem, this Ho Chi Minh who in the confusion following Japan's surrender had seized some buildings in Hanoi with a few hundred armed men, and then proceeded to impose a totalitarian state on his people with abundant assistance from Stalin and Mao and the French Communists. And in 1945 the Viet Minh already had the blood of many authentic Vietnamese nationalists on their hands, and would accumulate much more.

Ho Chi Minh made war not for an independent Vietnam but for a Stalinist Vietnam, although of course he successfully deceived most of his countrymen about that aim for many years. The war that began in 1946 was his chosen strategy for rallying the Vietnamese population behind the Viet Minh. Ho the "patriot" was willing to pay countless lives of his countrymen, not only through war, but through assassination, to have his way. And his successors wanted not to unite Vietnam but to purge it, as the massive executions following their victory demonstrate. North Vietnam was a totalitarian state, willing and able to impose incredible hardships on its people and silence its critics, a reality that many American journalists were inexplicably unable to comprehend. As Arnold Isaacs wrote:

> So immune did the [Communists] seem to normal human doubt and despair and want and fear that even some of their foreign supporters, on closer acquaintance, found them chilling. The same traits that inspired his admiration also caused a "subtle fear," admitted one European sympathizer, after living through the early months of the liberation; the qualities that made the revolution possible also seemed to bring its makers "to the borders of inhumanity."[24]

A South Vietnamese officer wrote that "within minutes of taking over the Cong Hoa Military General Hospital, the communist soldiers received orders to kick all 1,000 ARVN patients out onto the streets, even those who were on operating tables. Seriously wounded soldiers, whose limbs were torn and bleeding, some even with stomachs cut open and intestines exposed, were pulled out to the terrace in front of the hospital gate. Many died in a short time. I had never imagined that such barbarism would happen."[25] And after their conquest of the South, the Communists took great pains to desecrate the cemeteries in which ARVN soldiers had been buried.

Within a few years of the fall of South Vietnam, Stanley Karnow, certainly no friend of the South Vietnamese, found that "inefficiency, confusion, pilferage and venality are endemic" under "an inept and repressive regime incompetent to cope with the challenge of recovery."[26] Years after the conquest, Pham Xuan An, once a North Vietnamese Army colonel (and also a great source to U.S. reporters), expressed his despair over what a Communist victory had brought to Vietnam. "All that talk about liberation twenty, thirty, forty years ago," he lamented, "produced this, this impoverished, broken-down country led by a gang of cruel and paternalistic half-educated theorists."[27]

And, as Kissinger notes, "The Buddhist monks, whose quest for autonomy from the Saigon authorities had contributed to inducing the Kennedy Administration to overthrow the former South Vietnamese President Ngo Dinh Diem, were imprisoned [after the fall of Saigon] under the most brutal conditions."[28]

And Ho's insistence on a Communist Vietnam had a truly staggering blood cost. According to *Agence France Presse*, April 4, 1995, "the Hanoi government revealed on April 4 that the true civilian casualties of the Vietnam war were 2,000,000 in the North and 2,000,000 in the South. [Northern and VC] military casualties were 1.1 million killed and 600,000 wounded in 21 years of war. These figures were deliberately falsified during the war by the North Vietnamese Communists to avoid demoralizing the population."

The end of the war was not the end of the killing and dying. One very careful statistical analysis concludes that close to 100,000 South Vietnamese suffered "extrajudicial execution" after 1975, proportionately equal to the execution of 1,500,000 Americans in 2015.[29]

THE MEDIA AND THE CONSTITUTION

During the Vietnam conflict the Americans, leaders and citizens, were repeatedly and profoundly misinformed by the news industry regarding the problems facing President Diem, the meaning of the Tet Offensive, the quality of ARVN, even the New Hampshire Democratic presidential primary. These documented shortcomings of the media (attested to by, among others, distinguished professional journalists) present a grave constitutional issue. The responsibility for framing U.S. foreign policy rests, according to the Constitution, primarily in the hands of the President of the United States and the U.S. Senate. But many lawmakers and others in the Beltway believed that the media shaped the opinions of the electorate. Thus policy makers were intensely vulnerable to often inexperienced journalists, many of whom embodied American unwillingness or inability to familiarize themselves with either foreign cultures or foreign languages, who were responsible to no electorate, but were quite able and eager to present the public with the latest photogenic obscenity. Many years later, Robert Kaplan would observe: "The power of the media is wilful and dangerous because it dramatically affects western policy while bearing no responsibility for the outcome."[30]

For but one concrete example of this dangerous phenomenon, consider the interview of Harry McPherson, special counsel to President Johnson, that appeared on the PBS series "Vietnam: A Television History" in 1983; McPherson actually said that while he and others in the White House were receiving essentially encouraging reports from the U.S. Embassy, from the U.S. military with its hundreds of advisers among South Vietnamese troops, and from the Central Intelligence Agency with its countless sources of information, what they saw on the nightly television news shows contradicted all these reports, and he and others believed that the television stories were more accurate.[31]

As we have seen, the inexperienced and misinformed reporters of the elite media blew the artificial "Buddhist crisis" out of all proportion. Thus, the American news industry cannot escape its responsibility for the murder of President Diem, which opened the floodgates to more "Buddhist crises," repeated coups, and eventually the massive U.S. military intervention, with all its consequences.

What if North Vietnam had been subject to the same critical and even hostile media scrutiny that the South Vietnamese endured for twenty years? Or, what if there had been no images of burning monks or the street execution of a terrorist? Or, what if, during World War II, or before that, Stalin's Russia, America's ally, had experienced media treatment similar to that inflicted on South Vietnam?

And Arthur Dommen presents yet another example of the fundamental failures by the news industry to inform the American electorate regarding Vietnam:

> The propaganda of the Socialist Republic of Vietnam had adroitly converted its military victory over the demoralized ARVN [in 1975] into a victory over the United States. The "puppet regime" was simply airbrushed out so that the party's propaganda could claim that the valiant Vietnamese, led by the all-wise party, had defeated the Americans after having defeated the French, and that these victories were in the tradition of Vietnamese resistance against the Chinese and the Mongols. The propaganda was so successful that in the United States a young generation grew up believing in "the American defeat in Vietnam."[32]

The multibillion-dollar news business has not corrected these and other profound and dangerous (and more recent) misperceptions, or even admitted any responsibility for them.

THE FAILURE OF "PEOPLE'S REVOLUTIONARY WAR"

Because of the South Vietnamese debacle of 1975, one of the most important "lessons" of the Vietnam conflict is also probably the most overlooked: Communist guerrilla insurgency, "People's Revolutionary War"—that supposedly invincible Maoist weapon of the 1960s[33]—failed. The United States, of all the post-industrial democracies, is arguably the most culturally alien to underdeveloped societies. Nevertheless, however expensively and destructively, the Americans and their allies beat the Viet Cong guerrillas, despite the fact that the latter possessed sanctuaries and received plenty of outside assistance. Any list of the causes of the defeat of the Viet Cong would surely include irresistible American firepower, sweeping land reform, increasingly effective and determined South Vietnamese resistance, and the Communists' fatal abandonment of classical guerrilla tactics in the Tet Offensive. All this is why the Northern conquest of South Vietnam required the departure of the Americans and a full-scale, all-out invasion by conventional Northern armed forces.

THE LASTING EFFECTS OF THE WAR

Hanoi proved that violence pays and superpowers are vulnerable to it. After 1975 U.S. credibility approached the zero mark, encouraging the Iranian seizure of the Tehran embassy and the Soviet invasion of Afghanistan.[34]

The Johnson Administration made a disproportionate and destructive commitment to the Vietnam conflict. To reverse this policy would therefore have been intelligent. But the Americans changed their minds about the war largely because they misunderstood the Tet Offensive. They then decided that reversing a wrong decision justified abandoning the millions of South Vietnamese who had assumed a public anti-Communist stance, not to speak of the hundreds of thousands who had lost their lives. The bill for this cruel desertion remains unpaid. Sir Robert Thompson wrote acidly that "perhaps the major lesson of the Vietnam war is: do not rely on the United States as an ally."[35]

In the decade following the fall of Saigon, some expressed the opinion that the twenty-year struggle to save South Vietnam had not been in vain, because it gave the states of Southeast Asia a clear view of what Communism really was and the time to take internal measures against it. In effect, by delaying the fall of the dominoes, the war permanently prevented it. Whatever the merits of this view, it is probably of little comfort to the South Vietnamese people, whose tremendous efforts and sacrifices reaped only abandonment, poverty, emigration, and despair.

But in fact that conflict, so disastrous for the South Vietnamese, did have the most profound effects on the course of world politics, in a way that perhaps no one could have predicted. The Soviet Union of Leonid Brezhnev believed, or at least proclaimed, that the self-inflicted American catastrophe in Vietnam signaled a true shift in "the correlation of forces";[36] that is, the tides of world politics were definitely flowing toward the Communist shore. Soviet self-confidence increased and its foreign policy became more aggressive, from Angola and Libya to Ethiopia and Nicaragua. It seemed to many Washington observers that Soviet military and intelligence advisers were showing up everywhere, accompanied by a Soviet military buildup that appeared ominous.[37] In December 1979, with the invasion of Afghanistan, Soviet ground forces for the first time in the Cold War crossed a border outside the recognized Soviet bloc.

This unprecedented Soviet forward policy produced at least two fateful consequences. First, the Soviet Union's intercontinental activism required it to commit not only prestige but also resources. The CIA estimated that between 1981 and 1986 Soviet support to its clients in Afghanistan, Angola, and Nicaragua alone cost $13 billion, with another $6 billion a year just for Cuba.[38] This turned out to be far more than the Soviet Union could afford. There was a second consequence of all this highly visible (and in Afghanistan, resoundingly unsuccessful) Soviet military expansionism. Coming as it did on the heels of the debacle in South Vietnam and the U.S. national humiliation in Iran, it helped turn political opinion in the United States in favor of greatly increased spending on defense and intelligence.[39] The build-up began in the last year of the Carter Administration. It culminated in the Reagan Administration's strategy of cracking the power of the USSR through overwhelming technological challenges, a strategy massively assisted by the profound moral defiance of the Polish Communist regime on the part of a Polish people inspired by John Paul II, a combination of pressures that was unexpectedly and spectacularly effective.

Thus, history presents us one of its most staggering ironies: we can trace clear linkages between the fall of the South Vietnamese Republic and the implosion of the Soviet Empire.

NOTES

1. On the unrepresentative nature of the Viet Minh in 1945, see Dennis J. Duncanson, *Government and Revolution in Vietnam* (New York: Oxford University Press, 1968), p. 161; Peter M. Dunn, *The First Vietnam War* (New York: St. Martin's, 1985), p. 23; John T. McAlister, *Vietnam: The Origins of Revolution* (Garden City, NY: Doubleday Anchor, 1971), p. 128; William Duiker, *The Communist Road to Power in Vietnam* (Boulder, CO: Westview, 1981), p. 118.

2. Marguerite Higgins, *Our Vietnam Nightmare* (New York: Harper and Row, 1965), p. 132.

3. Anne Blair, *Lodge in Vietnam* (New Haven, CT: Yale University Press, 1995), p 158.

4. Timothy Lomperis, *The War Everyone Lost—and Won: America's Intervention in Vietnam's Twin Struggles* (Baton Rouge, LA: Louisiana State University Press, 1984), p. 162.

5. See The Military History Institute of Vietnam, *Victory in Vietnam: The Official History of the People's Army of Vietnam, 1954–1975*, trans. Merle L. Pribbenow (Lawrence, KS: University Press of Kansas, 2002).

6. Bruce Palmer, Jr., *The Twenty-Five-Year War: America's Military Role in Vietnam* (Lexington, KY: University Press of Kentucky, 1984), p. 183; Bui Tin, *From Enemy to Friend: A North Vietnamese Perspective on the War* (Annapolis, MD: Naval Institute Press, 2002), pp. 82–86. "The natural mobility of sea power facilitates deception for operational surprise . . . because of the multiplicity of routes that ships, but not armies, can take"; Colin S. Gray, *The Leverage of Sea Power: The Strategic Advantage of Navies in War* (New York: Free Press, 1992), p. 287.

7. Lewis Sorley, *A Better War: The Unexamined Victories and Final Tragedy of America's Last Years in Vietnam* (New York: Harcourt Brace, 1999), pp. 323–324.

8. Sorley, *A Better War*, pp. 323–324.

9. The Democrats lost five of the six presidential elections following the Tet Offensive.

10. Lewis Sorley, *Reassessing Vietnam* (Lubbock, TX: Texas Tech University, 2006), p. 2.

11. Ira A. Hunt, Jr., *Losing Vietnam: How America Abandoned Southeast Asia* (Lexington, KY: University Press of Kentucky, 2013), p. 167.

12. Toby Haynesworth and J. Edward Lee, eds., *White Christmas in April: The Collapse of South Vietnam, 1975* (New York: Peter Lang Publishing, 2000), p. 67.

13. Martin Windrow, *The Last Valley: Dien Bien Phu and the French Defeat in Vietnam* (Cambridge, MA: Da Capo, 2004), p. 188.

14. John T. McAlister, *Vietnam: The Origins of Revolution* (Garden City, NY: Doubleday Anchor, 1971), p. 281.

15. Sorley, *Reassessing Vietnam*, p. 30; see Hammer, *Death in November*, p. 96.

16. Arthur Dommen, *The Indochinese Experience of the French and the Americans* (Bloomington, IN: Indiana University Press, 2001), p. 85.

17. *Peace Is Not at Hand* (New York: McKay, 1974), p. 9. Thompson relentlessly hammers this point: "The great majority of the people of South Vietnam fought first against the Vietcong and then against the North Vietnamese Army" and "the GVN was supported in its war aims by over 90 percent of the population and the communists by less than 10 percent." *Peace Is Not at Hand*, p. 17, p. 127.

18. Malcolm Salmon, "After Revolution, Evolution," *Far Eastern Economic Review*, December 12, 1975, pp. 32–34.

19. See W. Courtland Robinson, *Terms of Refuge: The Indochinese Exodus and the International Response* (London: Zed, 1998). "Nothing has dramatized the revulsion against poverty and repression more vividly that the massive exodus from Vietnam—one of the largest migrations in modern times. Nearly a million people have risked their lives to escape from the country, most by sea"; Stanley Karnow, *Vietnam: A History* (New York: Viking, 1983), p. 34.

20. Dommen, *Indochinese Experience*, p. 974.

21. Jacqueline Desbarats and Karl Jackson, "Vietnam 1975–1982: The Cruel Peace," *Washington Quarterly*, vol. 8, no 5 (1985). Sorley says 250,000 died in the camps; *A Better War*, p. 458, n. 24. After their victory "the Communists proceeded to shunt four hundred thousand South Vietnamese civil servants and army officers as well as doctors, lawyers, teachers, journalists, and other intellectuals into 'reeducation' centers—and the concentration camps still [1981] hold between fifty and a hundred thousand people"; Karnow, *Vietnam*, p. 29.

22. Quoted in Sorley, *Better War*, p. 457, n. 21.

23. Robert Thompson, *Make for the Hills: Memories of Far Eastern Wars* (London: Leo Cooper, 1989), p. 173.

24. Arnold R. Isaacs, *Without Honor: Defeat in Vietnam and Cambodia* (Baltimore, MD: Johns Hopkins University Press, 1983), p. 487. Isaacs continues: "The Vietnamese Communists were not gentle or humanitarian. They were the makers of a totalitarian system who had inflicted great violence in the implacable pursuit of their goals." "To such men and women as the Vietnamese Communists, 'Liberation' might mean several things—but never freedom of the individual human consciousness to doubt, question, dissent, argue, or search for a private path to truth . . . to their ungentle hands, Vietnam's future was now committed"; *Without Honor*, pp. 13 and 487.

25. Nguyen Cong Luan, *Nationalist in the Vietnam Wars* (Bloomington, IN: Indiana University Press, 2012), p. 460.

26. Karnow, *Vietnam*, pp. 31 and 127.

27. *Vietnam Magazine*, August 1990, p. 6. "The party of which I was so proud and in which I put so much trust had turned out to be a stranger, a machine producing weird, stupid and uninformed policies"; Bui Tin, *From Enemy to Friend: A North Vietnamese Perspective on the War* (Annapolis, MD: Naval Institute Press, 2002), p. 120.

28. Henry Kissinger, *Years of Renewal* (New York: Simon and Schuster, 1999), p. 546.

29. See Jacqueline Desbarats and Karl D. Jackson, "Vietnam 1975–1982: The Cruel Peace," *Washington Quarterly*, vol. 8, no. 4 (Fall 1985), and Jacqueline Desbarats, "Repression in the Socialist Republic of Vietnam: Executions and Population Relocation," in *The Vietnam Debate*, ed. John Norton Moore (Lanham, MD: University Press of America, 1990).

30. Robert D. Kaplan, *Warrior Politics: Why Leadership Demands a Pagan Ethos* (New York: Random House, 2002), p. 129.

31. "Vietnam: A Television History," episode 7, "Tet: 1968," produced by WGBH, 1983.

32. Dommen, *Indochinese Experience*, p. 970.

33. Douglas Pike wrote that "the Vietnamese Communists conceived, developed and fielded a dimensional new method for making war: that in forty years they honed this method into a brilliantly innovative strategy that proved singularly successful against three of the world's great powers; and most important, that it is a strategy *for which there is no known proven counterstrategy.*" *PAVN* (Novato, CA: Presidio, 1986), p. 213 (italics in orial).

34. Thompson, *Make for the Hills*, p. 206.

35. Thompson, *Peace Is Not at Hand*, p. 200.

36. Martin Malia, *The Soviet Tragedy* (New York: Free Press, 1994), pp. 374ff. "The degree to which this perception predominated was so great that it is difficult to communicate to a generation that never experienced it"; Timothy Lomperis, *From People's War to People's Rule: Insurgency, Intervention and the Lessons of Vietnam* (Chapel Hill, NC: University of North Carolina Press, 1996), p. 315. In particular, the Vietnamese Communists were supposed by some experts to have perfected a strategy "for which *there is no known proven counterstrategy*"; Douglas Pike, *PAVN*, p. 213, italics in original.

37. Robert M. Gates, *From the Shadows: The Ultimate Insider's Story of Five Presidents and How They Won the Cold War* (New York: Simon and Schuster, 1996), p. 174.

38. Gates, *From the Shadows,* p. 427.

39. Gates, *From the Shadows*, pp. 175ff.

Appendix

Could South Vietnam Have Endured?

If, as we have repeatedly demonstrated in this volume, so many millions—the great majority—of South Vietnamese did not wish to be conquered by the North, why did the state of South Vietnam collapse so quickly and unexpectedly in the spring of 1975? The answer, of course, is that a war is not an election: South Vietnam fell not because of the wishes of its population but because just as the war had clearly become a conventional conflict, the type of war that Americans are excellent at fighting or supporting, the U.S. Congress embarked upon a program of mercilessly slashing vital military assistance to the South Vietnamese (actually small sums in comparison to the many billions the U.S. would lavish upon Israel and Egypt, among others). In light of those congressional actions—in light of the fact that ARVN no longer had the ammunition and gasoline to hold its positions in northern and central South Vietnam—the South Vietnamese leadership decided to retrench its forces into Military Regions III and IV. This was a very good idea in itself, but because of its timing and hastiness the retrenchment ended in total disaster.

The cutting of assistance to South Vietnam was rooted in a perception in the U.S. Congress and the media that the war was interminable. This perception is hard to understand: actually, large numbers of Americans had been in Vietnam only between 1965 and 1970, and most of those were in non-combat units. From the fall of 1972, the South Vietnamese were fighting on their own. Thus the actions of Congress were not about "bringing our boys home" but about reducing the South Vietnamese armed forces to helplessness.

The American decision to abandon South Vietnam is closely related to the profoundly flawed strategy which American forces had been pursuing

after 1965. For South Vietnam to have survived would have required a radically different system of defense. This chapter outlines such a system.

WHAT WAS THE MAIN PROBLEM?

Countless authors have quoted, with good reason, the following statement by
the famous Prussian military philosopher Carl von Clausewitz (1780–1831):
"The first, the most far-reaching act of judgment that the statesman and
commander have to make is to establish the kind of war on which they are
embarking; neither mistaking it for, nor trying to turn it into, something that
is alien to its nature."[1] U.S. policies in Vietnam, from 1961 to 1975, embodied the complete negation of this sage advice.

As this book is written, very few if any still deny that the source of the
war in South Vietnam, in terms of inspiration, direction, organization, and
supply (of both materiel and personnel), lay in Hanoi. To end Hanoi's propa-
gation of the war would not have required the total defeat of North Vietnam;
it is close to a certainty that multipoint amphibious assaults on North Vietnam by American and South Vietnamese forces would have quickly convinced the Northern Politburo to enter into serious peace negotiations. But
President Johnson and his advisers rejected any option of that kind, primarily
because of fear of Chinese intervention. This fear, while known today to
have been unfounded, was not unreasonable: between 1965 and 1968 over
three hundred thousand Chinese military personnel went to North Vietnam in
engineering and antiaircraft units. The peak year was 1967, when 170,000
Chinese troops were present there, most of them antiaircraft personnel.[2]

Another sound plan to defend South Vietnam would have been to go into
Laos and block the Ho Chi Minh Trail (eventually a highway down which
poured a torrent of men and materiel) and, ideally, to occupy a bridgehead in
southern North Vietnam (Quang Binh province). But the Johnson Administration most unwisely rejected this type of forward defense strategy, mainly
because of domestic political calculations, and therein lay the genesis of the
eventual collapse of South Vietnam (and of the Johnson Administration as
well). This fundamental decision against a forward defense forced the
Americans and their allies to assume the strategic defensive—letting the
enemy invade South Vietnam. In that situation, the American commander in
South Vietnam, General William Westmoreland, chose to employ the tactical
offensive—vigorously pursuing that enemy on the ground inside South Vietnam. Combining the strategic defensive and the tactical offensive was arguably the worst possible American choice. From this combination emerged the
so-called "attrition strategy"—killing more enemy personnel than could be
replaced—and the "body count" phenomenon, probably the biggest public-
relations debacle in U.S. history. Attrition ignored the essence of sound

counterguerrilla warfare by concentrating on locating and destroying main-force Viet Cong and North Vietnamese units instead of protecting the civilian population. Moreover, because the Communist side usually controlled both the timing and the scale of combat, and because North Vietnam was able to send great numbers of troops into the South and was willing to impose enormous casualties on its own population, the attrition strategy had very slim chances of succeeding before the impact of uncensored media coverage began to disturb the American people at home. (Nevertheless, attrition was working: the huge casualties suffered by the Communist side account for the fatal switch by the Viet Cong from classic guerrilla tactics to conventional operations—the Tet Offensive of 1968.) At the same time, a huge American army went through South Vietnam on one-year tours of duty, so that by the time a soldier learned anything about Vietnam he was sent home (officers often served only six-month tours). This American approach to counterinsurgency killed friendly civilians, devastated the environment, multiplied U.S. casualties, and upset the American electorate by providing a bonanza to sensationalist U.S. media.[3]

ALTERNATIVE CONCEPTS

Workable alternatives to and insightful critiques of the Johnson Administration's military policies were available but largely ignored.

For years before 1969, the Marines, drawing upon their long experience with insurgency gained in Central America and the Caribbean, had developed their own counterinsurgency program, the Combined Action Platoons (CAPs), "the most imaginative strategy to emerge from the Vietnam conflict."[4] This approach emphasized civilian security—cutting off the access of the guerrillas to the civilians in the villages. A typical CAP would permanently assign a Marine rifle squad of 14 men, all volunteers, to a particular village, where it trained a local militia platoon of 38 men. By 1970 114 CAPs were operating, all of them in the exceedingly dangerous MR I, immediately south of the North Vietnamese border. At its height the program counted 2100 Marines (plus 126 Navy hospital corpsmen). Very few villages protected by a CAP were overrun by Communist forces. General Westmoreland did not like the CAPs. He devoted exactly one paragraph in his memoirs to the program, stating that he did not have enough troops "to put a squad of Americans in every village and hamlet."[5] It is not clear why the General made that statement. To place a rifle squad of Marines in, for example, two thousand villages would have required 28,000 men, about 5 percent of total American military personnel in Vietnam in 1968.

Additionally, in July 1965 the Army Chief of Staff commissioned a study that was completed by March 1966: a nine-hundred page document titled *A*

Program for the Pacification and Long-Term Development of South Vietnam (PROVN for short).[6] Studying the history and culture of Vietnam and interviewing numerous U.S. army officers about their experiences in that country, PROVN's officer-authors concluded that "without question, village and hamlet[7] security must be achieved throughout Vietnam" by means of "effective area saturation tactics in and around populated areas." PROVN correctly identified the cutting of the all-important Ho Chi Minh Trail as a key requirement. It also urged unification of American programs and personnel in South Vietnam under the U.S. ambassador, and direct American involvement with key South Vietnamese government functions. In part because it criticized attrition and the search-and-destroy tactics underlying it, PROVN received a cool reception from General Westmoreland.[8] Little was done to implement its recommendations until 1969, when General Creighton Abrams took over command in South Vietnam. Abrams well understood the essentials of counterinsurgency, but by 1969 the Americans had already begun a massive pull-out from South Vietnam, ironically at the very time when the conflict there had become largely a conventional one.

Neither the PROVN study recommendations nor (especially) the CAPs program ought to be considered as panaceas, but they did show that there was widespread understanding of the weaknesses of administration policy in Vietnam. The need for a different strategy was obvious to many.

The clear-and-hold operations that worked so well in Malaya would be essential to any successful strategy to save South Vietnam. As set forth by Sir Robert Thompson, the principal exponent of this approach,[9] clear-and-hold, means driving the guerrillas out of first one designated particular area and then another, by systematically inundating that area with troops, police, and auxiliaries. Both CAPs and PROVN incorporated this essential concept.

In South Vietnam, however, clear-and-hold operations in themselves would not have been sufficient for victory, because the guerrillas were only one aspect of the conflict; the other was the slow-motion invasion of South Vietnam by North Vietnamese military units by way of Laos (an invasion that became super-fast-motion in 1972 and 1975). That was why numerous analysts made a convincing case, both during and after the conflict, that cutting the Ho Chi Minh Trail running through Laos was the key to stopping the invasion[10] of South Vietnam. In such an operation U.S. and ARVN forces would have deployed on a roughly east-west axis across Laos from South Vietnam to the Thai border, about one hundred miles, roughly the distance between New York City and Philadelphia.[11]

A realistic and realizable strategy to save South Vietnam, therefore, would have been rooted in clear thinking about that country's geography, and specifically, about how the allies could deal with the Northern troops and supplies coming through Laos, without going into Laos themselves, although a defense line across Laos would certainly have been the optimal choice.[12]

Ideally, such a strategy would have been one that made the Ho Chi Minh Trail irrelevant, while at the same time optimizing U.S. strengths, minimizing damage to Vietnamese society, sealing off the civilian population from North Vietnamese and Viet Cong forces, placing the principal responsibility for dealing with guerrillas on the South Vietnamese forces, and calming congressional apprehensions about a "wider war;" Above all, a viable strategy would have both reduced U.S. casualties and made unnecessary the 1975 decision of the South Vietnamese Army to retrench into the provinces of the deep south, the decision that brought about the fall of South Vietnam. Was it possible to construct a strategic approach that would produce all, or at least most, of these effects?

GEOGRAPHY AS DESTINY

Napoleon observed that to know a country's geography was to know its foreign policy. In the case of South Vietnam, to understand its geography is to understand its fate.

The Communist insurgency in the Philippine Republic (1946–1953) had failed largely because that country is an archipelago; thus the insurgents were effectively cut off from supplies and reinforcements. South Korea had successfully escaped Communist conquest (1950–1953) in large part because it is a peninsula; thus most of the fighting there took place along a limited and well-defined front line. In another peninsula, British forces successfully and fatally isolated Malaya's post–World War II Communist insurgents from outside assistance. But South Vietnam was neither an archipelago nor a peninsula. Too big, too poorly configured, and too exposed to invasion to be defended in its entirety, South Vietnam's geography would prove to be its doom. A successful defense of South Vietnam, therefore, depended on acknowledging the primacy of geographical reality: since one could not *isolate* that country, the answer would have been to *reconfigure* the country. That is, a realistic strategy would be based on defining which areas of South Vietnam were essential to be held, and which were not. This would not have been a difficult task. The great majority of the South Vietnamese population was concentrated in Greater Saigon and the Mekong Delta (Military Regions III and IV), plus a few urban enclaves along the central coast. The northern boundary of Military Region III—roughly 12 degrees north latitude—clearly marked the demographic frontier between the areas of heavy population and the rest. (Please consult the map of South Vietnam at the beginning of this book.)

As we have argued, establishing a line across Laos to block the Ho Chi Minh Trail would almost certainly have been the most effective U.S. choice for holding South Vietnam, but the Johnson Administration ruled out such a move. Therefore the defense of the demographic frontier, plus some coastal enclaves, becomes the next best option, and is the heart of the strategy proposed here. Allied forces would have withdrawn from the northern and central provinces of South Vietnam, with some well-trained South Vietnamese guerrilla units remaining behind in the highlands. The ancient capital city of Hue had tremendous historical importance to all Vietnamese. Allied forces would therefore need to hold it as an enclave, along with Da Nang, supported by the U.S. Navy. Each place would clearly serve as a potential launching area for amphibious flanking attacks on the coast of North Vietnam: Da Nang would be in effect a South Vietnamese Inchon (except that U.S. forces would already be there). The refugees who would flood into those coastal cities could be sea-lifted south. [13]

U.S. forces, much reduced in numbers, and some ARVN, would deploy along the demographic frontier and along the border between Military Region III and Cambodia—a total of about 375 miles, the length of the northern border of the State of Colorado. (The Morice Line which the French constructed between Algeria and Tunisia in the 1950s was much longer. [14]) Mobile reserves would support this deployment. With allied troops guarding the demographic frontier, ARVN and the Territorials would deal with what Viet Cong elements remained active behind (i.e., south of) that frontier. CAPs would defend highly exposed districts. [15] With far fewer U.S. troops in country, the South Vietnamese forces could receive weapons equal in quality to those of the Communists much earlier than they actually did. Military Regions III and IV (historic Cochin China), plus the coastal enclaves, would together comprise a viable state, containing a population larger than Australia's in an area twice the size of Switzerland. Ranging over this territory would be the unchallengeable might of allied air power.

Establishing and defending the demographic frontier would have additional major benefits for the allies. For one, the number of U.S. forces in Vietnam, and their casualty rates, could be greatly reduced: instead of a part-conscript army of more than half a million, American forces in Vietnam would be far fewer, more professional, perhaps completely volunteer—the end of the disastrous one-year tour policy. Employing conventional, conservative tactics, those forces would incur far fewer losses: no more hunting the enemy all over the country, no more "search and destroy," no more body counts, no more booby trap casualties. The war in South Vietnam would now have true front lines. With the enemy on one side and civilians on the other, American firepower could have free play. With the allies retrenched into Military Regions III and IV and the coastal enclaves, the Ho Chi Minh Trail would become irrelevant, and the bombing of North Vietnam unnecessary. Confronted by a true front line, Hanoi would have two choices: either to accept this de facto new partition and abandon the struggle, or else to mount massive assaults in the teeth of overwhelming allied fire superiority from the land, sea, and air; that would be attrition indeed.

And still more advantages: by creating an authentic rear area, with allied firepower directed toward the enemy and away from civilians, the demographic frontier strategy would have made possible thorough clear-and-hold operations in the regions of dense population, and created a stable setting for serious social and economic improvements in the lives of the South Vietnamese.

SOME OBJECTIONS

But, critics may observe, wouldn't a demographic strategy, because it is essentially defensive, concede the all-important initiative to the enemy? In an immediate sense, the answer is yes, it would. But the lessons of classical strategic theory and a consideration of the actual combat conditions faced by the allies in South Vietnam both cast revealing lights on this objection.

First, in *The Art of War*, Sun Tzu wrote that "invincibility lies in the defense."[16] Clausewitz pointed out that "the defensive form of warfare is intrinsically stronger than the offensive" and "it is easier to hold ground than to take it."[17] During the American Civil War, General Robert E. Lee achieved perhaps his greatest victory at Fredericksburg, where he was on the defensive. It would be quite to the advantage of the allies if the North Vietnamese chose to assault the defenses of the demographic frontier. First, they would be mounting attacks against the devastating firepower of entrenched American positions. Second, they would be offering themselves as textbook targets not only to American B-52s, the weapon they hated and feared above all others, but also to massive bombardment by the U.S. Navy, notably including the sixteen-inch guns of the USS *New Jersey*. That would have shown Sun Tzu's "invincibility of the defense" in the most drastic terms.

But the most important observation against the "defensive posture abandons the initiative" position is this one: American forces under the command of General Westmoreland, no matter what he thought, *were on the defensive anyway, both strategically and tactically*. The allies, by concentrating their efforts in northern and central South Vietnam, were permanently outflanked by the Ho Chi Minh Trail: on the whole, the enemy chose the time and place and scale and intensity of the fighting, all this at the cost of greatly inflated allied casualties.[18] How to reduce or eliminate the effects of the Trail was the real question. The demographic strategy option would have allowed the allies, not the enemy, to choose the locus of battle, because exits from the Ho Chi Minh Trail used by the enemy would have been north of the frontier.

Other critics, while agreeing in general with this assessment, might find fault with the plan's call for giving up territory in Military Regions I and II.

The Americans did not send a great military force to South Vietnam in order to hand over big chunks of that state's territory to the enemy. But exchanging land for time is a well-known stratagem that has often been highly successful in diverse circumstances. Lee defended Virginia, not distant and sparsely populated Texas. The Russians retreated in face of the onslaughts of Napoleon and Hitler, and emerged victorious in both instances; so did the Chinese who retreated before the Japanese. Consider also that a fundamental operational principal of the well-known method for dealing with guerrillas called clearing-and-holding is to concentrate first on establishing solid control of one's base areas, even if that entails letting the guerrillas operate freely in outlying areas, for the time being. Clearly, a strategic regroupment need not be the equivalent of a political concession.

In addition, we need to recall that in 1954 Washington had acquiesced in giving up control of the northern half of Vietnam to the Communists, against the vehement protests of the U.S.-recognized government of Bao Dai, which claimed—with unassailable justification—to be the de jure legitimate rulers of *all* of Vietnam. It had been an agreement between the French army and the Viet Minh that established the borders of what became known as South Vietnam; no moral or legal or military obligation required either South Vietnam or the U.S. to defend every inch of the territory within those artificial (and indefensible) borders, especially those areas closest to North Vietnam and outflanked by the Ho Chi Minh Trail.

THE DECISIVE CONSIDERATION

Arguably the most decisive benefit of the demographic strategy is this: we have seen that the ARVN attempt to retrench to the south in 1975 brought about the final catastrophe (chapter 8); but if ARVN had been entrenched along the demographic frontier in 1967 or 1969 or even 1972, that catastrophe would never—could never—have occurred.

For years ARVN had pursued a very inadvisable policy of stationing its soldiers far from their home areas and allowing their families to follow them. That was the key to the final debacle. In January 1975 most of ARVN was in the sparsely populated Central Highlands, and in the dangerously exposed Military Region I right below the 17th parallel. President Thieu's realization that the bulk of South Vietnamese forces needed to be withdrawn into the south was sound, and indeed should have been carried out years earlier. But the 1975 retrenchment turned into a disaster for two main reasons. One was completely inadequate planning, a South Vietnamese cultural failing. The other, much more important, was the presence of the families of ARVN troops in the areas to be left behind. That ARVN soldiers wished to prevent their families from falling into Communist hands is perfectly understandable.

But their attempts to achieve that end by leaving their units and gathering up their families resulted in the disintegration of much of ARVN and hence the collapse of the South. Basil Liddell Hart observed: "So long as their families are safe, [men] will defend their country, believing that by their sacrifice they are safeguarding their families also. But even the bonds of patriotism, discipline and comradeship are loosened when the family itself is menaced."[19]

But with the demographic strategy in place, the soldiers' families would stay put in their true homes—MR III and MR IV—with ARVN deployed to defend them. If before 1975 ARVN units had redeployed farther south, in an orderly manner, with their families on one side of them and the Communists on the other, retreat, desertion, or surrender would have become hardly thinkable. Consider the 18th ARVN Division. Nobody had ever imagined that it was much of a fighting unit, but in the last days of the war, after its dependents had been evacuated southward, the 18th put up a defense of the city of Xuan Loc that was truly exemplary. (Please see the discussion of desertion in ARVN in chapter 4.)

SUMMARY OF THE ARGUMENT

The United States had several options for defending South Vietnam. The first option, the Strategic Offensive and the Tactical Offensive—invading North Vietnam—would have been costly in terms of casualties on the ground, controversial at home, and unnecessary to save South Vietnam.

The second option, the Strategic Offensive and the Tactical Defensive— blocking the Ho Chi Minh Trail by establishing and holding a defensive line across Laos—would have been the best choice to ensure a viable South Vietnam, but the Administration believed it would be too expensive in domestic political terms.

The third option, the Strategic Defensive and the Tactical Offensive— allowing the enemy freely to invade South Vietnam and then pursuing him across unfamiliar terrain selected by him—was the policy of the Johnson Administration, and ended in complete disaster, even though that policy had in fact defeated the guerrilla insurgency itself.

The fourth option, the Strategic Defensive and the Tactical Defensive— retrenching to the southern demographic frontier—is the one advocated here. While admittedly only the second-best option, it would nonetheless most likely have preserved, at a quite limited cost, a viable South Vietnamese state, much like the South Korean state the U.S. has been helping to defend for close to seven decades.

NOTES

1. Carl von Clausewitz, *On War*, ed. and trans. by Michael Howard and Peter Paret (Princeton, NJ: Princeton University Press, 1976), Book One, chapter 1, p. 88.

2. Chen Jian, "China's Involvement in the Vietnam War, 1964–1969," *China Quarterly*, no. 142 (June 1995), p. 378; Allen S. Whiting, *The Chinese Calculus of Deterrence: India and Vietnam* (Ann Arbor, MI: University of Michigan Press, 1975); Xiaobing Li, *A History of the Modern Chinese Army* (Lexington, KY: University Press of Kentucky, 2007), p. 217.

3. General Westmoreland is not without his spirited and informed defenders. See, for example, Dale Andrade, "Westmoreland was Right: Learning the Wrong Lessons from the Vietnam War." *Small Wars and Insurgencies*, vol. 19, no. 2 (June, 2008). See also Gregory A. Daddis, *Westmoreland's War: Reassessing American Strategy in Vietnam* (New York: Oxford University Press, 2014). For a scathing evaluation of Westmoreland, see Lewis Sorley, *Westmoreland: The General Who Lost Vietnam* (Boston: Houghton Mifflin Harcourt, 2011).

4. Al Hemingway, *Our War Was Different: Marine Combined Action Platoons in Vietnam* (Annapolis, MD: Naval Institute Press, 1994), p. 178.

5. William C. Westmoreland, *A Soldier Reports* (New York: Da Capo, 1989), p. 166.

6. Washington, DC, Department of the Army, March 1962.

7. A hamlet is a subdivision of a village.

8. General Westmoreland does not even mention PROVN in his memoirs. But General Victor Krulak, commander of Fleet Marine Force, Pacific, and Robert Komer, in charge of U.S. pacification efforts, liked PROVN a great deal. See Lewis Sorley, "To Change a War: General Harold K. Johnson and the PROVN Study," *Parameters*, vol. 28 (Spring 1998); see also *The Pentagon Papers*, vol. IV, pp. 369, 371, 374, 376.

9. Sir Robert Thompson, *Defeating Communist Insurgency: The Lessons of Malaya and Vietnam* (New York: Praeger, 1966); *No Exit From Vietnam* (New York: David McKay, 1969); *Peace is Not at Hand* (New York: David McKay, 1974).

10. Invasion is the proper word. If all the North Vietnamese who came down the Ho Chi Minh Trail over a period of years had entered South Vietnam all together in a two-week period, it would have looked like the North Korean invasion of 1950.

11. Norman B. Hannah, *The Key to Failure: Laos and the Vietnam War* (Lanham, MD: Madison Books, 1987); Harry Summers, *On Strategy: A Critical Analysis of the Vietnam War* (Novato, CA: Presidio, 1982); Sir Robert Thompson, "Regular Armies and Counterinsurgency," in Ronald Haycock, ed., *Regular Armies and Insurgency* (London: Croom, Helm 1979).

12. And what if the North Vietnamese had committed the cardinal error of trying to outflank the blockage of the Ho Chi Minh Trail by invading Thailand? So much the better!

13. General Thi would not agree with this idea: he thought that enclaves in MR 1 would tie up ARVN troops necessary to defend a truncated SVN, and could easily be bypassed by the enemy. Lam Quang Thi, *Twenty-Five-Year Century*, p. 366.

14. During the insurgency in Algeria (1954–1962), the French determined to limit to the greatest possible degree outside help to the Algerian guerrillas, especially from neighboring Tunisia. To that end the French constructed the famous Morice Line, extending for hundreds of miles along the Tunisian border. The Line consisted of an electrified wire barrier with minefields on both sides and watchtowers at regular intervals. On the Algerian side the French built a constantly patrolled road protected by barbed wire. The whole system involved eighty thousand troops. Attempts to break through the electrified fence set off signals at monitoring stations, to which the French responded almost immediately with artillery, aircraft, and mobile ground units. Early efforts to break through the Line cost the guerrillas so many casualties that serious attempts to infiltrate from Tunisia came to an end.

15. For the CAPs, see F. West, *The Village* (New York: Harper and Row, 1972), and *Small Unit Action in Vietnam* (Quantico, VA: U.S. Marine Corps, 1967); and Stuart A. Herrington, *Silence Was a Weapon: The Vietnam War in the Villages* (Novato, CA: Presidio, 1982).

16. Sun Tzu, *The Art of War*, Trans. Samuel B. Griffith, foreword by Basil Liddell Hart, (New York: Oxford University Press, 1963), p. 85.

17. Clausewitz, *On War*, Book VI, chapter 1.

18. See the geographical distribution of U.S. casualties in Thomas C. Thayer, *War without Fronts: The American Experience in Vietnam* (Boulder, CO: Westview, 1985).

19. Basil Liddell Hart, *Strategy* (London: Faber and Faber, 1967), p. 153.

Bibliography

Ahern, Thomas L., Jr. *CIA and the House of Ngo: Covert Action in South Vietnam, 1954–1963.* Washington, D.C.: Center for the Study of Intelligence, 2000.

Anderson, David L. *Trapped by Success: The Eisenhower Administration and Vietnam, 1953–1961.* New York: Columbia University Press, 1991.

Andrade, Dale. *America's Last Vietnam Battle: Halting Hanoi's 1972 Easter Offensive.* Lawrence, KS: University Press of Kansas, 2001.

———. "Westmoreland was Right: Learning the Wrong Lessons from the Vietnam War." *Small Wars and Insurgencies*, vol. 19, no. 2 (June 2008).

Andrews, William R. *The Village War: Vietnamese Communist Revolutionary Activities in Dinh Tuong Province, 1960–1964.* Columbia, MO: University of Missouri Press, 1973.

Bao Dai. *Le Dragon d'Annam.* Paris: Plon, 1980.

Bartholomew-Feis, Dixie. *The OSS and Ho Chi Minh: Unexpected Allies in the War against Japan.* Lawrence. KS: University Press of Kansas, 2006.

Bass, Thomas A. *The Spy Who Loved Us: The Vietnam War and Pham Xuan An's Dangerous Game.* New York: Public Affairs, 2009.

Bator, Victor. *Vietnam: A Diplomatic Tragedy: The Origins of U.S. Involvement.* London: Faber and Faber, 1965.

Bergerud, Eric M. *The Dynamics of Defeat: The Vietnam War in Hau Nghia Province.* Boulder, CO: Westview, 1991.

Bergot, Erwan. *La bataille de Dong Khe: La tragédie de la R.C. 4 :Indochine 1950.* Paris: Presses de la Cite, 1987.

Berman, Larry. *No Peace, No Honor: Nixon, Kissinger and Betrayal in Vietnam.* New York: Free Press, 2001.

Bigeard, Marcel-Maurice. *Ma guerre d'Indochine.* Paris: Hachette, 1994.

Billings-Young, Melanie. *Decision against War: Eisenhower and Dien Bien Phu, 1954.* New York: Columbia University Press, 1980.

Blair, Anne. *Lodge in Vietnam: A Patriot Abroad.* New Haven, CT: Yale University Press, 1995.

Blaufarb, Douglas S. *The Counterinsurgency Era: U.S. Doctrine and Performance.* New York: Free Press, 1977.

Bodard, Lucien. *The Quicksand War: Prelude to Vietnam.* Boston, MA: Little, Brown, 1967.

Bodin, Michel. *La France et ses soldats: Indochine, 1945–1954.* Paris: L'Harmattan, 1996.

Bodinier, Gilbert, ed. *La Guerre d'Indochine, 1945–1954: Le retour de la France en Indochine. Textes et documents.* Vincennes: Service historique de l'Armée de Terre, 1987.

Boyer de La Tour, Pierre. *Le martyre de l'armée française: De l'Indochine à l'Algérie.* Presses du Mail, 1962.

Braestrup, Peter. *Big Story*. Boulder, CO: Westview, 1977.

Brigham. Robert K. *ARVN: Life and Death in the South Vietnamese Army*. Lawrence, KS: University Press of Kansas, 2006.

Brocheux, Pierre. *Ho Chi Minh: A Biography*. New York: Cambridge University Press, 2007.

Bui Diem, *In the Jaws of History*. Boston: Houghton Mifflin, 1987.

Bui Tin. *Following Ho Chi Minh: Memoirs of a North Vietnamese Colonel*. Honolulu: University of Hawaii Press, 1995.

————. *From Enemy to Friend: A North Vietnamese Perspective on the War*. Annapolis, MD: Naval Institute Press, 2002.

Bunker, Ellsworth. *The Bunker Papers: Reports to the President from Vietnam, 1967–1973*. Ed. Douglas Pike, 3 vols. Berkeley, CA: University of California Press, 1990.

Butler, David. *The Fall of Saigon*. New York: Simon and Schuster, 1985.

Buttinger, Joseph. *A Dragon Defiant: A Short History of Vietnam*. New York: Praeger, 1972.

————. *Vietnam: A Dragon Embattled*, Vol. 1, *From Colonialism to the Viet Minh*. New York: Praeger, 1967.

————. *Vietnam: A Dragon Embattled*, Vol. 2, *Vietnam at War*. New York: Praeger, 1967.

————. *Vietnam: A Political History*. New York: Praeger, 1968.

Cable, James. *The Geneva Conference of 1954 on Indochina*. New York: St. Martin's, 1986.

Cady, John F. *The Roots of French Imperialism in Eastern Asia*. Ithaca, NY: Cornell University Press, 1954.

Callison, Charles Stuart. *Land-to-the-Tiller in the Mekong Delta: Economic, Social and Political Effects of Land Reform in Four Villages of South Vietnam*. Lanham, MD: University Press of America, 1983.

Cantwell, Thomas R. "The Army of South Vietnam: A Military and Political History, 1955–1975." Doctoral dissertation. Sydney, Australia: University of New South Wales, 1989.

Cao Van Vien and Dong Van Khuyen. *Reflections on the Vietnam War*. Washington, DC: U.S. Army Center of Military History, 1980.

Carles, Pierre. *Des millions de soldats inconnus. La vie de tous les jours dans les armées de la IVeme République*. Paris: Lavauzelle, 1982.

Catton, Philip. *Diem's Final Failure: Prelude to America's War in Vietnam*. Lawrence, KS: University Press of Kansas, 2003.

"Causes, Origins and Lessons of the Vietnam War." Hearings before the Committee on Foreign Relations of the United States Senate. Washington, DC: U.S. Government Printing Office, 1973.

Chaffard, Georges. *Les deux guerres du Vietnam: De Valluy à Westmoreland*. Paris: Table Ronde, 1969.

Chanoff, David, and Doan Van Toai. *Portrait of the Enemy*. New York: Random, 1986.

Chapman, Jessica M. "The Sect Crisis of 1955 and the American Commitment to Ngo Dinh Diem." *Journal of Vietnamese Studies*, vol. 5, no. 1 (Winter 2010).

————. *Cauldron of Resistance: Ngo Dinh Diem, The United States, and 1950s Southern Vietnam*. Ithaca, NY: Cornell University Press, 2013.

Chapuis, Oscar. *The Last Emperors of Vietnam. From Tu Duc to Bao Dai*. Westport, CT: Greenwood, 2000.

Chau, Tran Ngoc. "From Ho Chi Minh to Ngo Dinh Diem," in Harvey C. Neese and John O'Donnell, eds., *Prelude to Tragedy: Vietnam, 1960–1965*. Annapolis, MD: Naval Institute Press, 2001.

Chen Jian. "China and the First Indochina War, 1950–1954." *China Quarterly*, 133 (March 1993).

————. "China's Involvement in the Vietnam War, 1964–1969." *China Quarterly*, no. 142 (June 1995).

Chesneaux, Jean, Georges Boudafrel, and Daniel Hemery. *Tradition et révolution au Vietnam*. Paris: Editions Anthropos, 1971.

Clarke, Jeffrey J. *Advice and Support: The Final Years, 1965–1973*. Washington, DC: U.S. Army Center of Military History, 1988.

Clayton, Anthony. *The Wars of French Decolonization*. London: Longman, 1994.

Bibliography

187

Clodfelter, Michael. *Vietnam in Military Statistics.* Jefferson, NC: McFarland, 1995.

Colby, William. *Lost Victory: A Firsthand Account of America's Sixteen-Year Involvement in Vietnam.* Chicago, IL: Contemporary Books, 1989.

Collins, James Lawton, Jr. *The Development and Training of the South Vietnamese Army, 1950–1972.* Washington, DC: U.S. Army Center of Military History, 1975.

Currey, Cecil B. *Edward Lansdale: The Unquiet American.* Washington, DC: Brassey's, 1988.

Daddis, Gregory A. *Westmoreland's War: Reassessing American Strategy in Vietnam.* New York: Oxford University Press, 2014.

Dalloz, Jacques. *La guerre d'Indochine 1945–1954.* Paris: Editions de Seuil, 1987.

Dang Van Viet. *De la RC4: La campagne des frontières.* Lectoure: Capucin, 2000.

Dansette, Adrien. *Leclerc.* Paris: Flammarion, 1952.

Daughton, J. P. *An Empire Divided: Religion, Republicanism, and the Making of French Colonialism, 1880–1914.* New York: Oxford University Press, 2006.

Davidson, Phillip B. *Vietnam at War: The History, 1946–1975.* Novato, CA: Presidio, 1988.

Davison, W. P., and J. J. Zasloff. *Profile of the Viet Cong Cadres.* Santa Monica, CA: RAND, 1966.

Dawson, Alan. *55 Days: The Fall of South Vietnam.* Englewood Cliffs, NJ: Prentice-Hall, 1977.

Defense Attaché Office. *RVNAF: Final Assessment.* Washington DC: U.S. Government Printing Office, 1975.

De Gaulle, Charles. *The War Memoirs,* Vol. 3, *Salvation.* Tr. Richard Howard. New York: Simon and Schuster, 1960.

Democratic Republic of Vietnam. *Ten Years of Fighting and Building of the Vietnamese People's Army.* Hanoi: Foreign Languages Publishing House, 1955.

———. *Thirty Years of Struggle of the Party.* Hanoi: Foreign Languages Publishing House, 1960.

Department of the Army. *A Program for the Long-Term Pacification and Long-Term Development of South Vietnam.* Washington, DC: Department of the Army, 1966.

Desbarats, Jacqueline. "Repression in the Socialist Republic of Vietnam: Executions and Population Relocation," in *The Vietnam Debate,* ed. John Norton Moore. Lanham, MD: University Press of America, 1990.

Desbarats, Jacqueline, and Karl D. Jackson. "Vietnam 1975–1982: The Cruel Peace." *Washington Quarterly,* vol. 8, no. 4 (Fall 1985).

Devillers, Philippe. *Histoire du Vietnam de 1940 à 1952.* 3rd ed. Paris: Editions du Seuil, 1952.

Dinfreville, Jacques. *L'Opération Indochine.* Editions Internationales, 1953.

Divine, Robert. *Eisenhower and the Cold War.* New York: Oxford University Press, 1981.

Doan Van Tuai and David Chanoff. *The Vietnamese Gulag.* New York: Simon and Schuster, 1985.

Dommen, Arthur. *The Indochinese Experience of the French and the Americans: Nationalism and Communism in Cambodia, Laos and Vietnam.* Bloomington, IN: Indiana University Press, 2001.

Don, Tran Van. *Our Endless War.* San Rafael, CA: Presidio, 1978.

Dong Van Khuyen. *The RVNAF.* Washington, DC: U.S. Army Center of Military History, 1980.

Donnell, J. C. *Viet Cong Recruitment: How and Why Men Join.* Santa Monica, CA: RAND, 1967.

Dougan, Clark, and David Fulghum. *The Vietnamese Experience: The Fall of the South.* Boston: Boston Publishing, 1985.

Duiker, William J. *Ho Chi Minh.* New York: Hyperion, 2000.

———. *The Comintern and Vietnamese Communism.* Athens: Ohio University Center for International Studies, 1975.

———. *The Communist Road to Power in Vietnam.* 2nd ed. Boulder, CO: Westview, 1981.

———. *The Rise of Nationalism in Vietnam, 1920–1941.* Ithaca, NY: Cornell University Press, 1976.

———. *Sacred War: Nationalism and Revolution in a Divided Vietnam.* Boston, MA: McGraw-Hill, 1995.

———. *U.S. Containment Policy and the Conflict in Indochina.* Stanford, CA: Stanford University Press, 1994.

Duncanson, Dennis J. *Government and Revolution in Vietnam.* New York: Oxford University Press, 1968.

Dunn, Peter M. *The First Vietnam War.* New York: St. Martin's, 1985.

Elliott, David W. P. *The Vietnamese War: Revolution and Social Change in the Mekong Delta, 1930–1975.* 2 vols. Armonk, NY: M. E. Sharpe, 2003.

Elsbree, William H. *Japan's Role in Southeast Asian Nationalist Movements, 1940–1945,* Cambridge, MA: Harvard University Press, 1953.

Eisenhower, Dwight D. *Mandate for Change, 1953–1956.* Garden City, NY: Doubleday, 1963.

Ely, Paul. *L'Indochine dans la Tourmente.* Paris: Plon, 1964.

———. *Lessons of the War in Indochina,* vol. 2. Santa Monica, CA: RAND, 1967.

Engelmann, Larry. *Tears Before the Rain: An Oral History of the Fall of South Vietnam.* New York: Oxford University Press, 1990.

Fairbairm, Geoffrey. *Revolutionary Guerrilla Warfare: The Countryside Version.* Harmondsworth, England: Penguin, 1974.

Fall, Bernard. *Hell in a Very Small Place.* Philadelphia, PA: Lippincott, 1967.

———. *Street without Joy.* Harrisburg, PA: Stackpole, 1994.

———. *The Two Vietnams: A Political and Military Analysis,* 2nd ed. revised. New York: Praeger, 1967.

———. *The Viet Minh Regime: Government and Administration in the Democratic Republic of Vietnam.* New York: Institute of Pacific Relations, 1956.

———. "The Political-Religious Sects of Vietnam." *Pacific Affairs* 28 (September 1955).

Fallaci, Oriana. *Nothing, and So Be It.* New York: Doubleday, 1972.

Fanning, Louis. *Betrayal in Vietnam.* New Rochelle, NY: Arlington House, 1976.

Fenn, Charles. *Ho Chi Minh: A Biographical Introduction.* New York: Scribner's, 1973.

Ferrell, Robert H., ed. *The Eisenhower Diaries.* New York: Norton, 1981.

Fishel, Wesley, ed. *Problems of Freedom: South Vietnam since Independence.* New York: Free Press, 1961.

———. *Vietnam: Anatomy of a Conflict.* Itasca, IL: Peacock, 1968.

Ford, Ronnie E. *Tet 1968: Understanding the Surprise.* London: Frank Cass, 1995.

Foreign Relations of the United States, 1952–1954. Vol. 13, *Indochina,* parts 1 and 2. Washington, DC: GPO, 1982.

Foreign Relations of the United States, 1955–1957. Vol. 1, *Vietnam.* Washington, DC: Government Printing Office, 1985.

Foreign Relations of the United States, 1958–1960. Vol. 1, *Vietnam.* Washington, DC: Government Printing Office, 1986.

Foreign Relations of the United States, 1961–1963. Vols. 1–4, *Vietnam.* Washington, DC: Government Printing Office, 1988–1991.

Foreign Relations of the United States, 1952–1954. Vol. 16, *The Geneva Conference.* Washington, DC: Government Printing Office, 1981.

French, David. *The British Way in Counterinsurgency (1945–1967).* Oxford, England: Oxford University Press, 2011.

Gaiduk, Ilya. *The Soviet Union and the Vietnam War.* Chicago: I.R. Dee, 1996.

Gates, Robert M. *From the Shadows: The Ultimate Insider's Story of Five Presidents and How They Won the Cold War.* New York: Simon and Schuster, 1996.

Gelb, Leslie. "Vietnam: The System Worked." *Foreign Policy,* Summer 1971.

Gilbert, Marc Jason, and Willkiam Head, eds. *The Tet Offensive.* New York: Praeger, 1996.

Gillespie, John. "Self-Interest and Ideology: Bureaucratic Corruption in Vietnam." *Australian Journal of Asian Law,* vol. 3 (May 2001).

Goodman, Allan E. *An Institutional Profile of the South Vietnamese Officer Corps.* Santa Monica, CA: RAND, 1970.

Goscha, Christopher E. "'La guerre par d'autres moyens': Réflexions sur la guerre du Viet Minh dans le Sud-Vietnam de 1945 à 1951." *Guerres Mondiales er Conflits Contemporains,* n. 206 (2000).

———. *Vietnam: Un état né de la guerre, 1945–1954.* Paris: Armand Colin, 2011.

Goscha, Christopher E., and Christian F. Ostermann, eds. *Connecting Histories: Decolonization and the Cold War in Southeast Asia, 1945–1962.* Washington, D.C.: Woodrow Wilson Center Press, 2009.

Grandclement, Daniel. *Bao Dai ou les derniers jours de l'empire d'Annam.* Paris: Lattes, 1997.

Gras, Ives. *Histoire de la Guerra d'Indochine.* Paris: Denoel, 1992.

Gray, Colin S. *The Leverage of Sea Power: The Strategic Advantage of Navies in War.* New York: Free Press, 1992.

Greenstein, Fred I., and Richard H. Immerman. "What Did Eisenhower Tell Kennedy about Indochina? The Politics of Misperception." *Journal of American History,* September 1992: 568–587.

Grintner, Lawrence E. "How They Lost: Doctrines, Strategies and Outcomes of the Vietnam War." *Asia Survey,* 15 (December 1975).

Gurtov, Melvin, and Konrad Kellen. *Vietnam: Lessons and Mislessons.* Santa Monica: RAND, 1969.

Haley, P. Edward. *Congress and the Fall of South Vietnam and Cambodia.* Rutherford, NJ: Fairleigh Dickinson University Press, 1982.

Hammer, Ellen J. *A Death in November: America in Vietnam, 1963.* New York: Dutton, 1987.

———. *The Struggle for Indochina, 1940–1955: Vietnam and the French Experience.* Stanford, CA: Stanford University Press, 1966.

Hammond, William M. *Public Affairs: The Military and the Media, 1962–1968.* Washington, DC: U.S. Army Center for Military History, 1988.

———. *Public Affairs: The Military and the Media, 1968–1973.* Washington, DC: U.S. Army Center of Military History, 1996.

Hannah, Norman B. *The Key to Failure: Laos and the Vietnam War.* Lanham, MD: Madison Books, 1987.

Hanson, Peter. "Bac Di Cu: Catholic Refugees from the North of Vietnam and Their Role in the Southern Republic, 1954–1959." *Journal of Vietnamese Studies,* vol. 4, no. 3 (October 2009).

Hatcher, Patrick Lloyd. *Suicide of an Elite: American Internationalists and Vietnam.* Stanford, CA: Stanford University Press, 1990.

Haynsworth, Toby, and J. Edward Lee, eds. *White Christmas in April: The Collapse of South Vietnam, 1975.* New York: Peter Lang Publishing, 2000.

Heduy, Philippe. *La guerre d'Indochine, 1945–1953.* Paris: Société de production littéraire, 1981.

Hemingway, Al. *Our War Was Different: Marine Combined Action Platoons in Vietnam.* Annapolis, MD: Naval Institute Press, 1994.

Henderson, William D. *Why the Viet Cong Fought: A Study in Motivation and Control in a Modern Army in Combat.* Westport, CT: Greenwood, 1979.

Henderson, William, and Wesley Fishel. "The Foreign Policy of Ngo Dinh Diem." *Vietnam Perspectives,* vol. 4 (August 1966): 3–30.

Hennessy, Michael A. *Strategy in Vietnam: The Marines and Revolutionary Warfare in I Corps, 1965–1972.* Westport, CT: Praeger, 1997.

Herring, George C. *America's Longest War: The United States and Vietnam, 1950–1975.* 4th edition. Boston, MA: McGraw-Hill, 2002.

Herrington, Stuart. *Peace with Honor? An American Reports on Vietnam, 1973–1975.* Novato, CA: Presidio, 1983.

———. *Silence Was a Weapon: The Vietnam War in the Villages.* Novato, CA: Presidio, 1982.

Herschensohn, Bruce. *An American Amnesia: How the U.S. Congress Forced the Surrenders of South Vietnam and Cambodia.* New York: Beaufort Books, 2010.

Hickey, Gerald C. *Village in Vietnam.* New Haven, CT: Yale University Press, 1964.

Higgins, Marguerite. *Our Vietnam Nightmare.* New York: Harper and Row, 1965.

Hirschman, Charles, Samuel Preston, and Vu Manh Loi, "Vietnamese Casualties during the American War: A New Estimate." *Population and Development Review* 21 (December 1995).

Ho Chi Minh. *On Revolution.* Ed. Bernard Fall. New York: Praeger, 1967.

———. *Selected Writings.* Hanoi: Foreign Languages Publishing House, 1977.

Hoang Ngoc Lung. *The General Offensives of 1968–1969.* Washington, DC: U.S. Army Center of Military History, 1981.
———. *Intelligence.* Washington, DC: U.S. Army Center of Military History, 1982.
Hoang Van Chi. *From Colonialism to Communism: A Case History of North Vietnam.* New York: Praeger, 1964.
Hoang Van Thai. *How South Vietnam Was Liberated.* Hanoi: The Gioi, 1992.
Honey, J. P. *Genesis of a Tragedy: The Historical Background to the Vietnam War.* London: Benn, 1968.
Horn, Keith. *Battle for Hue: Tet 1968.* Novato, CA: Presidio, 1983.
Hosmer, Stephen T. *Viet Cong Repression and Its Implications for the Future.* Santa Monica, CA: RAND, 1970.
Hosmer, Stephen T., Konrad Kellen, and Brian M. Jenkins. *The Fall of South Vietnam: Statements by Vietnamese Military and Civilian Leaders.* New York: Crane, Russak, 1980.
Hue Tam Ho Tai. *Millenarianism and Peasant Politics in Vietnam.* Cambridge, MA: Harvard University Press, 1983.
———. *Radicalism and the Origins of the Vietnamese Revolution.* Cambridge, MA: Harvard University Press, 1996.
Hughes, Geraint. "A 'Post-War War': The British Occupation of French Indochina, September 1945–March 1946." *Small Wars and Insurgencies* 17 (2006).
Hung Nguyen Tien. "Communist Offensive Strategy and the Defense of South Vietnam." In Lloyd J. Matthews and Dale E. Brown, *Assessing the Vietnam War.* Washington, DC: Pergamon-Brassey's, 1987.
Hung Nguyen Tien and Gerald S. Schecter. *The Palace File.* New York: Harper and Row, 1966.
Hunt, Ira A., Jr. *Losing Vietnam: How America Abandoned Southeast Asia.* Lexington, KY: University Press of Kentucky, 2013.
Hunt, Richard A. *Pacification: The American Struggle for Vietnam's Hearts and Minds.* Boulder, CO: Westview, 1995.
Hunt, Richard A., and Richard H. Shultz, Jr., eds. *Lessons from an Unconventional War.* New York: Pergamon, 1982.
Isaacs, Arnold R. *Without Honor: Defeat in Vietnam and Cambodia.* New York: Vintage, 1984.
Jenkins, Brian M. *Why the North Vietnamese Will Keep Fighting.* Santa Monica, CA: RAND, 1972.
———. *A People's Army for South Vietnam.* Santa Monica, CA: RAND, 1971.
Joes, Anthony James. *Urban Guerrilla Warfare.* Lexington, KY: University Press of Kentucky, 2007.
———. *Victorious Insurgencies: Four Rebellions That Shaped Our World.* Lexington, KY: University Press of Kentucky, 2010.
Johnson, Chalmers. *Autopsy on People's War.* Berkeley, CA: University of California Press, 1973.
Johnson, Lyndon B. *The Vantage Point.* New York: Holt, Rinehart, Winston, 1971.
Joint Chiefs of Staff. *The History of the Joint Chiefs of Staff: The Joint Chiefs of Staff and the War in Vietnam, 1960–1968,* Parts I–III. Washington, D.C. Historical Division, Joint Secretariat, Joint Chiefs of Staff, 2009.
Jones, Howard. *Death of a Generation: How the Assassinations of Diem and JFK Prolonged the Vietnam War.* New York: Oxford University Press, 2003.
Jumper, Roy, and Marjorie Weiner Normand. "Vietnam." In George McTurran Kahin, ed., *Government and Politics in Southeast Asia.* Ithaca, NY: Cornell University Press, 1964.
Kaplan, Lawrence S., Denise Artaud, and Mark Rubin, eds. *Dien Bien Phu and the Crisis of Franco-American Relations, 1954–1955.* Wilmington, DE: Scholarly Resources, 1990.
Karnow, Stanley. *Vietnam: A History.* New York: Viking, 1983.
Keegan, John. *Dien Bien Phu.* New York: Ballantine, 1974.
Kellen, Konrad. *A Profile of the PAVN Soldier in South Vietnam.* Santa Monica, CA: RAND, June 1968.
———. *A View of the VC.* Santa Monica, CA: RAND, 1969.

———. *Conversations with Enemy Soldiers in Late 1968/Early 1969: A Study of Motivation and Morale*. Santa Monica, CA: RAND, 1970.

Kelly, George. *Lost Soldiers: The French Army and Empire in Crisis, 1947–1962*. Cambridge, MA: MIT Press, 1965.

Kiem Do and Julie Kane. *Counterpart: A South Vietnamese Naval Officer's War*. Annapolis, MD: Naval Institute Press, 1998.

Kissinger, Henry. *White House Years*. Boston: Little, Brown, 1979.

Koch, Jeannette. *The Chieu Hoi Program in South Vietnam 1963–1971*. Santa Monica, CA: RAND, 1973.

Kolko, Gabriel. *Anatomy of a War*. New York: Pantheon, 1985.

Komer, Robert W. *Bureaucracy Does Its Thing: Institutional Constraints on U.S.-GVN Performance in Vietnam*. Santa Monica, CA: Rand, 1972.

Lacouture, Jean. *Pierre Mèndes-France*. Trans. George Holock. New York: Holmes and Meier, 1984.

———. *Vietnam Between Two Truces*. Trans. Konrad Kellen and Joel Carmichael. New York: Random House, 1966.

Ladejinsky, Wolf. "Agrarian Reform in the Republic of Vietnam." In *Problems of Freedom: South Vietnam since Independence*. Ed. Wesley R. Fishel. New York: Free Press, 1961, 153–175.

Lam Quang Thi. *Autopsy: The Death of South Vietnam*. Phoenix, AR: Sphinx Publishing, 1986.

———. *Hell in An Loc: The 1972 Easter Invasion and the Battle That Saved South Vietnam*. Denton, TX: University of North Texas Press, 2009.

———. *The Twenty-Five-Year Century: A South Vietnamese General Remembers the Indochina War to the Fall of Saigon*. Denton, TX: University of North Texas Press, 2001.

Lancaster, Donald. *The Emancipation of French Indochina*. London: Oxford University Press, 1961.

Langlais, Pierre. *Dien Bien Phu*. Paris: Éditions France-Empire, 1963.

Laniel, Joseph. *Le drame Indochinois*. Paris: Plon, 1957.

Lansdale, Edward Geary. *In the Midst of Wars: An American's Mission to Southeast Asia*. New York: Harper and Row, 1972.

Larteguy, Jean. *L'adieu à Saigon*. Paris: Presses de la Cité, 1975.

Le Gro, William. *Vietnam from Ceasefire to Capitulation*. Washington, DC: U.S. Army Center of Military History, 1981.

Leites, Nathan. *The Vietcong Style of Politics*. Santa Monica, CA: RAND, 1969.

Lenin, V. I. *Selected Works*. Moscow: Progress Publishers, 1977.

Lessons from the Vietnam War. London: Royal United Services Institute, 1969.

Le Thi Que, A. Terry Rambo, and Gary D. Murfin. "Why They Fled: Refugee Movements during the Spring 1975 Communist Offensive in South Vietnam." *Asian Survey* 16 (September 1976).

Lebra, Joyce. *Japanese-Trained Armies in Southeast Asia*. New York: Columbia University Press, 1977.

Lewy, Guenter. *America in Vietnam*. New York: Oxford University Press, 1978.

Lipsman, Samuel, and Stephen Weiss. *The Vietnam Experience: The False Peace, 1972–1974*. Boston: Boston Publishing, 1985.

Lockhart, Bruce. *The End of the Vietnamese Monarchy*. New Haven, CT: Yale Center of International and Area Studies, 1993.

Lockhart, Greg. *Nation in Arms: Origins of the People's Army of Vietnam*. Boston: Allen and Unwyn, 1989.

Logevall, Frederik. *Embers of War: The Fall of an Empire and the Making of America's Vietnam*. New York: Random House, 2012.

Lomperis, Timothy J. *From People's War to People's Rule: Insurgency, Intervention, and the Lessons of Vietnam*. Chapel Hill: University of North Carolina Press, 1996.

———. *The War Everyone Lost—and Won: America's Intervention in Vietnam's Twin Struggles*. Baton Rouge, LA: Louisiana State University Press, 1984.

Luan Cong Nguyen. *Nationalist in the Vietnam Wars*. Bloomington, IN: Indiana University Press, 2012.

Luttwak, Edward. *The Grand Strategy of the Byzantine Empire*. Cambridge, MA: Harvard University Press, 2009.

MacDonald, Peter. *Giap: The Victor in Vietnam*. New York: Norton, 1993.

Maigre, José. "Le general Nguyen Van Hinh et la création de l'armée vietnamienne." *Revue historique des armées*, no. 194 (January 1994).

Maneli, Mieczyslaw. *War of the Vanquished*. Trans. Maria de Gorgey. New York: Harper and Row, 1971.

Marc, Henri, and Pierre Cony. *Indochine français*. Paris: Éditions France-Empire, 1946.

Marchand, Jean. *L'Indochine en guerre*. Paris: Pouzet, 1955.

Marr, David G. *Vietnamese Anticolonialism, 1885–1925*. Berkeley CA: University of California Press, 1971.

———. *Vietnamese Tradition on Trial, 1920–1945*. Berkeley, CA: University of California Press, 1984.

———. *Vietnam 1945: The Quest for Power*. Berkeley, CA: University of California Press, 1995.

McAllister, James, and Ian Schulte. "The Limits of Influence in Vietnam: Britain, the United States and the Diem Regime, 1959–63." *Small Wars and Insurgencies*, vol. 17, n. 1 (2006), pp. 22–43.

McAlister, John T. *Vietnam: The Origins of Revolution*. Garden City, NY: Doubleday Anchor, 1971.

McAlister, John T., and Paul Mus. *The Vietnamese and Their Revolution*. New York: Harper and Row, 1970.

McGarvey, Patrick J. *Visions of Victory: Selected Vietnamese Communist Military Writings 1965–1968*. Stanford, CA: Hoover Institution, 1969.

McKenna, Thomas P. *Kontum: The Battle to Save South Vietnam*. Lexington, KY: University Press of Kentucky, 2011.

Merom, Gil. *How Democracies Lose Small Wars*. Cambridge, England: Cambridge University Press, 2003.

Michigan State University Social Science Research Bureau. *Problems of Freedom: South Vietnam since Independence*. Glencoe, IL: Free Press, 1961.

Military History Institute of Vietnam, The. *Victory in Vietnam: The Official History of the People's Army of Vietnam, 1954–1975*. Trans. Merle L. Pribbenow. Lawrence, KS: University Press of Kansas, 2002.

Miller, Edward. *Misalliance: Ngo Dinh Diem, the United States, and the Fate of South Vietnam*. Cambridge, MA: Harvard University Press, 2013.

———. "Vision, Power and Agency: The Ascent of Ngo Dinh Diem. 1945–1954." *Journal of Southeast Asian Studies* vol. 35 (October 2004), pp. 433–458.

Miller, John Grider. *The Co Vans: U.S. Marine Advisors in Vietnam*. Annapolis, MD: Naval Institute Press, 2000.

Modelski, George. "The Viet Minh Complex." In *Communism and Revolution: The Strategic Uses of Political Violence*, ed. Cyril Black and Thomas P. Thornton. Princeton, NJ: Princeton University Press, 1964.

Mountbatten, Louis. *Report of the Combined Chiefs of Staff by the Supreme Allied Commander: Southeast Asia, 1943–1945*. London: H. M. Stationery Office, 1951.

Moyar, Mark. "Political Monks: The Militant Buddhist Movement during the Vietnam War." *Modern Asian Studies*, vol. 38, no. 4 (October 2004).

———. *Triumph Forsaken: The Vietnam War, 1954–1965*. New York: Cambridge University Press, 2006.

Mueller, John E. *War, Presidents and Public Opinion*. Lanham, MD: University Press of America, 1985.

Mus, Paul. *Vietnam: Sociologie d'une guerre*. Paris: Éditions du Seuil, 1952.

Navarre, Henri. *Agonie de l'Indochine*. Paris: Plon, 1956.

Newman, John M. *JFK and Vietnam: Deception, Intrigue and the Struggle for Power*. New York: Warner, 1992.

Ngo Quang Truong. *Territorial Forces*. Washington, DC: U.S. Army Center of Military History, 1981.

———. *The Easter Offensive of 1972*. Washington, DC: U.S. Army Center of Military History, 1980.

Ngo Van Chieu. *Journal d'un combattant Vietminh*. Paris: Éditions du Seuil, 1955.

Nguyen Cao Ky. *Buddha's Child: My Fight to Save Vietnam*. New York: St. Martin's, 2002.

———. *Twenty Years and Twenty Days*. New York: Stein and Day, 1976.

Nguyen Duy Hinh. *Vietnamization and the Ceasefire*. Washington, DC: U.S. Army Center of Military History, 1980.

Nguyen Lien-Hang. *Hanoi's War*. Chapel Hill, NC: University of North Carolina Press, 2012.

Nighswonger, William A. *Rural Pacification in Vietnam*. New York: Praeger, 1966.

Nixon, Richard. *RN: The Memoirs of Richard Nixon*. New York: Simon and Schuster, 1990.

Nolan, Keith. *Battle for Hue: Tet 1968*. Novato, CA: Presidio, 1983.

Nolting, Frederick. *From Trust to Tragedy: The Political Memoirs of Kennedy's Ambassador to South Vietnam*. New York: Praeger, 1988.

O'Ballance, Edgar. *The Indo-China War, 1945–1954: A Study in Guerrilla Warfare*. London: Faber and Faber, 1964.

Oberdorfer, Don. *Tet!* Garden City, NY: Doubleday, 1971. Reissued 1984 by Da Capo.

O'Donnell, Kenneth P. *Johnny, We Hardly Knew Ye*. Boston: Little Brown, 1972.

O'Neill, Bard E. *Insurgency and Terrorism: From Revolution to Apocalypse*. Washington, DC: Potomac, 2005.

O'Neill, Robert J. *General Giap*. New York: Praeger, 1969.

Osborne, John. "The Tough Miracle Man of Asia." *Life*, May 13, 1957, 156–176.

Palmer, Bruce, Jr. *The Twenty-Five-Year War: America's Military Role in Vietnam*. Lexington, KY: University Press of Kentucky, 1984.

Palmer, Dave Richard. *Summons of the Trumpet: U.S.-Vietnam in Pespective*. San Rafael, CA: Presidio, 1978.

Pan, Stephen, and Daniel Lyons. *Vietnam Crisis*. New York: East Asian Research Institute, 1966.

Pannikar, K.M. *Asia and Western Dominance*. New York: John Day, 1950.

Paret, Peter. *French Revolutionary Warfare from Indochina to Algeria: An Analysis of a Political and Military Doctrine*. New York: Praeger, 1964.

Parrish, Robert D. *Combat Recon: My Year with the ARVN*. St. Martin's, 1991.

Pedroncini, Guy, and Philippe Duplay, eds. *Leclerc et l'Indochine 1945–1947*. Paris: Albin Michel, 1992.

Pellissier, Pierre. *Dien Bien Phu*. Paris: Perrin, 2004.

Penniman, Howard R. *Elections in South Vietnam*. Washington, DC: American Enterprise Institute, 1972.

Pentagon Papers, The. The Senator Gravel Edition. Boston, MA: Beacon Press, 1971.

People's Army of Vietnam. *Vietnam: The Anti-U.S. Resistance War for National* Salvation. Hanoi: PAVN Publishing House, 1980.

Peterson, Michael E. *The Combined Action Platoons: The U.S. Marines' Other War in Vietnam*. New York: Praeger, 1989.

Pham Kim Tuan. *The ARVN: A Stoic Army*. Washington, DC: U.S. Army Center of Military History, 1983.

Phillips, Rufus. *Why Vietnam Matters: An Eyewitness Account of Lessons Not Learned*. Annapolis, MD: Naval Institute Press, 2008.

Pike, Douglas. *War, Peace and the Viet Cong*. Cambridge, MA: MIT Press, 1969.

———. *A History of Vietnamese Communism, 1925–1976*. Stanford, CA: Hoover Institution, Stanford University, 1978.

———. *PAVN: People's Army of Vietnam*. Novato, CA: Presidio, 1986.

———. *The Vietcong Strategy of Terror*. Cambridge, MA: M.I.T. Press, 1970.

———. *Viet Cong: The Organization and Techniques of the National Liberation Front of South Vietnam*. Cambridge, MA: M.I.T. Press, 1966.

Pimlott, John. "Ho Chi Minh's Triumph." In *War in Peace*, ed. Ashley Brown and Sam Elder. London: Orbis, 1981.

Pimlott, John, ed. *Vietnam: The History and the Tactics*. New York: Crescent, 1982.

Pirey, Charles-Henri de. *La Route Morte: RC41950*. Paris: Indo Éditions, 2002.

Podhoretz, Norman. *Why We Were in Vietnam*. New York: Simon and Schuster, 1984.

Pohle, V. *The Viet Cong in Saigon: Tactics and Objectives during the Tet Offensive*. Santa Monica, CA: RAND, 1969.

Popkin, Samuel. *The Rational Peasant: The Political Economy of Rural Society in Vietnam*. Berkeley, CA: University of California Press, 1979.

Post, Ken. *Revolution, Socialism and Nationalism in Vietnam*. Vol. 4. Aldershot, England: Dartmouth Publishing, 1990.

Pouget, Jean. *Nous étions à Dien Bien Phu*. Paris: Presses de la Cité, 1964.

Prados, John. *Blood Road: The Ho Chi Minh Trail and the Vietnam War*. New York: John Wiley, 1999.

Prochnau, William. *Once Upon a Distant War: Young War Correspondents and the Early Vietnam Battles*. New York: Times Books, 1995.

Qiang Zhai. *China and the Vietnam Wars, 1950–1975*. Chapel Hill, NC: University of North Carolina Press, 2000.

Race, Jeffrey. *War Comes to Long An: Revolutionary Conflict in a Vietnamese Province*. Berkeley, CA: University of California Press, 1972.

Radvanyi, Janos. *Delusions and Reality: Gambits, Hoaxes and Diplomatic One-upmanship in Vietnam*. South Bend, IN: Gateway, 1978.

Randle, Robert F. *Geneva 1954: The Settlement of the Indochinese War*. Princeton, NJ: Princeton University Press, 1969.

Record, Jeffrey. *Beating Goliath: Why Insurgencies Win*. Washington, DC: Potomac Books, 2007.

———. "External Assistance: Enabler of Insurgent Success." *Parameters* 36 (Autumn 2006).

———. *Making War, Thinking History: Munich, Vietnam, and Presidential Use of Force from Korea to Kosovo*. Annapolis, MD: Naval Institute Press, 2002.

———. *The Wrong War: Why We Lost in Vietnam*. Annapolis, MD: Naval Institute Press, 1998.

Reston, James. *The Artillery of the Press: Its Influence on American Foreign Policy*. New York: Harper and Row, 1966.

Rice-Maximin, Edward. *Accommodation and Resistance: The French Left, Indochina, and the Cold War*. Westport, CT: Greenwood, 1986.

Robbins, James S. *This Time We Win: Revisiting the Tet Offensive*. New York: Encounter, 2010.

Rocolle, Pierre. *Pourquoi Dien Bien Phu?* Paris: Flammarion, 1968.

Rolph, Hammond. "Vietnamese Communism and the Protracted War." *Asian Survey* 12 (September 1972).

Roy, Jules. *The Battle for Dien Bien Phu*. New York: Harper and Row, 1965.

Rusk, Dean. *As I Saw It: A Secretary of State's Memoirs*. London: Tauris, 1991.

Sainteny, Jean. *Histoire d'une paix manqué: Indochine, 1945–1947*. Paris: Amiot-Dumont, 1953.

———. *Ho Chi Minh and His Vietnam: A Personal Memoir*. Chicago, IL: Cowles, 1972.

Salan, Raoul. *Mémoires: Fin d'un empire, vol. 2: Le Viet-minh mon adversaire*. Paris : Presses de la Cite, 1971.

Salisbury-Jones, Guy. *So Full a Glory: A Biography of Marshal de Lattre de Tassigny*. London: Weidenfeld and Nicolson, 1954.

Santoli, Al, ed. *To Bear Any Burden*. New York: Dutton, 1985.

Schaffer, Howard B. *Ellsworth Bunker: Global Troubleshooter, Vietnam Hawk*. Chapel Hill, NC: University of North Carolina Press, 2003.

Scigliano, Robert. *South Vietnam: Nation under Stress*. Boston: Houghton Mifflin, 1964.

———. "The Electoral Process in South Vietnam: Politics in an Underdeveloped State." *Midwest Journal of Political Science*, vol. 4, no. 2 (May 1960).

Shaplen, Robert. *Bitter Victory*. New York: Harper and Row, 1986.

———. "The Cult of Diem." *New York Times Magazine*, May 14, 1972, 16–17, 40–58.

Short, Anthony. *The Origins of the Vietnam War*. London: Longman, 1989.

Simpson, Howard R. *Dien Bien Phu: The Epic Battle America Forgot*. Washington, DC: Brassey's, 1996.

Smith, George W. *The Siege at Hue.* Boulder, CO: Lynne Rienner, 1999.

Smith, R. B. *An International History of the Vietnam War,* Vol. I, *Revolution versus Containment, 1955–1961.* New York: St. Martin's, 1983.

———. *An International History of the Vietnam War,* Vol. II, *The Kennedy Strategy.* New York: St. Martin's, 1985.

———. *An International History of the Vietnam War,* Vol. III, *The Making of a Limited War, 1965–1966.* New York: St. Martin's, 1991.

Snepp, Frank. *Decent Interval.* New York: Random House, 1977.

Sorley, Lewis. *A Better War: The Unexamined Victories and Final Tragedy of America's Last years in Vietnam.* New York: Harcourt Brace, 1999.

———. *Reassessing Vietnam.* Lubbock, TX: Texas Tech University, 2006.

———. *The Vietnam War: An Assessment by South Vietnam's Generals.* Lubbock, TX: Texas Tech University Press, 2010.

———. *Westmoreland: The General Who Lost Vietnam.* Boston: Houghton Mifflin Harcourt, 2011.

Spector, Ronald. *Advice and Support: The Early Years of the U.S. Army in Vietnam.* New York: Free Press, 1985.

Statler, Kathryn. *Replacing France: The Origins of American Intervention in Vietnam.* Lexington, KY: University Press of Kentucky, 2007.

Strober, Gerald S., and Deborah H. Strober. *"Let Us Begin Anew": An Oral History of the Kennedy Presidency.* New York: Perennial, 1994.

Summers, Harry. *On Strategy: A Critical Analysis of the Vietnam War.* Novato, CA: Presidio, 1982.

Sun Tzu. *The Art of War.* Trans. Samuel B. Griffith. New York: Oxford University Press, 1963.

Tanham, George. *Communist Revolutionary Warfare: From the Vietminh to the Viet Cong.* New York: Praeger, 1967.

Tanham, George, and Dennis Duncanson. "Some Dilemmas of Counterinsurgency." *Foreign Affairs,* vol. 48, no. 1 (October, 1969).

Taylor, Maxwell D. *Sword and Plowshares.* New York: W. W. Norton, 1972.

Thayer, Thomas C. *War without Fronts: The American Experience in Vietnam.* Boulder, CO: Westview, 1985.

Thomas, Martin. *The French Empire at War, 1940–1945.* Manchester, England: Manchester University Press, 2007.

Thompson, Robert. *Defeating Communist Insurgency: The Lessons of Malaya and Vietnam.* New York: Praeger, 1966.

———. *Make for the Hills: Memories of Far Eastern Wars.* London: Leo Cooper, 1989.

———. *No Exit from Vietnam.* New York: McKay, 1969.

———. *Peace Is Not at Hand.* New York: McKay, 1974.

Thompson, Robert. "Vietnam." In *War in Peace,* ed. Ashley Brown and Sam Elder. London: Orbis Publishing, 1981.

Thompson, W. Scott. "The Indochina Debacle and the United States." *Orbis* 19 (Fall 1975).

Thompson, W. Scott, and Donaldson D. Frizzell, eds. *The Lessons of Vietnam.* New York: Crane Russak, 1977.

Todd, Olivier. *Cruel April: The Fall of Saigon.* New York: Norton, 1990.

Tonnesson, Stein. *The Vietnamese Revolution of 1945: Roosevelt, Ho Chi Minh, and de Gaulle in a World at War.* Oslo: International Peace Research Institute, 1991.

Trinquier, Roger. *Modern Warfare: A French View of Counterinsurgency.* Westport, CT: Praeger, 2006.

Tran Dinh Tho. *Pacification.* Washington, DC: U.S. Army Center for Military History, 1980.

Tran Van Don. *Our Endless War.* San Rafael, CA: Presidio, 1978.

Tran Van Tra. *Concluding the Thirty-Years War.* Rosslyn, VA: Foreign Broadcast Information Service, 1983.

Trotsky, Leon. *The History of the Russian Revolution.* Ann Arbor, MI: University of Michigan Press, 1957.

Truong Chinh. *Primer for Revolt: The Communist Takeover in Vietnam. New York:* Praeger, 1963.

———. *The Resistance Will Win.* Hanoi: Foreign Languages Publishing House, 1960.

Truong Nhu Tang. *A Viet Cong Memoir.* New York: Vintage 1985.

Truong Vinh-le. *Vietnam: Où est la vérité ?* Paris: Lavauzelle, 1989.

Turley, G. H. *The Easter Offensive: Vietnam 1972.* Novato, CA: Presidio, 1985.

Turley, William S. *The Second Indochina War: A Short Political and Military History, 1954–1975.* New York: Mentor, 1987.

Turner, Robert F. *Vietnamese Communism: Its Origins and Development.* Stanford, CA: Hoover Institution Press, 1975.

———. "Myths and Realities in the Vietnam Debate." *World Politics,* vol. 149 (Summer 1986).

Turpin, Frédéric. *De Gaulle, les gaullistes et l'Indochine 1940–1956.* Paris: Les Indes savantes, 2005.

Van Nguyen Duong. *The Tragedy of the Vietnam War: A South Vietnamese Officer's Analysis.* Jefferson, NC: McFarland, 2008.

Van Tien Dung. *Our Great Spring Victory. An Account of the Liberation of South Vietnam.* New York: Monthly Review Press, 1977.

Vanuxem, Paul. *La Mort du Vietnam.* Paris: Editions de la nouvella aurore, 1975.

Veith, George J. *Black April: The Fall of South Vietnam, 1973–1975.* New York: Encounter, 2012.

Vo Nguyen Giap. *The General Headquarters in the Spring of Brilliant Victory.* Hanoi: The Gioi, 2002.

———. *Dien Bien Phu.* Hanoi: Foreign Languages Publishing House, 1964,

———. *Dien Bien Phu: Rendezvous with History: A Memoir.* Hanoi: The Gioi, 2004.

———. *How We Won the War.* Philadelphia, PA: Recon, 1976.

———. *People's War, People's Army.* New York: Praeger, 1962.

———. *Unforgettable Days.* Hanoi: Foreign Languages Publishing House, 1975.

Walt, Lewis. *Strange War, Strange Strategy.* New York: Funk and Wagnalls, 1970.

Warner, Denis. *Certain Victory: How Hanoi Won the War.* Kansas City: Sheed, Andrews and McMeel 1978.

———. *Not with Guns Alone.* Richmond, Victoria: Hutchinson of Australia, 1977.

———. *The Last Confucian: Vietnam, Southeast Asia and the West.* Harmondsworth, England: Penguin, 1964.

Warner, Geoffrey. "The United States and the Fall of Diem Part II: The Death of Diem." *Australian Outlook* (March 1975): 3–17.

Werner, Jayne Susan. *Peasant Politics and Religious Sectarianism: Peasant and Priest in the Cao Dai in Vietnam.* New Haven: Yale University Southeast Asian Studies, 1981.

Werner, Jayne S., and Luu-Doan Huynh, eds. *The Vietnam War: Vietnamese and American Perspectives.* Armonk, NY: M. E. Sharpe, 1994.

West, Francis. *The Village.* New York: Harper and Row, 1972.

Westmoreland, William. *A Soldier Reports.* New York: Da Capo Press, 1989.

White, Owen, and J. P. Daughton. *In God's Empire: French Missionaries and the Modern World.* New York: Oxfor University Press, 2012.

Whiting, Allen S. *The Chinese Calculus of Deterrence: India and Vietnam.* Ann Arbor, MI: University of Michigan Press, 1975.

Wiest, Andrew. *Vietnam's Forgotten Army: Heroism and Betrayal in the ARVN.* New York: New York University Press, 2008.

Wiest, Andrew, and Michael Doidge, eds. *Triumph Revisited: Historians Battle for the Vietnam War.* New York: Routledge, 2010.

Willbanks, James H. *Abandoning Vietnam: How America Left and South Vietnam Lost Its War.* Lawrence, KS: University Press of Kansas, 2004.

———. *The Tet Offensive: A Concise History.* New York: Columbia University Press, 2008.

Williams, Philip. *Crisis and Compromise: Politics in the Fourth Republic.* London: Longmans, 1964.

Windrow, Martin. *The Last Valley: Dien Bien Phu and the French Defeat in Vietnam.* Cambridge, MA: Da Capo, 2004.

Winters, Francis X. *The Year of the Hare: America in Vietnam, January 25, 1963–February 15, 1964.* Athens, GA: University of Georgia Press, 1999.
Wirtz, James. *The Tet Offensive: Intelligence Failure in War.* Ithaca, NY: Cornell University Press, 1994.
Woodruff, Mark. *Unheralded Victory: The Defeat of the Viet Cong and the North Vietnamese Army, 1961–1973.* Arlington, VA: Vandamere Press, 1999.
Woodside, Alexander B. *Community and Revolution in Modern Vietnam.* Boston: Houghton Mifflin, 1976.
Xiaobing Li. *A History of the Modern Chinese Army.* Lexington, KY: University Press of Kentucky, 2007.
Young, Marilyn, John Fitzgerald, and Tom Grunfeld. *The Vietnam War: A History in Documents.* Oxford, England: Oxford University Press, 2003.
Zasloff, Joseph. *Origins of the Insurgency in South Vietnam, 1954–1960: The Role of the Southern Viet Minh Cadres.* Santa Monica, CA: RAND, 1968.
Zhai, Quing. *China and the Vietnam Wars, 1950–1975.* Chapel Hill, NC: University of North Carolina Press, 2000.
Zi Jun Toong. "Overthrown by the Press: The U.S. Media's Role in the Fall of Diem." *Australasian Journal of American Studies*, vol. 27, no. 1 (July 2008).

Index

About the Author

Anthony James Joes (Ph.D., University of Pennsylvania) is professor emeritus of political science at Saint Joseph's University and visiting professor at the U.S. Army War College. He has made presentations to the Central Intelligence Agency, the Defense Intelligence Agency, the National War College, the RAND Corporation, the Foreign Policy Research Institute, and other organizations. He is the author of fourteen books, including *Victorious Insurgencies: Four Rebellions That Shaped Our World* (2010), *Resisting Rebellion: The History and Politics of Counterinsurgency* (2004), and *America and Guerrilla Warfare* (2000).